Ten Thousand Goddam Cattle

University of New Mexico Press • Albuquerque, New Mexico

A history of the American cowboy
in song, story and verse

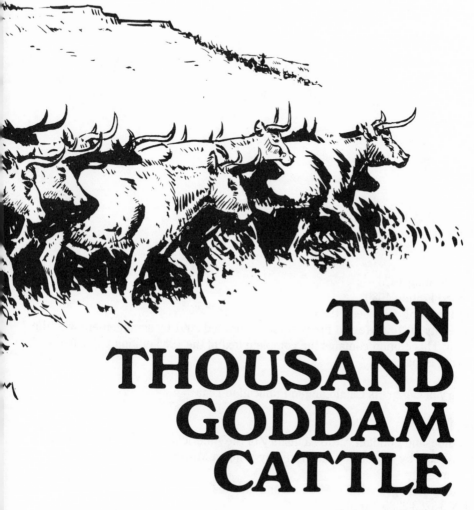

TEN THOUSAND GODDAM CATTLE

by Katie Lee

Illustrated by William Moyers

First Printing 1976
Revised Edition 1980
Third Printing (Revised) 1985
University of New Mexico Press edition reprinted 2001 by arrangement with the
author. This edition contains the complete text of the 1985 edition published by
Katydid Books.

Library of Congress Cataloging-in-Publication Data

Lee, Katie.
Ten thousand goddam cattle : a history of the American cowboy in song, story
and verse / by Katie Lee ; illustrated by William Moyers.
p.   cm.
Includes bibliographical references and indexes.
ISBN 0-8263-2335-9 (pbk.)
1. Cowboys—Songs and music—History and criticism. 2. Cowboys—West
(U.S.)—History. I. Moyers, William. II. Title.
ML3551 .L4 2001
782.421642—dc21   00-042313

To the memory of "Brandy"
  My very best and most beloved husband . . . and my last

Contents

Introduction

WE'RE GOING TO TALK ABOUT SONGS . . . and their cowboys.

As heard today, cowboy songs are a combination of additions, alterations and deletions. This book is an attempt to restore writer to lyric and composer to music. These are songs about the West, about the men who wrote them, about the space that sired the men before it vanished in noise and neon. A few cowboys are still around, old men now, hanging half in, half out, of a legend they helped to make, but holding their songs and poems clearly in memory. Their world was one of silver moonlit silence, of lonesome yips from the coyote pack, of thousands of bawling cattle, of uninterrupted prairies, rivers, canyons and mountains. A world of freedom and infinity. A world of sweat and discomfort.

When lonesome country goes, lonesome songs go too. All attempts to transplant them, unsullied, from their birthplace to crowded cities cause them to suffer. The city man has no touch with the sod, and while his attention may be caught by a nostalgic strain in the music without his knowing why, he can hardly comprehend the kind of aloneness that gave birth to the cowboy song. Nevertheless, the seeds of Western music were often planted by men whose roots had long been in other soil. Predominantly those seeds were Irish. We've heard it stated that America's musical heritage stems from the rhythms of the black people, but the blues were not the only, nor the first, music of the continent. The black man's music was adapted to a society, whereas the Irishman's was adapted to a terrain. The fast, rollicking jigs were often left intact, so far as their melodies were concerned, but they had great elasticity and when stretched and slowed fitted very well the gait of a walking or trotting cow pony. Finally, this music began to identify the cowboy who was surrounded environmentally with the other kind of stretch — space, and lots of time. A good many of the songs were conjured up long after the cowboy shook hands with St. Peter, were songs he never heard; yet again and again he is given credit for producing them as well as singing them.

And we're going to let the cowboy talk the way he talks, really, without laundering his lingo.

There are many dictionaries of his speech, yet somehow much of the rich color fades before it gets to the reader. We'll let the title of this book serve as an example — it comes from the cowboy's camp. The other title, *Ten Thousand Cattle Straying*, comes from a literary camp, and seventy-five years ago the Eastern dudes who were writing about the cowboy wouldn't have said shit if they'd had a mouthful of it. Also, at the time our cowboy was saying the most with his flamboyant tongue, decency was heading West with Victorian codes, breathing fire and damnation on the songs and verses of the nation's last great individual.

Oh, and there's that guitar he's supposed to have packed. He didn't.

Movie makers have given him that reflection. On cattle drives those gee-tars were non-existent. Once in a great while there might be a fiddle in the chuck (if the Cookie allowed such excess baggage), but if anybody thinks the mounted night nurse packed a guitar on his back or behind his saddle, he should hear what Shorty Mac McGinnis, an Arizona brush popper I know, had to say about that kind of reporting.

"Aw rite, s'posin' he *has* a geetar on night guard. S'posin' he's a settin' there on his hoss a'strummin'. The moonlight allofaquick catches on the shiny surface and flicks in the eye of some half-asleep steer. Whammy! The lid's off! An' what does he do with the geetar? Waa-a-al, he might could swang 'er round n' clout the rump of his hoss t'git a headstart on them boogered beeves, but chances'll take it the cayuse has already lit out like a fart in a windstorm and left the pore poke a'pickin' minor chords fer his requiem. Hell, I've knowed fellas what put their bandanas over the butts of their guns of a moonlit nite t' keep 'em from flashin' 'round!"

I was a one-year-old child, to the day, when we moved to Tucson, Arizona, and through all my years of listening to cowboy reminiscence, I've never heard one admit that he sang *to* the cows, or that the cows knew what singing was, or that they were soothed by what they heard. The point was to keep some noise going (most cowboys will attest that their style of singing amounts to that) so that sudden sounds of the night would go unnoticed by the nervous critters. Some sang, some hummed or softly whistled, those that felt like talking, talked, maybe played a mouth-organ, blew softly on a willow whistle, swore a quiet round of cuss words to keep themselves awake, or even squeezed a little concertina. But packing a guitar would have been the same as packing a piano on a pushcart.

The cowboy's brash, rebellious years were short. Two small decades made him immortal. He was America's last paladin, the idol of an age turned to legend. If time, or the passing of it, makes him a hero, absence of anything like that hero makes him a bigger one. The stories told here and the songs that celebrate them are from men who knew the land, who sopped it up like biscuits in gravy. The land made them what they were. My own years are expressed with a hand in the twentieth century and a heart in the nineteenth; thus a certain nostalgia prevails, a conscious yearning for important values slipping from our grasp never to return in any like form — a part of history that can't repeat itself because the land, the base that gave a sense of place, is gone. There will be a bit of personal history about the folksinger who teethed on these songs, who now a bit longer in the tooth, sees them as something more far-reaching than her regional heritage.

Most of the research for this book has been done unconsciously over a lifetime, but since the late fifties I've made a serious effort to record and present these songs and stories of my friends as near to their originals as is possible. It required a good deal of mileage. As an entertainer I have to eat, so I usually try to work in a couple of singing jobs along my research routes — and of course, I don't stop to see everybody I know on one trip. We could say, therefore, that the encounters presented herein cover a period of years. They cover a wide range of friends in places ranging wide throughout the West, and some of them, it sorrows me to say, are now on the "no-breakfast-forever" list.

Men like Shorty Mac and Buck, I have known since I was a teenager. Others

I've been led to or have sought out because they are the real thing and their songs deserve notice.

One song led me hundreds of miles in search of the place of its name and its "cowboy" composer — that story is woven throughout the book, culminating at the end. Bill Mekeel is an old friend in Santa Fe who helps me find this illusive place-in-song — Old Dolores; when maps and roads don't help he uses his old barnstorming techniques to uncover the rough land's secrets from the air. We will visit doughBelly Price (that *is* the way he spells it) whose earthy philosophy appears in his syndicated news column as well as on his tongue. On the side he sells real estate in Taos, New Mexico. Frank Ortiz y Davis, steeped in the Mexican-American tradition, brings forth some unusual facts along the Galisteo.

Gail I. Gardner and Billy Simon, grand old men of the bunch, live in Prescott, Arizona. They're responsible for a couple of the best loved cowboy lyrics and melodies in Western song history. A large family of ranchers (the four sons of Old Nick Perkins) live and ride beside the Verde River at Perkinsville, Arizona. Benny, one of the four, writes modern songs in the old cowboy tradition and maintains his part of the big spread where his grandfather homesteaded in the mid-eighteen hundreds. Old Nick is a man to reckon with!

Speed Richardson and Romy Lowdermilk, both in the Phoenix area, represent the cowboy's days in vaudeville and radio, as does singer-composer Slim Critchlow, who ended up in Oakland, California.

There's S. Omar Barker of Las Vegas, New Mexico, possibly the best living cowboy poet. I've had a good deal of correspondence with Mr. Barker, who laments the cowboy's passing. Remembering how it used to be, he resents much of what is now. Both modern-day singers and old have set music to his many verses.

And I will go home to Tucson to see Buck, who is almost a caricature, he's so typical of the cowboy. His salty phrases appear throughout. Like most men of his kind — the working cowboy — he has refused to ride against the grain of society and its cramping conditions; instead, he has moved beyond it and remained his own man. He's here to show how the songs get passed from one generation to the next, and to show how traditions of the past have left their mark on the cowboy personality of today.

I am attempting here more than just a book of songs. It does little good to go to some beautiful place with one or more of your senses missing — like smell, touch, sight, sound — you come away with no real essence of the place. The cowboy and his songs are nothing without some knowledge of what goes on around him and some insight into the way he thinks. I have, therefore, taken us deeper into the land that was, and is still, his home — the Catalina Mountains, the Rincons, are as much a part of Buck Watson as his gun and his wrinkles, his harmonica and songs. I want them to be *felt*. Most of the songs are created by, sung and traded among the cowboys, but a few are *Western* songs that haven't exactly slid off the back of a horse — *The South Coast, The Ballad of Alfred Packer, My Homestead, Old Arizona* — but they are deeply rooted in the West and its history, and when cowboys hear them, they like what they hear.

Cowboys taught me more than songs. From them I learned to ride, shoot, hunt, to spit ten feet into a stiff wind, to cuss, to live in and love the outdoors, to hate fences and respect rivers. They taught me how to drink whiskey and sing, or if I wanted to sing real good, how to sing and drink whiskey — in that order. They taught me old songs with new words, new tunes with old words; we made up songs and even un-made a few. I suggest that you read their songs and poems, interspersed throughout the narrative, slowly. They say more than you'd expect from a full century ago when a Victorian age was in its prime. They speak about things that are important to us, things we're reading in daily papers and magazines now, for the first time. The past history of the cowboy, briefly told, comes mostly from the mouth of Shorty Mac's Pa, who came to America during the Irish potato famine; the middle years from Shorty Mac; and much of the present from Buck. The songs are not in chronological order because I am telling a story which sustains a mood. For the same reason I seldom stop the proceedings to tell who wrote a song and when it was written or published. An asterisk placed inconspicuously beside the title tells the reader he can find this information in the compendium of songs — if he has the time and curiosity to look it up. There he can also learn to which of the five main periods the song belongs.

I have tried to paint the cowboy not at all, but to leave him as he was, and is yet, what's left of him, by letting him speak for himself in the lingo neither of us has found a reason not to use.

> The trail's a lane, the trail's a lane,
> How comes it, pard of mine?
> Within a day it slipped away
> And hardly left a sign.
> Now history a tale has gained
> To please the younger ears —
> A race of kings that rose, and reigned,
> And passed in fifty years!
>
> Charles Badger Clark
> *Sun and Saddle Leather*

* *When this symbol is found next to a song title see the Compendium of Songs for everything you ever wanted to know about the song and were afraid to ask.*

Ten thousand goddam cattle,
A-roamin' far and wide,
Shore wisht I had my sweetie here
A-layin' by my side,
A-layin' by my side.

M'gal, she up and left me,
I 'spect she's gone to stay —
She lit outta here a-runnin'
With a sonofabitch from Io-way,
With a sonofabitch from Io-way.

I'm a lone man, a real lone man.

Old Cowboy Song

Chapter 1

IN the country down below where the little piñons grow, and it's nearly allus half a day to water, there used to stand a town, where a crick come tumblin' down, from a mesa where she surely hadn't oughter. Her streets were bright with candle light, the whole town joined a chorus, and every man in sight let his cattle drift at night just to mosey to the town of Old Dolores.

Then things kind o' spin till the sun comes up agin, like the back o' some old yaller prairie wagon, and'd show ya dim and red, mebbe half a hundred head of our saddle ponies standin', reins a-draggin'; the red mud walls, the water falls, the whole wide world before us! But the 'dobe walls are gone and the goat bells in the dawn ain't a-jinglin' in the streets of Old Dolores.

The greaser girls'd fool on the plaza in the cool, and there's one . . . I used to meet her by a willer! But I guess most any girl gives a feller's head a whirl when the same's been using saddles for a piller. The wide-eyed stars, the long cigars, the smiles that waited for us! If there's any little well down inside the gates o' Hell, I know the boys have named it Old Dolores.[1]

Must have been some town!

I've seen it like that night after night, rising from the twisting cigarette smoke of a nightclub into the spotlight's beam, to become juniper smoke from those fires of long ago. The blackest nights passed quicker when I could sing of Old Dolores. Its melody pulled me out of those boozy, cloistered places and transported me to a spot overlooking the tiered mesas of the Southwest. The dream stretched on and on as my hunger grew to see it, until finally, after seven years of wondering, first about the author, then about the location, I left New

York in the early spring of 1960 and headed homeward to find the ghosts of Old Dolores.

In a way, I fancied myself a kind of Twentieth Century renegade, not quite the likes of my fellow man, not one who sought the goals of the masses, or one who sang as other singers do, for fame and bunches of money. I'd had the opportunity to do that but had shucked it for reasons I considered more important to the care and feeding of my soul. Searching for a place like Old Dolores was part of it.

I knew why Dolores called. A deep root of my heritage wanted to know the soil of that place, wanted to find why the town lived no more. In short, what had been so great about Old Dolores that after nearly one hundred and fifty years she lived on in song?

It's a sure thing she'd never have been heard from otherwise.

A-ll set! Go ahead!
Trailin' toward the West
Till the sunset's shinin' flag is furled.
Ay, our flag's the Western skies,
Flag that drew our fathers' eyes,
Flag that leads the white man 'round the world.[2]

Eighty years before I began my own search for the songs of the West, Shorty Mac's Pa began his. He kidney-packed his few belongings behind the saddle, stuck his foot in the stirrup, grabbed hair and swung himself up, elevating his spirit as well as his seat. Spitting a black fountain of tobacco juice to leeward, he picked up the reins, blew a soft whistle thru his teeth and said, "Let's go, Amigo." With shoulders relaxed, he made a bobbing bud of his head on the stem of his neck, wove his spine to the rhythm of the horse's gait, leaned in the stirrup to steer, or neck reined. For speed he pressed his knees against the horse's sides. For flight he jabbed in the rowels.

He wasn't pressed for time . . . in 1879.

Riding along he sniffed the smells of earth, or animals, his own sweat and tobacco, alert to sounds, using trails that had been there since his hairy ancestors swung down from the trees — animal trails. Preferring the easiest routes, the fewest fords, these animals found a way over prairies, through passes, around the humps, bumps and sawteeth of an uncompromising land. When the Indian took over the paths, he only creased them deeper, and maybe added a few lesser ones with his bare and moccasined feet. To the more accessible of these, red and white man added the horse, and by the time our pioneer rolled this way, so well defined were the existing trails, going along within a few miles of each other, that an extra wagon wheel turned them to roads. Where wagon, trapper and horse trails stopped, prospector's mule, burro and plodding boot continued until there was no place from peak to salt flat that some trace of man could not be found.

Deeply the buffalo trod it
Beating it barren as brass!
Now the soft rain-fingers sod it,

Green to the crest of the pass.
Backward it slopes into history!
Forward it lifts into mystery.
    Here is but wind in the grass.

Quick or the swift seasons fade it!
    Look on his works while they show.
This is the bison. He made it.
    Thus say the old ones who know.
This is the bison — a-pondering,
Vague as the prairie wind wandering
    Over the green or the snow.[3]

They entered a new-leafed forest, cool and dim. The horse swung his head
down and ripped off a mouthful of sweet grass. Shorty Mac's Pa stuck out his
hand, ripped off fresh leaves and chawed on the stems. Out of the tree tunnel
across a field of young weeds, over a hill, down to a lake filled with the spring
freshets, rimmed with wildflowers, to the edge of a tilled field bordered by
young fruit trees — a farm in the Iowa back country where he might rest for
the night, maybe work a day or so for some grub, then ride on till he connected
with the trail herd. A little farther west he'd start riding the chuck line.

Upon the old-time ranches there was always table space
    For any cowboy stranger droppin' in.
They never tried to judge him by the whiskers on his face,
    Nor make him state his attitude toward sin.

They set him down to share their chuck, they gave his horse a feed.
    What brought him there they didn't ask to know.
They just showed hospitality in every word and deed.
    They never asked him when he aimed to go.

He might not be a cowhand of the rangeland's very best,
    But if he showed he wasn't scared of sweat,
Nobody took exception to his stayin' as a guest,
    Nor grudged him any vittles that he et.

Sometimes a stranger cowboy only aimed to stay the night,
    To rest himself and horse while driftin' through,
But found the boss could use a hand, he liked the work all right,
    So wound up ridin' there a year or two.

The old-time western cowfolks never shut a stranger out
    In summer's balm or blizzard's wintry storm.
Their ways was rough, their gizzards tough — but don't you ever doubt —
    This world has known few hearts that was as warm![4]

Most cowboys only rode chuck in the lean season — winter — when they'd
been laid off after fall roundup and had spent most of their money that first
weekend in town, lost it at the tables, or to some pretty girl. Good thing for
Shorty Mac, his old man, and others like them, that line camp cooks kept coffee

3

and beans on the fire, that horse feed and a spare bunk could be found at ranches from Texas to Montana — especially around Christmas when a fellow felt like a lonesome polecat eatin' rat tails. It was called Good Ol' Western Hospitality, and there wasn't supposed to be any of it east of the Missouri.

"An' sometimes there wasn't some of it *west* of the Mizzou neither," Pa told Shorty Mac. "Summa them bunks was scabby with lice and bed ticks, the coffee like watered-down skunk piss. And don't let 'um tell you nobody never had to pay fer a meal out West, cuz it's a plum ballface lie! Them nesters, lots of 'em, lived like scarecrows and looked like 'em. Oh, there wasn't no *ranches* let you go hungry, but them psalm-singin' sodbustin', goatfaced, prayer-bayin' nesters! — mean ol' bastards, starved their animals and beat their kids an' made a cowpoke work slave labor for three hours b'fore they give up a chunk of meat tough enough to sole a boot!"

> 'Twas in one of them "Come in Stranger," joints,
>   That sure does lots of good,
> Where they give you a bed and a bowl of soup
>   For sawin' a cord of wood,
>
> When the hoss-faced guy and his Infinite
>   Was all that we got to chew,
> While waitin' the chicory, beans and pork,
>   And with nothin' else to do
>
> But to listen to one fed stomach talk
>   About the future of our souls;
> And he knew we dassent to sass him back
>   Or we'd lost our breakfast roll.[5]

With nothing but rolling hills and little brooks to cross, Shorty Mac's Pa made twenty-five miles that day.

I packed half a house in the trunk of Mr. Ford's first T-Bird, crawled into a plush seat under a chrome wheel, turned a key, took a slug of hot coffee from a thermos, pushed the throttle and said, "Let's go, Thunder."

I felt pressed for time . . . in 1960.

Can't say why, other than it seems to be a reflex condition like those spots on your knees and elbows that only have to be pressured slightly to react. I whizzed along the ironed-out asphalt like one of millions of bubbles in a black artery, isolated in my cell, bored with the mechanical thing, elevated by a kind of power status, over no vestige of Pa's former trail — too fast, man, too goddam fast — the only likeness: we both ride the chuck line.

> I'm ridin' the chuck-line this winter;
>   The bread-line they call it in town —
> But it ain't so onpleasant out this way;
>   Folks treat a man right when he's down;
> The latchstring is out at the cabins,
>   And every man makes the friend's sign;

4

> The chuck-line ain't bad in the Westland —
> In fact I'm a-thinkin' it's fine.[6]

Furthermore, I can ride it in any season. Friends are scattered everywhere ready to offer me some of that good Ol' Western Hospitality. If they don't I can always spend it in one of those wayside cells, airless and eyeless with a central air conditioning unit that smells of everybody's stale tobacco and booze. And I can drink mid-western skunk piss that passes for coffee and pay eighteen dollars the night for it just because I like it so much.

I made seven hundred and sixty miles my first day; coagulating with the other bubbles where the pulse-beats were strongest at a chuckline stop near Gary, Indiana. I didn't see much, or smell anything but exhaust fumes; nor cook over a campfire, not even an hibachi. Black leather clouds socked in the lake and flickering thru the trees were the lights of Bethlehem . . . Steel. But much better than sleeping in the rain.

Pa, Shorty Mac and I agree about sleeping in the rain. It hasn't changed much over the years even with our fancy water-repellent equipment. "One side of the sky'll turn black and a wind'll come up blowing off your tarpaulin, tossin' a cyclone of sand down yer neck. B'fore you can grab and secure the canvas, rain like glass darts punctures your dry roll bringing some mud spatters with it. The raking angle'll change, but not fer the better. It'll come down like the gutting stream from a fireman's hose and very soon you begin to feel a soggy, cold wetness, like you had the baby in bed with you and he just peed a god-dam lake! When you find there ain't no swear words yet invented to cover the situation, you either pretend you like it and git up and dance in the stuff or roll up in a wet ball and shiver out the night — there ain't no ignorin' it, it won't go away," Shorty Mac grumbled.

> Ev'rybody blue an' sour!
>   Not a sign o' sun in sight!
> Jest a steady, soakin' shower
>   When we ride to camp at night!
> Blankets sozzled, wet an' mussy;
>   Tarps all damp an' feelin' strange!
> Ev'ry puncher mad an' cussy!
>   Hopin' mornin' brings a change![7]

In the early fifties there weren't many turnpikes or Interstate highways, so I drove the little country roads from New York to L.A. and Maine to Miami. They were slow-going, narrow, and truthfully not very interesting — beaded with little *bergs, tons, Frts, Flls,* and *villes* — until you got west of Omaha and the Missouri where things began to open up. There are still some winding ribbons flung against the earth in gentle coils and folds, up the sides of mountains, dropped into canyons and stretched across barren deserts drying in the sun, but you have to know where the Interstate has hacked them off or you'll get plumb lost.

> And the little roads laugh at the straight-laced highway,
> Dreary in its pride and its bonds of wire fence:

5

Each roving saddle trail, wagon track, and byway —
"Come-a-gypsying," it calls. "Leave your smug pretense."[8]

Possibly I stretch a point to juxtapose my trips home, or westward, with those of the cowboy eighty years ago, but we left the eastern, more congested part of the country for the same reasons, and though he'd never recognize it now, we did cross the same continent.

THE WESTERN PLAINS*

Each night in my dreams
Somehow it seems
That I am back where I was born.
I'm just a country hick
From the country sticks,
And that's where I belong.
Now all your city life
And all your city ways
Are drivin' me insane —
I want to be alone
Where I feel at home,
Back on the Western Plains.

I want to drink my java
From an old tin can
While the moon is riding high.
I want to hear the call
Of the whippoorwill
I want to hear them coyotes cry!
I want to feel a saddled horse
Between my legs
Just ridin' him out on the range,
Just to kick him in the side,
Make him show his step with pride,
Back on the Western Plains.

I want to hear the thunder
As it booms and rolls
I want to feel the rain in my face,
Just a thousand miles
From your city life
Drawin' a cowhand's wage.
I want to ride the range
Beneath the stars above
With the cold moon shinin' down,
I want to cook my grub
Over cactus coals
Fifty miles from town.

Chorus:
Oh-lee-oh-lay-de-o
Oh-lee-oh-lay-de-o
Oh-lee-oh-lay-de-yodel-lay-de-ay-de-oo.

Shorty Mac's Pa was seven years old when the potato famine caused his family to leave Ireland and land on the eastern shore of North America. From that day on his one wiggling ambition was to get out West. He made it in 1859. Three times after that he'd tried going back East to see his parents, but he couldn't get out quick enough.

> New York's a human round-up
> Uv fun an' fuss an' care,
> But I'm 'er — suffercatin' —
> I want the broad blue air!
> I hate the shows of cities,
> They goes ag'in my youth;
> I lov' the tarnal mountains
> Wot pints to God an' Truth![9]

They called him a drifter, said his language was coarse, his manner rough, even implied he was some kind of outlaw, and started belting him with that religious stuff he's been weaned on. The more they talked the more ridiculous it sounded to a man whose day began and ended in plain sight of the Lord's wonders and whose conversation ranged from a little jangle with the Devil to a talk with the Big Boss up yonder. Not any use to argue with them. He had his own ways of looking at the Bible now, and they were somewhat different than he'd been taught. All over the East and Midwest were fanatic sects that had flowered, died, re-seeded and entrenched, growing weeds in Victorian soil, fighting among themselves for the rain of souls. And worse, trailing it with them in the wagons West like some bad-tasting medicine for freedom lovers. The rowdy, individualistic cowboys like Shorty Mac's Pa, who'd rid a fer piece for his kind of life, didn't make a clean getaway. The puritanical aggregate turns up in their songs and poems with a quick pang of conscience:

> It was there I took to drinking,
> I sinned both night and day,
> And there within my bosom
> A feeble voice did say . . .[10]

or maudlin homesickness:

> I loved the old farm and its gnarled apple trees,
> The daisies and buttercups there;
> Then life was all music and flowers and bees,
> For I dwelt amid castles of air . . .[11]

in his attitude toward the purity of womanhood:

> She is fairer than the flowers
> That dream of tropic seas,

7

> She is purer than the zephyrs
> That woo the orange trees . . .[12]

and concern for his reception in heaven:

> Just keep an eye on all that's done and said,
> Just right me sometimes when I turn aside,
> And lead me on the long dim trail ahead
> That stretches upward toward the Great Divide.[13]

I never knew Shorty Mac's Pa. He died in 1912, but Shorty said, "He never sung them sappy songs. He sung *Chisholm Trail* 'n *The Cowboy's Lament* 'n *I'm a Rambler, I'm a Gambler*. Fer sadders he'd moan *Omie Wise* er *Pretty Polly* er *Bury Me Not on the Lone Prairie*. On the trail it was *Ten Thousand Cattle*, er *Night Herding Song*, and lotsa Irish lullabies." Mighty heady verses in some of those originals. Still, Shorty Mac was a gentleman, downright chivalrous around women. He had a strong basic religion that wasn't to be messed with, and he didn't just pick those codes out of thin air. He was taught some things by his Pa, who was going through important changes at the time his music was taking root in the West.

Running briefly back over the cowboy's history, we'll find that he and his songs went through four — make that five counting the modern — distinct periods. The first songs were borrowed from other cultures and gave no hint of his heroics. He sang a mournful sea song to keep his longhorns from getting all het up. What the words said didn't matter, but neither did they seem out of place in a sea of prairie grass. When he got around to making changes, little poetic genius was required to alter *The Ocean Burial:*

> "She hath been in my dreams." . . . his voice failed there.
> They paid no heed to his dying prayer.
> They lowered him over the vessel's side,
> Above him rolled the cold, cold tide.

to *The Dying Cowboy:*

> "O bury me not." . . . and his voice failed there,
> But we took no heed of his dying prayer.
> In a narrow grave just six by three
> We buried him there on the lone prairie.

The ocean song wasn't particularly old. It's said to have been written around 1839 in New York by a Congregationalist minister and set to music in 1850.[14] The tune was not the one the cowboys used; theirs was Irish. *I'm a Rambler, I'm a Gambler,** for instance, is pure Gaelic in character; Gaelic, stemming from Moorish, which fed Spanish, and Spanish which (as we will see later) completes a cycle at the Mexican border in the mid-eighteen hundreds.

> I'm a rambler, I'm a gambler
> I'm a long way from home.
> If the people they don't like me
> Let 'um leave me alone.

8

Oh, it's dark and it's rainin'
And the moon gives no light;
My pony, he won't travel
This dark road at night.

Unsaddle your pony
And feed him some hay,
Then come sit here beside me
For as long as you'll stay.

My pony, he ain't hungry,
And he won't eat your hay;
I am bound for Wyoming
He can graze on the way.

When you get to Wyoming
A letter you'll see —
If you get into trouble
Just you write and tell me.

I once had a sweetheart
Her age was nineteen;
She was the flower of Belton
And the rose of Saline.

But her parents was against me
Now she is the same;
If I'm writ in your book, love,
Just you blot out my name.

I'm a rambler, I'm a gambler
I'm a long way from home,
If the people they don't like me
Let 'em leave me alone.

The second phase came when the cowboy's life was drastically changed.
When the land he had conquered began to have value for things with roots, the nesters and sodbusters came to fence him out of it. Not only did he lose his job, he lost the need to perform his role of the first white man to inhabit the *whole* Western wilderness, not just isolated forts and trading posts. This put him uptight psychologically. He had departed the conventional pattern when he left the East, or his homeland; he now departed from it harder trying to maintain a hold on what he considered to be his territory. Naturally, he became a target. Newspapers and pulps began making gross exaggerations, calling him everything except what he was, a hard-working stiff with a lust for life in open country. Those doing the writing had never seen a cowboy and couldn't possibly know the sheer drudgery of his task. Yet from these very newsmen, songs (printed now, not word-of-mouth) began to radiate. Cowboys didn't have time to sit around the campfire after riding herd all day and say, "Hey, any you fellers got a pencil? I wanna write a folk song." Here and now was their concern; the fact

that it rhymed with *steer* and *cow* was immaterial. Nor was the range abundant with poets who might defend their way of life — at least, not then.

Poems turned songs, like *Lolita, Lavender Cowboy,* and *Dobe Bill,* are by no means inferior as far as songs go, but misrepresentational as far as cowboys went. Such material continued to be written from then on by more or less the same class of people, the age-of-sentimentality dreamers, not the doers. They made him the hero of the stampede, the outrider, wizard of the six-gun and reata, Robin Hood, rebel and misfit; an image hard to live down, and many of them didn't try. The epic that follows is typical of the "paper hero." It sounds like a three-reel western of the Hoot Gibson era, stuck together with gobs of sentimental glue. Two-Gun Blake's a scoundrel, a snake and a cur instead of a sonofabitch, a rat and a bastard: he slaps the Killer instead of belting him in the chops. Dobe's an international cowboy: he's got a Greek gun, an Indian horse, and a Mexican hat, and you can always point to the leetle feller and say, "Thar goes a hombre who loves his hoss . . . dearly!"

DOBE BILL*

Dobe Bill he come a-ridin' from the canyon in the glow
Of a quiet summer evenin' from the town of Angelo
Ridin' easy on the pinto that he dearly loved to straddle,
With a six-gun and sombrero that was wider than his saddle.

And he's hummin' as he's ridin' of a simple little song
It's a rumblin' through the cactus as he's gallopin' along.
"I'm a hootin'-shootin' demon, and I has my little fun
With my pinto called Apache, and Adolphus, that's my gun!"

Straight to Santa Fe he drifted and he mills around the town,
Sorta gettin' of his bearin's while he pours his likker down.
And he's watchin', always watchin' every hombre in the place
Like he's mebbe sorta lookin' for a certain hombre's face.

Then one night he saunters, careless, to the place of Monte Sam
And he does a little playin', like he doesn't give a damn,
All at once it's still and quiet like a calm before a blow
And the crowd is tense and nervous and the playin's
    mighty slow.

At the bar a man is standin', feared wherever he is known;
Two-Gun Blake, the Pecos Killer with assurance all his own.
Then the eyes of Blake the Killer catch the glance of Dobe Bill
And they hold each one the other with the steel of looks that kill.

Walkin' calmly toward the Killer, Bill advanced with steady pace.
Then he grinned, and quick as lightnin' slapped him squarely
    in the face.
"Shoot, you snake," he whispered hoarsely, "Draw! you lily-
    livered cur!
You was always strong for killin', now I'm here to shoot for her!"

10

Some there was claimed they saw it as the Killer tried to draw,
But no one knows for certain just exactly what they saw.
And the man who stood there lookin' at the killer as he lay,
Murmured, "Nell, I kept my promise, I have made the
    scoundrel pay!"

Dobe Bill he went a ridin' from the town of Santa Fe
Of a quiet Sunday mornin', goin' happy on his way,
Ridin' happy on the pinto that he dearly loved to straddle,
With a six-gun and sombrero that was wider than his saddle.

And he's hummin' as he's goin' of a simple little song
That's a-boomin' through the cactus as he's gallopin' along,
"I'm a-goin' down the valley, through the mesquite and
    the sand.
I'm a-rarin'-flarin' Bucko, not afraid to play my hand.
I'm a-hootin'-shootin' demon, and I has my little fun,
With my pinto called Apache, and Adolphus — that's my gun!"

In 1874 some dude had to go invent barbed wire. As this stuff unwound, mile after mile off the spools, Mr. Cowboy's usefulness as a night nurse ended. A short twelve years later his trail-herding days shuffled to a stop. The long drives from Texas to Montana were over. In their place railroads spread like lights in series, dashing across the continent, carrying the cattle he once had driven.

The cowboy's third and most productive musical period begins here. After the fences he had time to do things beside rope cattle, brand, wrangle horses, de-horn steers, and de-ball bulls. He discovered talents he didn't know he had. The bunkhouse replaced the trail camp and in it such items as a fiddle, a jew's harp, banjo, mouth-organ (called a French harp then), a concertina, and even a guitar could be found. He started putting down words about how things *used* to be, and you know what that means — it means he forgot a lot of the bad stuff and waxed nostalgic about the nearly insignificant. No longer isolated, this cowboy caught a dose of creeping civilization and began believing his press. He even went out and did some of those things just to live up to the image.

He composed a lot of sentimental garbage, but along with it came the finest song-poems he ever produced, and they came from first-hand knowledge, not some hack's daydream. Add to these the cowboy's innate sense of the ridiculous, his dry humor, his picturesque manner of expression, and you have some of the best folk songs in the world.

Most of them never saw print.

His unique vernacular was often too blue for printer's ink, and these songs "never went anywhere," as we say in the trade, except in a circulatory motion among the cowhands themselves. Not that it mattered. He didn't like singing for dudes anyway. The good songs were passed from the Canadian border to Mexico; a copyright being about as common as chocolate sauce on a fried egg. They covered his religion, his sex life, his trade, his frustrations, his love affairs, his tricks, his adventures, and his rank opinion of outsiders. They were written by cowboys who'd gotten an education in the East, by those who'd no education

11

but the range, by Eastern men who became Westerners forever, by English, Scots, Irish, Blacks, the lot, but they had one thing in common — an abiding love of, and devotion to, the West.

"He'll do to ride the river with!"
(Bridging the years between,
Men shall use those words again —
And wonder what they mean.)[15]

Chapter 2

WHERE DID I FIRST HEAR *Old Dolores?*

We sat on the floor around the fireplace at my mother's house in Tucson, 1953, I think, with drinks and guitars, recorders and harmonica. We were having a "hoot," which is what we called such get-togethers in those days. A kind of song-trading affair.

Singing Sam Agins, a friend who sings at dude ranches there during the winter, sat with crutches beside him, his huge shoulders and arms bent into a Martin Dreadnought guitar, strumming.

"Katie," he said, "heard a helluva song this summer — your kinda song. I'll make you a trade for *Ten Thousand Goddam Cattle.*"

"Oh, you will, eh? Let's hear it first. I don't trade that one off for just any old thing."

When the last notes of *Old Dolores* had died away, I broke a spellbound silence, not with the usual "Where'd you get it?" but with "Where *is* it?"

"Who knows? Mexico, I guess. I got the song from some kids who were herding sheep near Estes Park, Colorado. Hauled my tape recorder outta the van and taped them on the spot b'fore they could get away."

If any more information was offered about the song that night, I don't remember — other than opinions from the group about its ring of authenticity. I know I sang it through with Sam three times; from then on knew it letter perfect. At some later date we began pulling the song apart for clues. Both decided it was the Dolores south of the Mexican border in Sonora. One of the mission towns in Father Kino's chain — first line told us that, *In the country down below where the little piñons grow,* but a year or so later, I checked it out and there were no piñons. There wasn't any *red mud* either, and no *whole wide world before us,* to say nothing of the *crick.* I hunted Sam up after that foray south of the border and told him we'd been barking up the wrong horse.

"I got a lead while you were back east in the saltmines," he told me. "A professor of folklore at the University of Colorado in Boulder, Ben Gray Lumpkin, says the dean of the law school there wrote it."

"Dean of the law school! The hell you say — that song was written by a cowboy, ain't nobody going to tell me different."

"Well, maybe he was a cowboy before he was a dean."

"Not impossible, but where's the town? Has to be at the four or five thousand foot level to have piñons."

Sam laughed at me. "Why the hell don't you write the professor and quit guessing? The dean ought to know where the place is he's writin' about — 'course he coulda made it up."

"No, he didn't make it up! That's no imaginary town, it's real."

"Okay, it's a real town, it's five thousand feet elevation, it's near the border and it was writ by a cowboy-dean."

And that's the way we left it.

> Westward from the greener places
>   Where the rivers glint and twine
> Stretch the gold-and-purple spaces
>   Of the country that is mine;
> And to the lilac Rockies lifting
>   Toward the deeper blue above,
> There is neither flaw nor shifting
>   In the title of my love.[16]

Sun was high, spring bustin' everywhere, birds singing, and a good trail allowed as how Pa didn't have to watch the horse's every footfall. Besides, Pa McGinnis had been this way before. He pulled a new sack of Bull Durham from his vest pocket, from under the trademark extricated a coupon and tucked it away for safe keeping. From another pocket he took a palm-sized book about a quarter inch thick — one he had redeemed with other coupons — a classic. Down its side was lettered SHAKESPEARE and across the front, *Macbeth.* By the time he got to Ogallala he'd be able to quote near half of it, plus many more pages from a couple dozen such books he carried in his rig. Him and other boys would have contests who could quote the most from memory. On night herd he'd have to keep himself from laughin' out loud because it struck him so all-fired ridiculous to be riding around spouting the profound words of one of the greatest authors ever born, to a bunch of the dumbest critters that ever lived. (E. Haldeman Julius's *Little Blue Books*[17] made many a cowpoke literate!) Pa humphed to himself. This was for sure his last trip back East; not even the extra pay he got for nursing the steer shipment to Chicago would coax him to go again. Those people back there, raised on prunes and proverbs, thought he was illiterate just because he was a working cowhand. Hell, he could outquote the lot of 'em, and not just Shakespeare, but Milton and Homer and

14

Wordsworth and Burns, and lots more. And great long passages from the Bible when and if he had a mind to.

> Folks say we got no morals — that they all fell in the soup;
> And no conscience — so the would-be goodies say.
> And perhaps our good intentions did just up and
>   flew the coop,
> While we stood around and watched 'em fade away.

> But there's one thing that we're lovin' more than
>   money, grub, or booze,
> Or even decent folks what speaks us fair,
> And that's the grand old privilege to chuck our
>   luck and choose
> Any road at any time for anywhere.[18]

Pa was only one of the Irish immigrants who poured into the country during the nineteenth century. They worked on railroads, planted potatoes, fought in saloons, mined and sang. Pa went west to the Union Pacific where he hired out as a terrier — *And drill, ye terriers, drill!* — joined in common labor with every nationality but the indigene. The trans-continental U&P was completed at Promontory Point in northern Utah in 1869; simultaneously and conveniently history arranged for the big herds to be gathered in Texas and Mexico and walked north as far as the Canadian border. The Irisher, fresh out of a job, left hammer, pick and drill for reata, spurs and chaps, learned to ride a horse, drove cattle, did his fighting on the plains, and kept right on singing about it.

This is not to say that only the Irish herded cows, worked on railroads and sang, but it is to point out that they were a flexible lot while adapting to a country unlike theirs in any way. The Cornish, Welsh, Chinese and German kept their language, held to tradition, while the Irish cowboy not only changed the names of places in Ireland to the new towns in the West (i.e. "the flower of *Belton*, the rose of *Saline*" in *I'm a Rambler, I'm a Gambler*) but slowed his jigs to keep pace with the lazy habits of a cow. On night herd he hummed lullabies or sentimental songs of the times — many of those Irish as well. Now and then the blues crept into a lyric from the Negro drovers — more than history credits; about one in every eight — but in spite of that influence, the music stayed Irish in character.

Shorty Mac said his Pa sang *The Cowboy's Lament*, originally an Irish jig of the eighteeenth century, but he didn't let it go at that; he added: "After them ol' boys lost several hundred head to stompedes they smartened up one night and decided, 'Sa-a-a-y, we gotta slow that goddam song down!' In so doin' they got a nice lullaby, but the old words was so undelicate and sounded so turrible at that tempo — they was about a pore bloke with a venereal disease, ya know — that they had t'think up some new ones." It's true. And there were several versions of this venerable venereal song even then. Some for boys: *As I Walked Out Past Tom Sherman's Barroom* and *The Poor Unfortunate Rake*. Some for girls: *The Bad Girl* and *A Young Girl Cut Down In Her Prime*. They were all pretty sad doses, no matter what side you were on.

15

The spring days of Pa's ride west passed pleasantly. He'd average maybe twenty-five miles each day, depending on the amount of rain, the number of people he'd meet on the trail, the hospitality of the chuck line, and depending too, on the towns he passed through. In those days coming to a settlement was an event! Unless a guy was on the run, he didn't just whip through at a high gallop with his eyes shut. He needed that town.

Ogallala for instance.

Ogallala on the South Platte. A town with a history bloodier than a stuck boar! The Dodge City-Western and Oregon trails converged here, and when the cowboys hit town they hit her so hard she had to rebuild. Several times. There were the girls and the music and the whiskey, the well-done steaks, the new clothes, a bath and meals at a *table*. The streets rolled up their dust around the land office, the swindler, the fighter and freighter, the gunslinger, gambler and rustler, preacher and outlaw, all milling, indistinguishable in the noise and bustle, until nobody knew which was which when a gun fired. And nobody stayed to find out. When the dust of the deed settled, it settled on the cowboys because there were more of them, they were drunker, and without a horse under them they didn't react quick.

THE RUSTLER*

We found his smokin' brandin' fire
In a holler dark and dim,
And we follered his faint and lonesome tracks
All the way to the mesa's rim.
We rode through the cool of a canyon's gloom,
Then over the range, then down,
And the foam flew hot from our swingin' reins
As we loped to the border town.

All grey in the dusk at the hitchin' rail
There loomed his lean cayuse.
The flanks was streaked with dirt and sweat,
The reins was a hangin' loose.
The Rustler stood at the lamplit bar
All framed in a golden glow,
And someone sang to the silver strings
In the moonlit patio.

He stared us down as we all came in
Then slammed his glass down on the bar.
A Spanish girl came clickin' her heels
To the beat of a wild guitar.
Her ruby lips were set in a smile
As she twirled in her dance near the flame.
A crash! and the room was dark and still
Her whisper said his name.

We drew our guns in the darkness there
Shootin' fire left and right,

16

Then we heard the thud of a pony's stride
As it galloped away in the night.
A lamp went up in the 'dobe bar
And a shadow lay on the sill.
We saw an arm and an upturned face,
Girlish, and white, and still.

All grey in the dusk at the hitchin' rail,
There loomed his lean cayuse.
The flanks all streaked with dirt and sweat,
And the reins still a-hangin' loose.
But no Rustler stood at the lamplit bar
All framed in the golden glow,
And no one sang to the silver strings
In the moonlit patio.

In Ogallala's noise and dust, Shorty Mac's Pa stopped to get his horse shod, to eat something besides camp beans and stew, to wait for the trail boss he'd be working for, and to see some unguarded women and down a little red eye. But mostly he just wanted to walk around town, see the sights of what he called "not all that civilized," and *talk* to the kind of people who gave him the kind of answers he wanted to hear. More than likely it took Pa the better part of five weeks to get from Chicago to Ogallala. The cows, the cowboys and trail boss would all rest and re-supply there for two weeks, then go north to the Yellowstone. On the way back to Texas his stop-over might not be so gentle.

We acquired our hasty temper from our friend,
    the centipede.
From the rattlesnake we learnt to guard our rights.
We have gathered fightin' pointers from the famous
    bronco steed
And the bobcat teached us reppertee that bites.
So when some high-collared heerin' jeered the garb
    that I was wearin'
'Twasn't long till we had got where talkin' ends,
And he et his illbred chat, with a sauce of derby hat,
While my merry pardners entertained his friends.

Sing 'er out, my buckeroos! Let the desert hear the news.
Tell the stars the way we rubbed the haughty down.
We're the fiercest wolves a-prowlin' and it's just our
    night for howlin'
When we're ridin' up the rocky trail from town.[19]

Wasn't too many years after that, in the 1880s, that the "cleanup crews" in their Righteous Wagons filed through the dusty streets, single-tree to tailgate, and laid decency, law and order, and The Word of the Lord on Ogallala. Other towns that dotted the cattle trails got the same white-washing.

17

Town that was fiery and careless and Spanish,
　　Boy that was wiry and wayward and glad —
Over the border to limbo they vanished;
　　Progress and order decreed they were bad.

Latigo Town, ay, Latigo Town,
　　Pursy with culture and civic renown,
Never censorious progress can banish
　　Dreams of the glorious youth that we had![20]

It takes me two days to cover Pa's five weeks of trail through Illinois and Iowa.
　　Beyond there the short-grass country begins — grasses that feed cattle. They alternate with waving wheat and space, a thing we could see very little of back in the folded hills of hog farm country. The winding road has straightened. Nebraska, as flat as an old maid's chest, her stark white grain elevators teething the horizon, basks languidly in the sun as she yawns toward the Great Divide. Each mile unrolls endless bolts of grain, rippling with the westerlies, seeming to be in flight, but hemstitched to earth inside neat rows of fenceposts.

I rode across a valley range
　　I hadn't seen for years.
The trail was all so spoilt and strange
　　It nearly fetched the tears.
I had to let ten fences down
And each new line would make me frown
　　And hum a mournin' song.

Oh, it's squeak! squeak! squeak!
　　Here 'em stretchin' of the wire!
The nester brand is on the land;
　　I reckon I'll retire,
While progress toots her brassy horn
　　And makes her motor buzz,
I thank the Lord I wasn't born
　　No later than I was.[21]

A thick meander of tall fresh green appears off to the right as I curve gently into the South Platte. Under a high noon sun we find a little town stretched out like the long belly of a lazy cat taking a siesta. Its houses are spaced wide, its trees the color of trees that get less water and more sun. False store fronts rise above sheltered sidewalks, giving the place a western look, a kind of scattered-on-the-air appearance when heat waves rise and shimmer through it. The air is light and dryer than it has been up to now, and there is no tunnel of green shade over Main Street. The streets are white and glittering. Everything is very still. Only the tires hum a little as we roll out the west end of town and I turn around to peer at the sign giving the name of this place which I haven't noticed coming in.
　　It's OGALLALA!

18

This town was rougher than a tall stud at a trot? Shorty Mac's Pa would have been a mite upset.

> Sing 'er out, my bold coyotes! leather fists and
> leather throats,
> For we wear the brand of Ishm'el like a crown.
> We're sons o' desolation, we're the outlaws
> of creation —
> Eeyow! a-ridin' up the rocky trail from town![22]

Westward from the South Platte River valley the land rises slowly, insistently as if toward some great climax — heard more in the motor than seen with the eye. Each dip unfolds to yet a higher plain, monotonously, until after we've stopped thinking about it, and entirely without warning . . .

There they are!

The Rockies. The one physical feature that more than any other makes Westerners different from Easterners. Not better, or wiser, or more sensitive, just different. If we are born and raised west of these monsters, the land tends to form us before we have the chance to reform the land. Beyond here is a marked change. Flatlanders become mountain men, farms become ranches, valleys drop away to gorges, there are fewer questions and half as many answers; rivers aren't so wet, lakes are mostly dry. And on the westward side folks seem more secure in the knowledge of who and what they really are, rather than what a social system has named them.

> South, where the sullen black mountains guard
> Limitless, shimmering lands of the sun,
> Over blinding trails where the hoofs rang hard,
> Laughing or cursing, we rode and won.
> Drunk with the virgin white fire of you,
> Hotter than thirst was desire of you;
> Straight in our faces you burned your brand,
> Marking your chosen ones, young, young, land.[23]

Stopping at the side of the road, I get out to watch a deep purple shadow chew up the valley as the sun drops toward the peaks fifty miles away. A soft but steady wind rises and combs the hill where I stand, bringing smells of earth, dust, and rain. Three thunder showers hang over the long chain of ranges falling beneath billowing sunlit cumulus like old men's whispy gray beards trailing on Colorado Springs, Denver and Loveland.

> They tell me there is countries where there ain't no purple hills
> And every hoss is white or black or bay,
> Where colors is dependable, and evenin' never spills
> Paint buckets from the sun through shadders gray.
> Old Pinto pony, you and me ,the desert and the West,
> Are kinder splotched with colors I'll admit,
> But dang our pinto souls, old boy, we love each other best,
> And if you ask me why, I guess that's it![24]

19

One thing the Pulaski Skyway and the belch and upchuck of Newark and Manhattan gave me was a view from the dump, so to speak — a vantage point where I could view the West without vertigo and hear from its harshest critics, learned or otherwise, what was the matter with us out here. Said critics told me that the *real* America, the life blood, the creative guts of America, was in the cultural hub of New York City. That "out west" was only closed-mindedness, dog-in-the-mangerism and ostriching. That cowboys were a fake and cattle ranches a dying form of feudalism.

Well, goddam!

I've got a strong sense of place, and that stung. Of course they put me on the defensive, but they also made me realize I was ignoring an important part of my heritage — the songs I'd called "corny" and the way of life I'd put down as "unsophisticated." And it seemed to me, the criticizers (few of them had ever *lived* in the West, none of them born there) had left something out. Isn't it important what these mountains *do* to you? How they make you feel?

Small. Very small. Even seen from a plane they're formidable. They look mean sometimes, and mysterious. They're cruel and impersonal and treacherous, until we get to know them a little, learn how to survive in them. They can be strong and protective and peaceful. They can mould a person, or kill him. They're a way of life. Mountain men, desert rats, miners, cattlemen, cowboys, rivermen, sheepherders. *Westerners*, they'll tell you.

Standing on this hill I think of Pa and wonder how he felt about the Rockies. The only clue he left was that he never went East again.

The sun cuts through the back of a bruised-looking cloud, throwing out Jesus rays before it sinks behind Pikes Peak. The wind turns cold, a heavy blanket of deep blue unfolds in the valley, and many lights begin to fleck the nothingness so I know it isn't nothingness.

Cowboy, did you see *one* light when you dismounted on this grassy hill?

> One time way back where the year marks fade,
>   God said: "I see I must lose my West,
> The prettiest part of the world I made,
>   The place where I've always come to rest,
> For White Man grows till he fights for bread
> And he begs and prays for a chance to spread.
>
> Yet I won't give him all of my last retreat;
>   I'll help him fight his long trail through,
> But I'll keep some land from his field and street
>   The way it was when the world was new.
> He'll cry for it all, for that's his way.
> And yet he may understand some day."
>
> [Man] flung out his barb-wire fences wide
>   And plowed up the ground where the grass was high.
> He stripped off the trees from the mountain side
>   And ground out his ore where the streams ran by,
> Till at last came the cities, with smoke and roar,
>   And the White Man was feelin' at home once more.[25]

The Rockies, huge lumbering beasts with white blankets on their humps, move along beside us in the moonlight, scattering the cold neons of Colorado Springs under their feet. I smell the promise of high mountain air through the open window and feel the giants following me, leading me, West.

Chapter 3

EVERY NOW AND THEN I'm reminded that *Old Dolores* is responsible for a broken toe.

One night in Hollywood, after working on The Railroad Hour show all day, I'd hit the sack early and was asleep in minutes. The phone rang. I staggered out of bed in pitch dark, slammed into the metal leg of a table and busted my right number four cliff-hanger. Kee-rist! I saw all the stars in Hollywood before I hit the light switch and picked up the phone.

"Hi, honey," it said.

After the groaning and the tears, Hi-honey, a pre-med student at CU in Boulder, Colorado, told me why he'd called.

"I was in chemistry finishing a lab test when this gal who shares the table with me starts humming a song. It dawns on me after a couple verses that she's humming *your* song, *Old Dolores!* Says she learned it in her folklore class, so I got the name of the professor who. . . ."

"Jim. I've *got* the name of the professor — Ben Gray Lumpkin. Thanks for the broken toe."

"Oh, gee . . . well, I thought you didn't know where the song came from or anything . . . 'n you wanted to find out . . . 'n they're the same words, and . . . uh. Aw, honey, I'm sorry about your toe."

"And I've already written Lumpkin and received an answer. I've even written a second letter to the man he says composed the song — he lives near there in Georgetown, Colorado. Lumpkin says he's retired; he's not dean of the law school any more."

It wasn't more than a few days until I had a letter from the cowboy-dean, written in longhand with bulgy g's and y's and f's resting on the lines below, making the page afloat with bubbles:

Dear Miss Lee:

Your letter of April 27th on the song *Old Dolores* was forwarded to me during two months travels and I have just returned. I am sorry for the delay. I wrote the words to the song *Old Dolores* about 1912 and to an adaptation of *The Weaver* (or *Foggy Foggy Dew* as you suggest). I enclose a copy here. There was an article on it a year or so ago in the *Rocky Mountain News*. George A. H. Fraser, a retired lawyer in Denver, wrote an additional verse sometimes printed, as in the song book of the University Club of Denver called the *Golden Treasury*, but not in this copy I'm sending you. The song has been widely sung over radio but not as widely as another song of mine about the same date, *The Santa Fe Trail*. *Dolores* was suggested by a village, now I think deserted, in the Ortiz Mountains of New Mexico, southeast of Santa Fe. It was a well-known cattle drive point in the 1860s and 70s. A movie short was taken on the site, and I saw it in South America with Spanish words!

Sincerely,
James Grafton Rogers[26]

Pretty fancy moniker for a cowboy-dean. *New* Mexico. Not Old Mexico — written in 1912 — and the reason why the bridge sounds like the chorus of *Foggy Foggy Dew* is because it *is*. (Singing Sam and I had put the date around the turn of the century because it wasn't an all-verse song — that means it has a middle part with a different melody than the other couplets. The bridge is used in popular song construction and is a more sophisticated form.) And it was near Santa Fe in the Ortiz Mountains, up in the piñon-juniper country.

Well, *that* was pretty clear. I contacted my friend Bill Mekeel of Santa Fe asking him to get a search going for Old Dolores. Months later he hadn't found a sign of it or a sign of anyone who ever had, and it wasn't because he hadn't looked. It was a few years before I was able to get there for the first time myself, and by then Bill had resorted to the air. Every tall tree on the Ortiz range knew him, but he still couldn't find Old Dolores.

Meanwhile, I was content to sing it, picturing it as it must be; the faint image of the "dean" becoming even fainter, and the cowboy ever stronger. This trip west in Spring of 1960, laden with topographical maps, correspondence from the Britannica Library Research Service, the Museum of New Mexico, Folk Art Museum and State Historical Society, plus Professional Papers of the USGS, I didn't see how we could lose, not a whole town, anyway.

> There's a sayin' out West, and it's true, I'll allow,
> That a man who can't drink from the track of a cow
> Ain't much of a cowboy; for where punchers ride,
> There ain't babblin' brooklets on every side,
> For a waddy to drink from when joggin' around.
> He waters, like cattle, wherever it's found.[27]

Cimarron Creek lies in the Sangre de Cristo range of the Rockies' eastern slope, its bubbles flowing to the Canadian River. I lie in Cimarron Creek, buck-ass, on my way to Taos and Santa Fe to see doughBelly Price and Bill Mekeel.

A mania for dipping in creeks, rivers, oceans, ditches, any water that *moves,* stems from youthful association with drought and the stock tank. Many's the time I've had to ride drag on roundup instead of point or swing because those bums wouldn't wait for me to get out or join me like they should've — you can lead a smelly man to water but you can't make him get in.

"Where'n hell's Kitty?" yelled Buck.

"Back there splashin' round with the cow slobber in the stock tank," said Shorty Mac.

"Goddam'er, I told her she could stay the hell home if she was gonna pull that stunt again. I need a swing rider!"

"She mentioned in her delicate way, Buck, that you smelled like a skunk's posterior regions and oughta be in there with her."

"Oh, crap! I'm gatherin' a herd. I got no time t'cool my balls in that scum because some crazy female thinks I need a bath. I'm gonna smell six times worse b'fore we get this stock to the pens!" Angrily he spurred up the rocky bank.

"Maybe she'll drownd," Shorty Mac hollered gleefully.

"No such luck!" Buck snorted, disappearing in a cloud of dust over the top.

Places where you water cattle in southern Arizona aren't too often rivers, creeks, or even trickles. Sure, no self-respecting cowhand's going to bathe with the cows in some muddy waterhole, but after three days of roundup, sweating chalk moons in their shirt-pits and stiffening their collars with alkali dust and body salts, I had them figured for just plain onery. Stock tanks are made of cast iron, like miniature swimming pools with the deep end taken away, so there's no excuse they might drown — most of them can't swim — and there's only a *little* scum around the edges.

It finally took Shorty Mac to straighten me out. He said in spite of how they behaved they were a shy bunch, even though I protested he must be talking about the old crop of cowboys, not these of my day.

"Ne'er you mind that now, lissen t'me. It's born in the breed. Buck might be coaxed into that tank with you if you was *alone* with him, but wild elephants ain't a gonna drag him in with the rest of the boys standin' 'round gawkin' — and they ain't a gonna join him 'less he puts a gun on 'em. It goes a long way back. Dust and grime is part of a cowboy's pleasure, ya might say, it satisfies him to know he's done a helluva day's work and the dirt he's wearin' proves it. You ever consider how goddam much trouble it is to take a bath?"

I raised my eyebrows in mild surprise and said, snotty-like, "No trouble at all, for me."

"Why hell, you don't wear enough to wad a shotgun, and besides you gotta look at it like the breed does. S'posin' the cows watered earlier in the day and bedded down near grass; the poke had t'ride some more t' find hisself a stream. If he had to swim the herd any time during the day, he'd already had him a

24

bath. If they was bedded near water his splashin' round would crazy-up the herd — remember they wasn't like the bovines we got these days — and even on a dark night, cowboys is whiter'n spooks below the collar. In the seventies it was downright dangerous t'be takin' off your clothes, for a coupla reasons: Those fun-lovin' skunks *invented* the practical joke and there ain't nothin' so disarmin' to a man's dignity as being caught with his pants down, much less *off*. If there was hostile Indians or other evil doers about he'd be as good as daid! Gettin' the boots on is bad enough, but consider chaps, pants, socks, longhandles (summer *and* winter) shirt, vest, hat, well hell . . ."

Would you believe that from Texas to Montana, wherever cows were moved, *they* got more baths than the cowboys?

Cimarron's flow is not exactly soft and caressing this time of year, and before long its icy needles drive me out on a warm rock to dry — and think about what to do next.

It's long since I've been to Taos, or seen doughBelly Price. He's the sort of man a person could learn a new trick from every day. His youth was spent roaming around the country as if somebody stole his rudder — punching cows and banging himself up on the rodeo circuit — looking for a place to light that was softer than the ground. "The spring after I was fourteen years old," he wrote, "I had come to the conclusion that I was the best bronc rider in the world. Though no one else thought so didn't make any difference to me." Finally, doughBelly took one flip too many and landed behind a real estate desk, there to settle and sell the land he got fenced out of. On the side he writes a syndicated news column — *Wisdom & Insanity* — insanely punctuated, witty and wise. People who feel down on the world ought to go to Taos and listen to doughBelly talk; the only ailment they'll have after that is a sore stomach from laughing so hard.

Cowboy vernacular is motion, sound and vision thrown into colorful word pictures, scrambled, turned backward and upside-down, then spread out before the listener in phrases that make the most unlikely, and at the same time, the most thought-provoking comparisons. Unable to say simply, "Jake's skinny,"— "Handy's tall,"— or "Shorty laughed," he'll say:

"Jake's so skinny he can fall down through a flute and never strike a note."

"When Handy falls down he's halfway home."

"Shorty's ol' face looked like the wave on a slop bucket."

All of which relate to things he's had time to observe and save until he's ready to spring them into idiom. He will then turn extravagantly aside and seemingly ignore your reaction. His caustic observations are directed toward everything he sees and everyone he meets:

"Damn mud out there in the corral's slicker'n deer guts on a doorknob."

"This stew tastes like cut straw and road apples!"

"The liars in this gatherin' is thicker'n turds 'round a country schoolhouse."

"You're as fulla shit as last year's bird nest!"

"Ol' Duke succumbed to a throat injury and we put him to bed with a pick and shovel." (An acquaintance who was hanged)

"That nose-paint'd raise a blood blister on a rawhide boot!" (*Strong* whiskey)

25

"He's out there in the pond snuffin' up frog farts." (Swimming or bathing)
"She's got a mind like a diaper, changes it every hour." (Wimmin!)

From my warm rock beside Cimarron Creek to the village of Taos is a matter of half an hour. The "Come in, Sucker" sign on the window of his real estate office is still there, doughBelly's boots are propped on the desk and a signal of cigar smoke rises behind the magazine he's reading.

"Well, if it ain't the chantoozie come to spread joy and slobber on us little dunghillers! You just passin' through as usual, or are you gonna settle on us fer a spell?"

"As usual."

"Well, pull up yer butt and plunk 'er. You could leastways go to lunch with me. I feel like eatin' till my little navel sticks out like a pot handle. *You* look happy as a dead pig in the sunshine. What you got up your buckskin that you ain't tellin'?"

"Nothing, doughBelly, it just tickles me to sit here and listen to you."

"Well, here now, yer supposed t'drop some intelligence about the big outside world on us little dunghillers when ya come stompin' in here like this; you're 'bout as useless as fur on a snake!"

"I'll take you up on that lunch offer, doughBelly."

"Goody! I'll spring from *both* pants pockets an' your chantoozie friend, Jenny, from over t' the record shop can come too." Then remembering a former visit, he said, "You and she ever find out where that so-called Mexican song came from?"

"You mean *Firolera*. I did — don't know if Jenny knows, but it sure blew my theory all to hell." This exchange in regard to something that has mystified me for years.

I find it strange there isn't any Spanish, or Mexican, influence on the cowboy songs close to the border where I came from, or around Santa Fe, which was at one time the northern capital of New Spain. Their songs make reference in the *lyric* to gringos and greasers and tejanos, cholos and dark-eyed señoritas, and they had to hear, certainly, Mexican rhythms and chording, but they have never used those melodies or rhythms for their own words, as they did European melodies, or music hall songs. We all thought *Firolera* was a breakthrough, since it's sung in both Spanish and English.

LA FIROLERA*

Mi marido está en la cama
Y yo en la cabecera,
Con mi rosario en mi mano
Y pidiendo le a Dios que se muera.

Chorus:
Firoliro-li, Firoliro-li
Firoliro-lera,
Firoliro-la, ven aca
Firoliro-lera.

26

Ven aqui, Firoliro-li
Ven aca, Firoliro-la
Ya me amante esperando se está.

Ya mi marido se murió,
Y el Diablo se lo llevó
Ahora se estara pagado
Las patadas que me dió.

Repeat Chorus

My poor husband is sick with a fever
And I'm on my knees by his bed
With my rosary here in my hand
And I pray that he soon may be dead!

Chorus:
Firoliro-li, Firoliro-li
Firoliro-lera,
Firoliro-la, hurry up
Firoliro-lera.
Hurry up! Firoliro-li
Hurry up! Firoliro-la
Ya me amante esperando se está.

And now my poor husband has died,
And the devil has hauled him away
And I hope that he's paying with his hide
For the beatings he gave me each day.

Chorus:
(Same as above, except last line)
For my lover is waiting outside!

Jenny Wells Vincent joins us and we go to one of the local restaurants that serve tacos and Mexican beer, where I tell them that the "breakthrough" was a "teardown," as doughBelly would call it.

The song settled north of here in the San Cristobal Valley and was, I heard, sung by cowboys. That was enough for me; in a spot akin to those small pockets of the Ozarks where Elizabethan songs remained intact for centuries, it could be very old. I figured the title for a nonsense word because there is no such in Spanish.

Then the lightbulb went on.

In Toronto, Canada, of all places, a woman who had been part of my audience at the Fifth Peg one night informed me that her mother and aunt had sung that same melody with similar words in Piedmontese, a dialect of northern Italy. She quoted the refrain as "La canson verolero, vero lero lero," and said a *verolino* was a person who shifted from one place to another without forming deep roots or attachments. More recently, while living in Aspen, Colorado, an Italian ski instructor who frequented the gin mills for *après ski* serendipity, re-

27

called that the song is from an Italian operetta. And he had heard it in southern Italy as well.

So much for an authentic little Spanish *copla*.

"I don't reckon they done much face-lickin' down there across the border when them songs you're lookin' for got hatched," mused doughBelly. "When I was packin' a geetar, we sang respectable songs like *Blood on the Saddle, Strawberry Roan, I Ain't Got No Use For the Women* 'n such."

"Never sang *Lolita*, I don't suppose."

"I never even played with her as a child. Is she purdy?" Our lunch comes and he exclaims, "There, set yore little lunchgrabbers into that!"

LOLITA*

The caballeros throng to see thy laughing face
    Señorita!
But well I know thy heart's for me
Thy charm and grace
    My Lolita!

I ride the range for thy dear sake to earn thee gold,
    Señorita!
And steal the gringo's cows to make
A ranch to hold
    My Lolita!

In all this world there is no thing I will not do,
    Señorita!
To see thee laugh and dance and sing
Aye, and love me too,
    My Lolita!

The finest horse on all the range it will be thine,
    Señorita!
So easily the brand we change
From his to mine,
    Eh, Lolita?

I could not be so well content so sure of thee,
    Señorita!
But well I know you must relent
And come to me
    My Lolita!
    Ayi-i-i-iiiii-ha!

I bemoan the fact that it was a poem written by an English gentleman-writer-educator and adventurer, Captain Roger Pocock.

"If you are so plumb set on making this Ph.D. discovery which ain't been discovered yet, why don't you have some pencil-pushin' Profess-sewer to open your gate?" He bites off the end of a new cigar and lights up.

Jenny pours salt in her beer and responds, "She's tried the Profess-sewers but no theses abound on the subject."

Fanning away the first wave of smoke, I answer, "My first choice is the source — you guys who sing the songs of your profession."

"By the way," Jenny informs me, "did you know that our little potbellied friend here *appears* in a cowboy song?"

"You don't say. Will he sing it, I wonder?"

"Chantoozie, I ain't much of a songer any more. I just done that because I was told it was a colorful trait. Jenny here wrote the music for that poem — S. Omar Barker's *Adiós* — about as truthful a-soundin' piece as ever I heard, and she sings it mighty purdy too. I couldn't do it noways, it's a real tear jerker about our old wagonboss, Mac McMullen."

Jenny smiles her thanks at doughBelly and calls him a sentimental old goat. "Why don't the two of you come over to the shop after lunch and I'll sing it for you."

"Have t'git back to my fleecing job," he says, seriously. "There's a gang of feather-headed tourists in town this week just dyin' to part with their hard-earned E pluribus unim an' I got t'git me some."

He pays for our lunch out of both pockets and bowlegs down the street, great clouds of hemp smoke in his wake.

ADIOS *

In a valley high up in the mountains,
    With the wind like a knife on their cheeks
They carried Old Mac to his resting,
    When winter lay white on the peaks.

Behind come his fav'rite ol' pony,
    Led slow by an ol' Spanish friend.
The saddle and chaps, they was empty —
    Ol' Mac's trail had come to its end.

There wasn't no fancy procession —
    Just cowboys and Injuns and such —
Plain men of the saddle and mountains,
    And nobody said very much.

Ol' doughBelly Price done the preachin',
    Astride of his cream-yaller hoss.
All he said was a few words and simple
    About Mac, the ol' wagonboss.

"We've not come slicked up for a show-off,
    We've not brought no preacher to pray.
My words won't be fancy ones, neither,
    For Mac wouldn't want it that way.

"We all of us knew Mac McMullen,
    I couldn't say more if I'd try.
He was one of our own, but he's left us.
    We've gathered to tell him goodbye.

29

The range that he rode was a wide one,
    His friendships was many and deep;
So now that his saddle is empty,
    God rest him at ease in his sleep!"

'Twas thus near old Taos in the mountains,
    With the winter-white peaks looming close,
They carried a *man* to his resting,
    And quietly said, "Adiós!"

Barker, who is indeed a professional writer of *Western* verse, is not one of the uninformed. He's been a rancher, forest ranger, teacher, and ardent fighter for the Taos Indians, and he's highly respected by the cowboys. His poems are bone-ticklers and tear-jerkers in the proper idiom, telling it like it was, and is yet, in some far-away places that are still hard for people to get to on wheels. Probably his most celebrated poem is *A Cowboy's Christmas Prayer*,[28] though many other poems have been lifted from the pages of his books and sung. In a note to Jenny Wells Vincent, Mr. Barker expresses his appreciation of her singing of *Adiós:*

> I liked your singing of *Adiós* so well that I damn near cried! Elsa (his wife) is also delighted with the air and your true *corrido* style of singing it.

Jenny has given me a picture of that day at Mac's funeral. doughBelly is astride "his cream-yaller hoss." It is bleak and misty with patches of snow on the ground; a scene truly poignant with all his friends standing beside the grave. The song will be sung by many a cowboy whose *compadre* is "given a halo, gratis," indeed has been used recently to send off a cowboy friend of mine. The words may be changed a little, maybe, to fit the particular occasion, as I changed them, but the melody will remain pretty much intact, and not many of those who sing it will know, or care, that said melody was written by a lady in Taos, quite recently.

As I watch doughBelly, the indestructible, the humorist, the truthful little man with the bay window, bowleg his way back to the office, it never occurs to me that I might not see him again, but he "stacked his saddle" and his old geetar before I returned. He seemed ageless, as most cow folk, and how I savored the thought of spending more time with him. He could always make me think, make me laugh, give me a new slant, just by the way he put things. It was like him not to talk about himself unless pushed, so he may well have written some songs or verse he never told me about. I hope Mr. Barker one day writes another poem about the short-spoke "preacher" in *Adiós* — I'd like to try putting it to music. doughBelly is something to sing about!

The road from Taos to Santa Fe fixes itself to an ancient trail along the storied Rio Grande. It is late afternoon and dark shadows are gripped in the jaws of the gorge. Coming over the rise above Santa Fe to a full view of the city, one has the illusion it is the same as it was two hundred years ago — a Spanish-Indian Pueblo. Streets away from the square are narrow and winding — a charmed atmosphere, and therefore, I'm sure, economically unsound. Guarded by some of the city fathers, it has to date escaped the glass-plastic-highrise horror. It will be sad should they fail to preserve the only city of this kind in Ugly America.

We cut from the herd of road cattle onto a private trail and climb a cedared hill to where a soft-cornered Pueblo-style house blends with the landscape, its *vigas* pointing north and south, casting shadows of soft mauve against the bronze adobes. Down in the city, trails of disorganized lights begin to flick on as though children played the dot game, drawing lines to the numbers, one at a time. Shadows from the *vigas*, like lashes, glance eastward, and fade.

This is a three-day chuck-line stop. As I pull in the drive a colorful mobile of friends bursts from the back door to greet me, activated once more by the vagrant breeze of my passing.

> While the mountain shadows mingling lay like pools
>   above the sand,
> As the gentle Padre climbs the stair to ring the
>   mission bell,
> Making music o'er the silence of the eventide, aglow
> With the Spanish girls' serapes, red and yellow,
>   pink and blue —
> Will the pretty colors vanish in the swift and starry
>   change
> Of the sky from blue to velvet-black and silver
>   flame of stars —
> While across the brown adobe flitting shadows form
>   and pass.[29]

Chapter 4

When the dreamers of old Coronado
    From the hills where the heat ripples run,
Made a dust to the far Colorado
    And wagged their steel caps in the sun,
They prayed like the saint and the martyr
    And swore like the devils below,
For a man is both angel and Tartar
    In the land where the dry rivers flow.[30]

Four men pulled Shorty Mac's Pa off the man underneath and butted him up against the chuck wagon.

"McGinnis, you drunk 'er somethin'? He didn't call you nuthin' bad. We was settin' here drinkin' coffee, 'n we heared what Frenchy said."

"Yeah, cool down," said one of the other men, "you gonna fry yer freckles."

Pa's eyes snapped green fire under a matted mop of red hair. "He called me a buccaneer, that slab-sided little pelt-snatcher — in *my* book that's a goddam *pirate!* I never stole nuthin' from nobody!"

"He was jawin' about *all* us, Mac," said another of the four. "Sometimes I think you don't know sic'um."

"Then why ain't we all fightin' him. He's callin' us all the same as highjackers and thieves."

"*No he ain't!* Frenchy's purt' near what you call eddicated, an' what he was a-sayin' sounded mighty interestin' to me. You oughta flop on yer side and lissen to him oncet in a while."

They let go of Pa and helped Frenchy from the ground. After a little more explaining, Pa cooled off. Frenchy, who was more surprised than angry, shook hands, and they sat back down to listen to his tale of who the *first* cowboys were. This is the gist of that story.

In the 1490s the Spaniards brought Andalusian cattle from Spain to the West Indies. The herds were unloaded at Santo Domingo and other islands in the Caribbean, where they ran wild, adapted to the terrain, became fleet footed, and sometimes even fierce. Native Indians began hunting these cattle for profit — to sell the meat to Spanish galleons which were en route to or from their fanatic quest for gold. The first wild cattle hunters, half wild themselves, set up rude smokehouses along the shores of these islands, which they called *boucans*. Here they prepared the meat. When a ship was wrecked, the hunters found it even more profitable to band together and plunder. In time they acquired ships of their own, took to the high seas for piracy, and were called by their own Indian word, *boucaniers*. Buccaneers.[31]

In 1521 Gregoria de Villalobos brought a tiny seed herd of these same cattle to the shores of Mexico. They also thrived on Mexican coastal grasslands, and before long needed herdsmen. And who were they? Aztec Indians who had survived the Cortez slaughter to be branded with a G (for *guerra,* war) on their cheeks, and sold as slaves to wealthy Spaniards in New Spain.[32]

The cowboy carried a brand before the cows.

> Came the padres to soften the savage
> And show him the heavenly goal;
> Came the Spanish to piously ravage
> And winnow his flesh from his soul;
> Then miner and riotous herder,
> Over-riding white breed of the North,
> Brought progress, and new sorts of murder,
> And a kind of perpetual Fourth.[33]

No one, to this day, has sufficiently proven where and when the first cattle were herded by horses, and the difference between herding *wild* cattle and the bovines of Europe can be classed as two separate vocations. It is known that in Ireland men rode behind domestic cattle as far back as 1300 with long sticks to drive them from one place to another. But they weren't called cowboys. By the mid-1830s there were three million head of horses and cattle in the Texas-Rio Grande area. Some Indians, some Mexicans, some Caucasians, were riding around on horseback either "collecting" them or trying like hell to stay out of their way, and the men from Spain were swinging ropes and using branding irons long before then.

> Ay, the Border, bewildering Border
> Our youngest, and oldest, domains,
> Where the face of the Angel Recorder
> Knits hard between chuckles and pains,
> Vast peace, the clear sky's earthly double,
> Witch cauldron forever a-bubble,

Home of mystery, splendor and trouble
And people with sun in their veins.[34]

My head, feeling like a sounder dropped in deep water, rolls over on the pillow. The frame of reference swims, then settles to become a ceiling of whitewashed saguaro ribs lying across peeled pine saplings. Bubbles of consciousness surface slowly . . . the Indian House . . . Santa Fe . . . must be near noon.

Coffee. *Now!*

Making way over a patchwork of Indian rugs to the kitchen, I find a note from my hosts scrawled on the blackboard: "Bloody Mary on the stove, coffee in ice box. Mekeel bring reinforcements one o'clock."

I'm in the patio baking it out when Bill rolls up the drive. He steps through the gate with an armful of six-packs, looking as hung over from last night's face-lickin' as I.

One of my ex-husbands first met Mekeel in Liberia where he planted rubber, wore white linen shoes, white linen pants and drank scotch whisky. He won my affection when he told me about flying hunters to faraway places in New Mexico for big-rack deer and forgetting to come back after them. He has been Kay Starr's private pilot, a radio announcer, salesman and disc jockey, a social worker with the Indians, a promoter of the arts and of the Santa Fe Opera. He now holds down a big desk — Assistant Director of New Mexico Department of Aviation. Bill is witty, curious, has a cosmopolitan flair, a debonair manner, and mixes a *demolishing* drink!

"I say, Mekeel, we do not fly today, izzat right?"

"Not with me, we don't, baby. Unless the butterflies take off with me, I'm grounded."

I hear a significant sigh escaping from a punctured can as foam sprays lightly down my face. "I want that *in* me, not *on* me, pal."

"Reinforcements," he says, handing over the icy flagon.

After a satisfying glub-shudder-and-burp, I suggest, "We ought to drive to Galisteo and see what Ortiz y Davis knows about Old Dolores, huh?"

Bill sits on the adobe wall, his long legs stiff to the ground. "Know what I think about your town, Katie? Same thing that's happened around here before. People who own such property are afraid they'll be liable if someone falls in it, over it, or through it, so they bulldoze the muthuh to the ground."

"Suppose they have?"

"Well . . . you aren't going to like that, it'll spoil your illusions."

"Listen, Willie, I've sung *Dolores* for several years figuring it was written by a cowpoke, only to discover that cowpoke is a lawyer. Do you think I can get the first picture out of my mind? No way."

Bill says, "I wonder if anybody really cares who wrote it or where it is when you sing it?" His blue eyes look far away as if he had his own picture of the crumbled walls and didn't want to be pressed with technicalities.

"Probably not. But *I* do."

"Anyhow, it's not where your Mr. Rogers said. The Ortiz Mountains are south*west* of here, not southeast."

"I'm hip."

"I fly over that way at least a couple times a week and I tell you there's *no town* — a ranch or two, a bunch of old mine diggins, but no ruins."

"Have to be, can't all be gone; probably covered over with cedars."

"Won't give up, will you?"

"Nope. Let's take a run down to Galisteo."

Ay, the Border, the sun smitten Border,
    That fences the Land of the Free.
Where the desert glares grim like a warder
    And the Rio gleams on to the sea;
Where ruins, like dreamy old sages,
Hint tales of dead empires and ages,
Where a young race is rearing the stages
    Of ambitious empires to be.[35]

Frank Ortiz y Davis is at his bar-store-museum when we arrive in the early afternoon. I forget now who told me about him, but Bill pressed the idea some time back that he might be helpful in the hunt. We introduce ourselves and explain. I perch on a barstool in the dim cantina with my guitar and sing *Old Dolores* for him, watching him closely as I do so. He nods here and there, smiles broadly most of the time, and on completion says, "That ees very good song, I like eet. I never hear it before."

"But you know where it is, or was, the town — right?"

"Oh, chure, ober dair in de mountains," he says, and wanders his thumb in the first of those vague gestures I will become familiar with in my search. He tells me his ancestors *lived* in Old Dolores, that he is a descendant of the original land grantees.

"It's still there, then," I say, throwing an I-told-you-so look at Bill.

"I don' go there for long time. I *theenk* is still there. Beeg mine, lotta gold come outta Dolores."

"Where?"

"Cross de valley (another gesture). Hey! Look dees guitar. You like? Eet come from Dolores, maybe. . . . I theenk."

Frank goes to the wall over the bar and reaches down an ancient rawhide guitar with hair still on the hide. It nearly falls to the floor when I take it; surely it weighs fifteen pounds! The skin has buckled with dryness and age and pulled the frame out of shape, but I can see it is made of cottonwood. A ponderous neck sprouts ill-fitting tuning pegs and the holes for them seem to have been gouged out with the blade of a dull knife. The edges are laced together, the sound hole stitched around. And it really *could* have come from Old Dolores. I wonder what crazy kind of sound it made, and if that's all the poor soul could find to play?

It sometimes took more than a year to receive such expensive luxuries, but the wealthier people of Santa Fe ordered guitars, lutes, zithers, violins and even harpsichords, which had to suffer the mishaps of ship and stage, robbery and Indian firewood. Those who couldn't afford these treasures simply took to making their own. Indians in this section made crude instruments of cactus burls, put strings over them and simulated the violin — tone quality unimportant, so

35

long as they made noise. But the rawhide idea didn't originate with the American Indian or the Spanish; it was an Arab wig bubble many centuries old, brought to Spain during one of the invasions. It became a folk art near the Portugese border in the rather poor Extremadura section where Cortez and other Conquistadores were born.[36] Might Cortez's or Coronado's men have played something like the one in my hand?

"My God, Willie," I say passing it to him, "feel the weight of this thing!"

He takes it, returns it to its peg on the wall, "First time I ever saw a guitar with a brand on it."

"Just think how badly the maker must have wanted to play!"

And *what* did he play?

At the celebration last night I didn't just get juiced, I learned something; the dilemma of my Mexicanless-cowboy song was solved. Someone there turned me on to the works of a professor from the University of Texas. His fine book, *With His Pistol in His Hand*,[37] pretty much clears up the mystery.

What really happened was that the cowboy got his songs handed *back* to him.

> Ay, the Border, the bright, placid Border!
>   It sleeps, like a snake in the sun,
> Like a "hole" tamped and primed in due order,
>   Like a shining and full throated gun.
> But the dust-devil dances and staggers
> And the yucca flower daintily swaggers
> At her birth from a cluster of daggers,
>   And ever the heat ripples run.[38]

Border conflict lasted almost a whole century; if not with weapons, with words. The Irish-sired cowboy song was in its bloom of youth when cowboys first collected herds along the Rio Grande and drove them north to Canada, and the Cavalry riding that border was supposed to have sung *Green Grow the Rushes, Oh!* or the Americanized version, *Green Grow the Lilacs All Covered With Dew* (from which the word "gringo" is said to have derived, but didn't).[39] Shorty Mac's Pa was on the Kansas Trail when it opened in 1867 and claims he rode with Mexican, Scot, English, German, Negro and Canadian, and that on night guard "they was so many lingos floatin' on the breeze, them pore cows prob'ly wondered what country they was in." He also told Shorty Mac he couldn't separate one tune from another because, lacking the instrumental backing that furnished a characteristic rhythm for each country, they all sounded pretty much alike. Whistle some of the faster songs; there will be so little difference it will astound you. *The Irish Washerwoman, The Mexican Hat Dance, Get Along Little Dogies, La Bamba, Chisholm Trail, La Cucaracha, Turkey in the Straw.* So Mexicans were hearing American tunes of the mid-ninteenth century as well as older European folk tunes. What they did with them is what other countries all over the world have done in the case of border conflict, they succumbed to the influence of the invader.[40] (A Mexican jukebox will confirm that it's still happening — rock and roll with a huapango beat!) Americans produced no border balladry of significance, but the Mexicans made it traditional.

Then out from the peaceful old places
  Walked the Law, grave, strong and serene,
And the harsh elbow-rub of the races
  Was padded, with writs in between.
Then stilled was the strife and the racket
  That neighborly love might advance —
With a knife in the sleeve of its jacket
  And a gun in the band of its pants.[41]

Shorty Mac knew something about border ballads. He was forty-three when Pancho Villa staged his raids in 1914–15. I have heard him tell it so often I can nearly serve as a tape machine for his narrative:

"Most of the big cattle shufflin' was over, so three of us boys who'd had our ropes cut headed south lookin' for forty 'n found, and excitement. We ended up workin' fer a mine, shufflin' mules and keepin' a packtrain in shape bringin' in supplies. We bached with three Americans and twenty Mexicans and in between supply runs to Chihuahua, I'uz usually practicin' how to shoot the ass out of a gnat.

"It's a-gittin' long about the fall of the year, an' Pancho is messin' up the landscape with raids and plunder 'n such, gatherin' recruits, when come it high noon one day he snakes up on the mine and starts layin' down lead. Squawk and Bolo, my friends, was on a supply run, and as it happens I'm outta camp takin' a leak in the locoweeds, preparin' t' burn a little practice powder. When I hears the shots I bites dust all-of-a-quick, crawls under a bush an' waits for 'em to quit makin' the camp so smoky. After about fifteen minutes all the yellin' and thunderin' of hooves dies down, whereupon, I creeps slow and cautious up behind the cook shack and gives 'er a squint around the corner. Well, there was the biggest corpse and cartridge occasion I ever seen! Every last man 'cept one down in the shaft had Last Roundup'd or gone to Texas! Villa took all the stock, all the firearms, an' all the beans — all bein' left is my six-shooter and one blind, rat-tailed ol' burro. So me an' this other fugitive from the foray gets a-straddle that bull-headed desert canary and kicks, pushes and shoves our way to Chihuahua fer help. Had t'bury them pore duffers b'fore the buzzards got 'em."

Deterioration of the *corrido* (border ballad) and the Cowboy Song came about the same time in history — mid-twenties to late thirties — and for the same reasons, though I suspect America outdistanced Mexico in its zeal. That zeal had to do with the turning of a few dollars into many, which requires a certain amount of corruption of said material to make it understandable and attractive to the consumer. Radio and Tin Pan Alley put the bite on Cowboy Songs, often changing them beyond recognition.

The process continues. The larger the audience, the more corruption necessary, the more money a performer wishes to make, the less he can afford to care about what he does to the folk song. My own small practice has not been lucrative, but I have cut, or altered, verses and melodies for the short attention span of nightclub audiences all over the country, and I have used the Mexican beat in songs that never felt it before, partly to assist me with that audience, and

37

partly because I could feel it no other way. I was raised next to the Mexican border and learned to play guitar in Spanish before I learned to play in English.

The legend of "Black Bart the Po8" was too good to leave at rest, though in this case the tampering is not mine alone. In the early thirties it was dug up and made into a kind of "popular song" for the singing cowboy dudes on radio. This version suffered mightily because of the media, turning it into so much diluted water. Such lingo could not be sung over the air. In the early fifties two Hollywood friends attempted to write the "real story." Barbara James and David Zeitlin's melody was the old and often sung *corrido, El Hijo Desobediente*. They wanted their version to sound authentic (and it does, much more than the thirties attempt), so they called it *El Corrido de Bartolo Negro* and used as a chorus the actual poem set down for history in the words of the famed Po8. The rest of the song follows fact about as well as other bandito verses of the late 1800s, which is to say, never let the truth interfere with a good story.

"Black Bart, the Po8," as he signed himself, was a gutty little squirt who wore a tall hat and a flour sack with eye holes cut in it for disguise. After sacking the boxes and mailbags he'd leave snatches of terse verse in lieu of the loot, which kind of pushed Wells Fargo out of shape.

> here I lay me down to Sleep
> to wait the coming morrow
> Perhaps Success perhaps defeat
> And everlasting sorrow
>
> I've labored long and hard for bred
> for honor and for riches
> But on my corns too long yove tred
> You fine haired sons of bitches
>
> let come what will I'll try it on
> My condition cant be worse
> and if theres money in that Box
> Tis munny in my purse
>
> Black Bart the Po 8[42]

In 1875 he began operating out of California and for eight years, until he was bagged after his twenty-seventh robbery, he lived "out of the box." One story says he was a bank teller and knew when shipments of gold went in and out; another says that Wells Fargo offered him a retirement pension if he'd quit robbing the stage and settle down. Neither story has grounds. What follows seems less fictitious.

A young kid, friend of the driver of that twenty-eighth stage, was the only passenger on board the morning Bart planned and began to execute the holdup. He saw them coming in the distance, but at a bend in the road the boy got off to do a little hunting with his new Henry rifle, arranging to meet the driver on the other side of the hill. Bart stopped the stage, disarmed the driver, told him to take the horses over the rise, then started wrestling with the box which was bolted and locked to the floor of the coach. About then, the kid came over the hill, caught the signal from the stage driver, and together they inched back to where they could see Bart. Stooped over with the weight of the box, he was backing out of the stage. The kid shot at the most available target — thrice, missing two but scoring on the last — and the hooded figure departed with the speed and likeness of a comet, leaving hat, magnifying glass, field glasses case, and a *handkerchief*. A Fargo Pinkerton sniffed him out from there (via the laundry mark on his hankie) and the infamous bard served six years in San Quentin.[43] Hopefully, he used that time to improve his lyric style, which was as rusty as a graveyard hinge.

El Corrido de Bartolo Negro*

I sing not of the seas
Or robbing ships of their cargo
But of a man, if you please.
Who nearly broke Wells Fargo.
He made the drivers obey
When he came out on the rocks
And in a great voice he'd say,
"Hey, Mister, throw down the box!"

Chorus:
"Too long, in vain, I've toiled for bread,
For honor, fame and for riches,
But on my toes too long you've tread,
You fine haired sons of bitches!"

He'd come out of the hills,
The riverbeds or the prairie,
He'd take the box with the bills
And all the loot he could carry,
Then off he'd go to the woods
And leave the box where they'd find it;
He'd leave a note, not the goods,
Black Bart, the Po 8, he signed it.

Repeat Chorus

Eighty times this was done,
While Bart remained hale and hearty,
Until a coal miner's son
Shot him and ended the party.
In the jailhouse he did abide,
But not long enough for Wells Fargo;
They paid a pension till he died
To keep his paws off their cargo.

Here in Galisteo, in Frank Ortiz-y-Davis's small museum, the time machine cranks backward and border conflict seems very real. Laid before us is the story of Frank's heritage from pre-history, through Spanish, Mexican and American occupation. Primitive Indian instruments, a violin that came over the Santa Fe

Trail, Santos, furnishings from the room of a Spanish priest, knives, guns, lances, bows, saddles, braided horsehair reatas, and a collection of barbed wire that shows us the masterful defeat of the cowboy and his wandering herds.

And every man in sight
Let his cattle drift at night
Just to mosey to the town of Old Dolores.

Expecting a negative answer, I ask Frank if *he* knows why there are no Spanish-sounding cow songs in this area where so many people still speak Spanish?

"Chur, I know. Sheepmen don' seeng cowboy songs; they don't even *like* cowboys."

"Sheepmen?"

"Thees was sheep, not cattle country. Remember the Lincoln County Wars in the late 1870s? It was border fighting all over again on a smaller scale — cowboys killing sheepherders and driving their cattle up into this rich mountain grass because there wasn't no more grass down in Texas. It took the U.S. Army to stop those wars."

Mekeel picks up a strand of the old fashioned barbed wire and glances sidelong at me. "Why didn't *you* think of that?"

"Dumb I guess. That stuff in your hand put a stop to most of the driving north looking for grass."

"If you ask me, this stuff here is what started the wars."

"Right," says Frank. "The Texas cattlemen brought it here. They filed deeds on open range and fenced the Mexican's sheep out."

I notice a new twist to his speech and say, "Frank, what happened to your Mexican accent?"

He flashes a wide grin full of even white teeth, "You don't think I talk like that all the time, do you? That's for tourists. You guys aren't tourists, we're talkin' serious now."

Ay, the Border, the whimsical Border,
    Deep purples and dazzling gold,
Soft hearts full of mirthful disorder.
    Hard faces, sun wrinkled and old,
Warm kisses 'neath patio roses,
Cold lead as the luck-god disposes,
Clean valor fame never discloses,
    Black trespasses laughingly told![44]

The above interchange with Frank took place in the fall of 1960. Ten years later I returned to Galisteo with cinematographer Harry Atwood and a small crew from the University of Arizona Film Department to film the second picture in a series titled *The Last Wagon*,[45] based on the men, the music and the stories in this narrative. The museum had grown larger by then and Frank's son, Jose Ortiz-y-Pino III, was running the place. But Frank came to talk with me on film, to retell some of his stories, ask me for songs, and fill us with more good Mexican cerveza. He spoke with and without his accent, did everything he could toward putting his museum, store, local personnel, as well as his personal treasures, at our disposal. Father and son, to say nothing of customers, tripped over cables for the better part of two days, but we got some excellent footage of Frank behind the bar where first I'd found him, telling tales to tourists in his most colorful accent.

Not any more.

I received the news that Frank Ortiz-y-Davis had passed away on the third day of May, 1973.

The late afternoon sun is hidden behind a massive blue cloud when Bill Mekeel and I come out of the museum, saying our thanks and goodbyes to Frank. We drive leisurely back to Santa Fe on the dirt road, wondering about flying conditions tomorrow and the continuing search for Old Dolores.

"If the weather's shitty," says Bill, "you can drive to Los Cerrillos or Madrid and see if anyone there can give you a lead."

"Do you know that 'Real de Dolores' is the oldest gold mining district west of the Mississippi, that the Spanish worked the area about 1713, and that they were playing around with lead and silver near Cerrillos as far back as the mid-seventeenth century?"

"All that 'when' and 'what,' but no 'where,' " grumbles Bill.

"And in 1900," I add smartly, "Edison built a special machine to extract gold by electrolysis, shipped it by rail and wagon all the way to Dolores, never got it to work and shipped the whole rangoo back to New York at enormous expense — built a stamp mill too. Did you know that?"

"Too bad he didn't ship Dolores back there too, then we'd know where it was."

Rain clouds follow us down the valley, blot out the Ortiz mountains and drench us all the way to Santa Fe.

> The rain, gust-driven, veils the distant pines
> Upon the hill,
> Yet cannot hide the skeletons of mines
> And silent mill;
> And through an empty street the cold wind whines
> With hag voice, shrill.
>
> I pause and turn, upon the hillside's crown
> And vision gropes
> Where gleam the rain-washed cabin roofs far down
> The dark'ning slopes;
> But now the night has closed upon the town
> Of buried hopes.[46]

With morning, a strong wind gulps at the cedars, rolling gravel along the driveway, whipping sand against the west side of the Indian house.

We cannot fly again today.

And I am due at the Gardner's in Prescott tomorrow. Last night it was decided I should give Bill more time, with new information revealed by the topography maps, to ferret out the mysterious Dolores. Also, I should check the Territorial Governor's records for some clues, see Mr. Rogers in Georgetown for more firsthand information, however dim, and return in the fall when I'll have time for the final assault.

It is early morning when I turn on to Route 66. Three hundred and sixty-seven miles to the Ash Fork turnoff — an intestinal tract cluttered with the refuse of ad-mad America. Televise it, radio it, rhyme it, jingle it, and cover up the scenery with it. Not often, but now and then, showing from behind a sign we see where the wind carrying its sharp knife has etched and sculpted graceful forms from the soft pink sandstones, laid down milleniums ago in shallow seas.

Nearing Flagstaff we tail a shower that has left the air clean and pungent with a smell of pine. Long needles, heavily beaded with water, glitter gem-like in backlight from a sun swinging low in the five o'clock sky. West of Flag, the dark woolly clouds turn pink at the edges and explode over deep turquoise.

In Chino Valley windmills stand like cardboard cutouts stuck against a flame backing. Cattle dot up the range or stand bunched at water tanks, drooling into blood red mirrors. The air in each dip is cool and damp, at the top of each rise, warm and dry. Cottonwood and willow twist and turn with a stream that meanders, unroped into field, yard, and orchard, like a friendly and curious neighborhood pet. Dark green grasses in the fading light are crushed velvet.

Magic times in stretchy land. Dawn and sunset. Birth and death of a day.

The loom of Prescott appears on the southern sky, and soon lights float over the horizon like fishing scows, bobbing between far-shored mountains. There stand the "Sierry Petes" — the peaks that rare up in Gail Gardner's famous song.

Wonder if that ol' Devil is still up there a-bellerin' about them knots that's in his tail?

Chapter 5

THE SIERRY PETES*

Away up high in the Sierry Petes,
Where the yeller pines grows tall,
Ole Sandy Bob an' Buster Jig
Had a rodeer camp last fall.

Oh, they taken their hosses and runnin' irons
And mabbe a dawg or two,
An' they 'lowed they'd brand all the long-yered calves,
That come within their view.

And any old doggie that flapped long yeres,
An' didn't bush up by day,
Got his long yeres whittled an' his old hide scorched,
In a most artistic way.

Now one fine day ole Sandy Bob,
He threwed his seago down,
"I'm sick of this cow-pyrography,
And I 'lows I'm a-goin' to town."

So they saddles up an' hits 'em a lope,
Fer it warnt no sight of a ride,
And them was the days when a Buckeroo
Could ile up his inside.

Oh, they starts her in at the Kaintucky Bar,
At the head of Whisky Row,
And they winds up down by the Depot House,
Some forty drinks below.

They then sets up and turns around,
And goes her the other way,

43

An' to tell you the Gawd-forsaken truth,
Them boys got stewed that day.

As they was a-ridin' back to camp,
A-packin' a pretty good load,
Who should they meet but the Devil himself,
A-prancin' down the road.

Sez he, "You onery cowboy skunks,
You'd better hunt yer holes,
Fer I've come up from Hell's Rim Rock,
To gather in yer souls."

Sez Sandy Bob, "Old Devil be damned,
We boys is kinda tight,
But you ain't a-goin' to gather no cowboy souls,
'Thout you has some kind of fight."

So Sandy Bob punched a hole in his rope,
And he swang her straight and true,
He lapped it on to the Devil's horns,
An' he taken his dallies too.

Now Buster Jig was a riata man,
With his gut-line coiled up neat,
So he shaken her out an' he built him a loop,
An' he lassed the Devil's hind feet.

Oh, they stretched him out an' they tailed him down,
While the irons was a-gettin' hot,
They cropped and swaller-forked his yeres,
Then they branded him up a lot.

They pruned him up with a de-hornin' saw,
An' they knotted his tail fer a joke,
They then rid off and left him there,
Necked to a Black-Jack oak.

If you're ever up high in the Sierry Petes,
An' you hear one Hell of a wail,
You'll know it's that Devil a-bellerin' around,
About them knots in his tail.

"You ain't heared that song, you ain't much of a cowboy," I once heard an old bronc rider drawl.

Most of them probably can't sing it, but they recognize it as having come from the horse's mouth and maybe one out of fifty can say who wrote it. That's not the point — for them. I've watched the frayed end of a burning shuck tilt up in sunburned lips as they smiled, relating to the lingo and the happy thought that one of their kind finally put old Devil where he belongs . . . and maybe the happier thought that it took some forty-odd drinks to do it.

At dusk, when I walk in the front door of the old house on Mount Vernon Street to be welcomed by Gail and his wife Delia, the Old West flies right up and gives me a smack!

"You're Katie," he says, "come on in here and park yer soogans. Chow's on the stove, what'll you have to drink? This here's Delia."

"Hello, Mrs. Gardner."

"Delia!" he says.

"Hello Delia." From this moment, they seem like people I've known all my life.

The house is a territorial frame structure (Gail was a young man when Arizona was yet a territory — this is the house where he was born) with a great front porch complete with gliders chained to the ceiling. Inside, heavy square-rigged oak and walnut furniture, wooden floors and Navajo rugs, sofas, glassed-in hutches, hall trees and cane racks, stuffed deer heads, antlers, libraries, six bedrooms, an *upstairs* kitchen as well as one down, two living rooms, a fireplace, dining room and screened back porch — all for the two of them now, kids all grown and moved away. When I try to describe the style and period he says, "I calls it *Early Fred Harvey*."

"Why the kitchen upstairs?"

He smiles. "When I was married to Delie, we moved in here with my folks. Got along fine everyplace except the kitchen. Seems the fillies had different ways of doing things, so to keep the gals from lockin' horns, m'dad built a kitchen up there. After that things rippled along smooth as bear grass in the breeze."

Gail is not tall, about five-seven, and the first thing that takes you is a black patch over his left eye. He wears boots, always, legs so bowed you can drive a freight train between them, a little eyetooth sticks out and twinkles when he smiles, sun has burned him full of holes and freckles, his knuckles are knotted from pulling on ropes and reins, his butt pounded to a flat, back straight, shoulders square. Whatever the patch covers shows up on the double in the other eye, alert and full of mischief. (He now wears glasses with a black lens over that eye socket. The eye was removed many years ago, the result of radium treatments for sun cancer.)

"Now, what kinda bellywash d'ya drink?" he asks again.

"Oh, wine mostly."

"Wine, huh? Champagne do ya?"

"Well — uh — yes, I think I can choke some down."

He bowlegs it out to the fridge, pops the cork and pours me a glass of bubbly like it was an everyday occurrence; then he sits down at the kitchen table with a glass of whiskey while Delia makes salad.

I had written him from New York half hinting that he'd sent me an expurgated version of *Sierry Petes*, and gotten a reply which suggested a red-rumped steer bushed up and ready for a fight. When he found I was coming to straighten things out and re-establish authorship, printing his song as written with such stories he might want to tell me, he came off the prod.

"Katie and I come off the rim-rock and got strung out along the flats," he says to Delia. "She'll do t' take along."

"That's a cowboy's most laudatory phrase," between puffs on her cigarette. "He might just as well have kissed you."

I'd heard a rumor that he married a sheepman's daughter, so I asked him about it.

"Good gawd! No!" he bellered. "Her dad owned a *goat* ranch. I have enough trouble living that down."

"Tell her about Al Smith." She flicks imaginary tobacco from her bottom lip.

"Ol cowboy up near Ashfork," he nods, "had t'go to the funeral of one of his bunkmates, so b'fore they step to the coffin to view the remains he gets to the bar and juices up pretty fair. Each of the deceased's friends was to pass by and say something reverent about the dear departed. Ol' Al walked by, removed his hat, peered in, stood at the foot of the bier and said: " 'He died the way a good cowboy should — with a good horse on one end of his string and a bull yearlin' on the other. *He wasn't butted t'death by no goddam sheep!'* "

"Yeah, I got razzed pretty good when I married a goat-rancher's daughter. But I'd shore hate t'get out of it now, it'd take twenty freight cars just to haul my stuff out of here. When I was single and in the cow business all I had t'do to move was grab m' hat, piss on the fire, and call the dog."

OLD BACH*

I hears of a blowout up in town,
So I 'lows I'll take her in;
When it comes to slingin' a dancin' foot,
I'm thar like a quart o' gin.

I digs way down for my spike-tail clothes,
Then I curry-combs my hair;
I buys myself some yaller boots,
Which a gent should always wear.

When I prances up to a likely gal,
And gits me a good tight hold,
And skates her out on the ball-room floor,
I knocks them town sports cold.

Now I was a-havin' a right good time,
Just a-hittin' a long keen trot,
When a danged old gal horns into me,
And nails me on the spot.

I didn't like the looks of her eye,
An' when she turns on me her talk,
I seen that she meant business,
So I settles back to a walk.

Sez she, "Why Mr. Cowboy Man,
How lonely it must be,
To live way out on that there ranch,
And not have no company."

46

An' then she puts on what she thinks
Is a wise and knowin' grin.
"I'll bet you cook your own vittles too,
That's why you're a-gettin' thin."

Sez she, "Man is so helpless like,
They need a lot of care."
And the meanin' way she said it,
Why, it like to riz my hair.

Carsarn her bloomin' picture,
There was nothin' else to do,
Fer I seen I couldn't dodge her,
So I grabbed my hat and blew.

Don't want no woman around my ranch,
Closer'n half a mile,
Objectin' to chawin' tobacker,
And everything else worth while.

I've learnt to do without 'em fine,
I'm snug as a bump on a log.
An' a woman just nacherally wouldn't go
With me 'nd my horse 'nd my dawg.

He stands and motions to me. "Come on, I'll take you on the two-bit tour."
Whiskey in hand, he leads the way to the basement where his old working kak
hangs from a floor brace. The Indian-braided rawhide reins are worn smooth
from sweat and friction against the horse's neck, and little bristles of hair stick
in the webbing. "A lost art. There never was no better reins than these; they
never knotted 'er harded up 'er twisted on ya. Utes made 'em."

His rope hangs over the saddlehorn and a pair of brush-beaten, weather-
stained chaps lie across the saddle couch. He reaches up and gently runs his
hand over the cantle. Standing on the opposite side I see his eye glaze to far
away, hear a horse snort, a saddle creak, and smell warm sweaty leather.

"Betcha think I'm all sniffles and nostalgia about them days, don't you? —
instead of bein' plain relieved that it's over except the tellin'. That's the best, the
tellin'. Oh, sure, cowboyin' was fun. I'd like a little of that again maybe, if I was
younger, but that owning your own outfit is a different set of hobbles. It ain't
no goddam picnic when ya gets a dry summer and a bitchin' winter, cows dyin',
starvin' t'death, gettin' yerself all beat up, horses fallin' on you, turnin' over
comin' off the ridge and throwin' ya away. It's easy to laugh and joke about
them things that happened 'cause they're so far gone now, but there was a time.
. . . I wrote some verses about it once, you like to hear 'em?"

His arms across the saddle, one foot lopped back of the other, he stands singing, his voice like a familiar rusty gate hinge that lets you into the home corral.

You have read these cowboy stories,
About their life so wild and free,
I expect that you could tell me,
What a cowboy's life should be.
Oh, he rescues lovely maidens,
And he shoots the rustlers down,
He wears a fancy outfit,
And he paints up every town.

You can see him in the movies,
He's a high-falutin' swell,
A-ridin' wring-tailed pintos,
And always raisin' Hell.
But now let me tell you somethin',
'Bout this cowboy life so free,
It ain't no bed of roses,
You can take a tip from me.

Now there ain't no handsome cowboys,
Nowhere I've ever been,
For a real top-notch Buckeroo
Is just homelier than sin.
And all cowboys have their troubles,
A few of which I'll name,
To show you that cowpunching
Is a mighty sorry game.

When the roundup starts in April,
The first job you undertake
Is to shoe up all your horses
Till you think your back will break.
Now then you can be a "center,"
Or a "rimmy" if you will;
It don't make any difference,
You will have your troubles still.

When you take your dally-welties,
You can lose a lot of hide,
But if you fail to get 'em,
You have shorely got to ride.
Or you tie her hard and solid,
And then throw away the slack,
If your steers should hub a saplin',
You are shore to lose the pack.

When you get a wild bunch driftin',
Straight down for the home corral,
There will somethin' spook the leaders,

And your whole bunch go to Hell.
You build to an "orejana,"
For to tie him in a rush,
But your pony turns a knocker,
And he throws you in the brush.

Then you long-ear's in the thicket,
And your dogs have plumb give out,
So the only thing that you can do
Is cuss and cry and shout.
As you ride away and leave him,
You can hear the critter bawl,
And you know some feller'll git him
Before the rodeer comes next fall.

When you have a real hard winter,
And your cows all try to die,
You ride out every morning,
And to lift 'em up you try.
You can git one by the handle,
And you heave and lift and strain;
With a might awful struggle,
You can tail her up again.

Oh, you try to leave her standin',
But she charges you in high,
Then she breaks down in the middle,
So you leave her there to die.
On the ranch there's not a yearlin'
That is fat enough for meat,
And you're all burnt out on bacon,
And the beans ain't fit to eat.

When you've cowboyed for a lifetime,
Here is all 'twill do for you:
Some busted ribs and shoulders,
And a hip knocked down or two.
You have butted into cedars
Till your hair is hard to find,
And the malapais and granites
Have you all stove up behind.

If you ever have a youngster,
And he wants to foller stock,
The best thing you can do for him
Is to brain him with a rock.
Or if rocks ain't very handy,
You kin shove him down the well;
Do not let him be a cowboy,
For he's better off in Hell.

You may swear you'll never ride again,
And know you will not fail,
Till you hear a cavviada
Come a-jinglin' down the trail.
Then you pack up all your soogans,
And prepare to pull your freight,
For you know you're just a cowboy,
And your head ain't screwed on straight.

"That's how she was — no damn tattin' bee." He rams a hand into his pocket.

As he talks about living in Skull Valley, running his greasy sack outfit, of roundup, branding, fogging strays out of the brush and roping wild cattle, the lingo drifts into his speech like the warmth of an old campfire. He tells of building cattle traps to hold strays — was one of the very first to do so — of when he could get eleven calves out of ten cows, "but not now, cuz there's too many fences," and of the days before the cattle business went to hell, when they sold beef by the head instead of the pound.

"Hey, you guys," calls Delia, "come and get it!"

In candlelight the dining table is set with white linen, crystal, china and silverware; heirlooms brought to the territories at all costs, to validate the Westerner's cultural heritage, to bear witness he was not the heathen the Easterner described. "You get the full treatment first few times, then we hunker down in the kitchen like common folk."

During dinner he tells me how he wrote *The Sierry Petes*. On a train in 1917, going back East to get into the Air Service in World War I, passing through Kansas he saw a bunch of round-rumped cattle in the fields, not an earmark on one of them and farmers all round *on foot!* He'd just come from a camp gathering wild steers in Copper Basin, and the contrast between the lizard-tailed outlaws he'd been handling and those placid bovines set him to thinking about that camp.

"I was ridin' to camp at the old Dearing ranch near Thumb Butte one evening with the late Bob Heckle. We'd been celebrating in town and were pretty well jugged up, when one of us remarked that the devil got cowboys who did the things we'd been doing, and the other replied that if the devil monkeyed with us, we'd neck him to a black-jack oak just like a steer. Imagination took over from there, so I sat down at the desk in the club car and wrote on Santa Fe Limited stationery the verses of the *Sierry Petes*. Incidentally, the name comes from the Sierra Prieta Mountains, just west of Prescott. An old miner I knew in these mountains always called them the Sierry Petes, not peaks."

"I learned it as The Frisco Peaks. I've heard Chirichua Peaks, Dragoon Peaks, Montana Peaks and any number more."

"Don't doubt it; it's a fearfully pirated song, she got plumb away from me."

The rest of its history he'd sent me in that salty letter:

After the war I showed that poem and some others I'd written to some cowboy friends, among them Billy Simon. Bill decided to cook up an old tune for it and started singing it around cow camps and rodeos. This was the first time I got the idea that a lot of my poems would do for songs.

A Wickenburg dude wrangler by the name of George German was also a radio singer and he wanted my *Sierry Petes* and my *Moonshine Steer* to publish in a collection of old cow songs he was getting out for his radio station in Yankton, South Dakota, in 1929. George wasn't a cowboy so he bitched up the words somewhat to suit the sensitive ears of his radio audience, deleted the damns and hells and changed phrases he didn't understand. I suppose that is where those radio punks first got hold of it. I would hear it sung by some guitar plunker who didn't know which end of the cow gets up first — I would write the station a blast about copyright laws and the singing of a song without the author's permission. I stopped a good many of them but I couldn't stop them all. This will explain the different versions, together with the fact that one cowboy learned it from another without any written copies being passed around. Once I saw it in a college quarterly with the quotation: "A perfect example of early Western folklore, author unknown" — what the hell![47]

"You got m' tail all curled up with curiosity now, Papoose, where'd you learn it?"

"From Shorty Mac McGinnis in Tucson. I've sung it in places as far afield as Mexico City and the Blue Angel in New York, believe it or not."

His boyish grin spreads clear to his ears as he muses, "New York, eh? We sure do get around! I know about that part of the country all right, m' folks sent me back there to Dartmouth."

"*You* went to *Dartmouth?*"

"Sure. They thought I'd make a fine doctor or lawyer. But after I got a Bachelor of Science degree in math I decided I'd druther count cows, so I come back, worked in my dad's store for a bit, then bought in with a little greasy sack outfit in Skull Valley. When I finally quit cowboyin' I worked as postmaster. All ya got t'do to have a first class postmaster is get yerself an old cowboy and punch his brains out."

THE MAGIC JUG

You've heard that story of Buster Jig,
The old riata man,
How he jerked the knots in the Devil's tail,
And the Moonshine Steer he ran.

I'll bet you've often wondered,
And I know that you never knew
What kind of a hand was finally delt
To this drunken old Buckeroo.

Well he was a-siftin' off of a ridge
To lass a steer one day
When his hoss hung a foot in the crotch of a bush
An' throwed him clear away.

Ol' Buster Jig flew through the air
An' he hit with a Hell of a thump,

He knocked out all his doggone brains
On the butt of a cedar stump.

The cowboys they all gathered 'round
To view the sad remains,
They says, "He caint punch cows no more,
'Cause he ain't got no brains."

So they loaded him up an' packed him home
And they showed him to the boss,
Who says, "He weren't much good nohow,
So he won't be no loss."

"They tell me he's a Democrat,
And too damn tough to kill,
We'll git him one of them Government jobs,
He'll shorely fill the bill."

Ol' Buster Jig used to wear big corns
On the seat of a Porter saddle,
But now a padded swivel chair
Is all that he can straddle.

He sits all day behind a desk
And he never has no fun.
He shore would like to git in the brush
And bust a loop at one.

A neighbor of his, named Jerry E.,
Says, "This won't never do,
Although that boy ain't got good sense
He shouldn't feel so blue."

So Jerry ordered him a jug of Scotch
As big as the back of a hack,
With copper bands and a patent spout
All slung on a self-cockin' rack.

The jug it held the finest brew
That ever was known to fame,
And there on a plate beneath the jug
Was engraved old Buster's name.

When Buster Jig he seen that jug
He let out a great big cheer
He walled his eyes, an' he shook his hocks
Just like that Moonshine Steer.

Three or four drinks beneath his belt
And his spirit starts to roam
An' he sees hisself on the Sierry Petes
A-Foggin the wild bunch home.[48]

Before we turn in he takes me upstairs to see the silver trimmed rig he rides as head of the Sheriff's Posse, leading the rodeo parade. The leather is engraved, the silver trim is engraved, big silver conchos stud the martingale. It sits on a rack in his bedroom and glitters back at us, begging comparison to the cowboy legend — the hard-working soak that he really was, to the knight in shining armor he has become. I remember what Shorty Mac called those fancy saddles — horse jewelry, Texas trinkets, wampum, parade bangles. Gail is proud of it, I think because it is a gift from a beloved friend, now gone to distant ranges . . . but I am the one who touches it.

> Now here is a recipe, time-tried and true,
> For chuckwagon coffee, the buckaroo's brew:
> Use water and coffee in equalized parts.
> Then set on the fire. That's how the deal starts.
>
> Boil hard for two hours, then into it toss
> The well-rusted shoe of a clubfooted hoss.
> Gaze into the pot for a few minutes steady.
> If the hosshoe ain't floatin', your coffee ain't ready.[49]

Gail's breakfast call rattles the latch on my bedroom door. "Come and get it or I'll feed it to the coyotes!"

A steaming cup of the above-mentioned coffee waits on the kitchen table. One sip and I tell Gail, "Haven't tasted coffee like that since Shorty Mac's — strong enough to dissolve your toenails!"

"Yup, cowboys is fussy about the stoutness of their brew. When Bob Heckle and me was keepin' a brandin' camp fer strays near Thumb Butte one spring, we come down for supplies 'n found the whole dang town outta Arbuckles coffee, the only kind we would use. Well, I bought another brand, fergit what, and heads on back t' camp by our little stream up in the junipers. Next morning I rolls out, makes the coffee and calls Bob. As I recall he got a little fire-bellied in town and wasn't too spry come sunup. He takes a good round mouthful of that coffee and lets 'er fly — sprays all over me, the camp, the bacon 'n eggs, everything. I says, 'What the hell's the matter, you latch on to a scorpion?' He says, 'Christ! Where'd ya git that bellywash?' I told him they didn't have no Arbuckles. 'Jesus!' he spits, 'I cud stick a coffee bean up m'ass and wade through the crick and git stronger coffee than that!' " Gail puts a plate of golden hotcakes in front of me, "Those are extraordinary pancakes, guaranteed not to come apart in your stomach."

Today is a good day for staying inside — a restless spring wind whistles and whines under the eaves, swirling leaves and papers around the wide front porch — we sip coffee and get to the business I've come for: listening to the tapes and records of his much-pirated song. In his own collection he has but two printings and one record. I've brought a flock more. There are at least four *Folkways* albums,[50] with none of the singers giving him credit. On *Folk Songs of Idaho and Utah* is the Arizona song *Tying Knots in the Devil's Tail*, sung by Rosalie Sorrels, liner notes by Ken Goldstein. The notes touch off a blast from Gail right away with the observation that, "Perhaps the best of [the Cowboy's] expressions

53

and one which could successfully compete with the most colorful language created in any segment of American life, is the term 'cow-biography' which simply means working with cattle."

"Oh, it means workin' with cattle, does it?" he snorts. "Now ain't that nice to know, since it doesn't at all, even if *cow-biography* was the right word, which it ain't! Katie, there's a perfect example of how not knowin' can bitch the meaning and ruin the 'colorful language' all to hell. The word is *cow-pyrography*. As defined in Webster's, pyrography is the art of producing designs or pictures as on leather by burning with a hot iron or instrument. When I was a little button around the turn of the century the ladies had pyrography sets and burned pictures on leather sofa pillows or table covers. So, naturally, *cow-pyrography* is burning a design on a cow's hide. In the second printing of my *Orejana Bull*[51] I changed it to 'the smell of burnin' hair' because nobody knew what pyrography meant, and what the cowboys made of that word was fearful and wonderful indeed!"

"There *you* go tampering with the original."

"Hell, I didn't change it until 1950. By then there wasn't nuthin' more they could do with it."

At the end of Miss Sorrel's version, he says, "I can see how Buster Jig got changed to Jinks, Gawd-forsaken to Lord-forsaken, and hell of a wail watered down to awful wail, but how in chiggers did she ever find Hell-brim-muck? An' she says, lopped off his ears, why, that doesn't mean anything! When you brand a cow you ear mark him — ours was the swallerfork."

"She also says, 'they sets her up and turns her around' — most singers think that refers to drinks," I tell him.

"Well, it don't! The two front feet when training a cow horse are left unshod and are therefore tender. So when he stops his front feet go up in the air and he 'sets up.' If he slides on his front feet he'll split yer crotch."

"There are several lines that *always* get sung wrong, Cowboy, one's the line about *dallies*."

"My God, you'd think anybody lived west of the Mississippi would know what a dally is."

"Too many dudes living west of the Mississippi. I found a guy in Nevada who thought a dally was the pitch fork the devil carried."

"Hell he did! People should find out what they're singing. Dally-weltie is the Yavapai cowboy's corruption of the Spanish *dar la vuelta*, to take a turn or twist around."

"They don't care, they sing it because they happen to like it, and because it's good."

"When they git done with it, it ain't no damn good."

"Gail, you've written on a universal theme — the devil out collecting souls — everybody's with those boozed up cowboys, one hundred percent." I glance up at an artist's re-creation of the scene that hangs over the fireplace — "The essence is there in George Phippen's painting. You don't really have much to say anymore about the way it gets sung, it's part of folklore now. And in most cases even the cowboys didn't help you keep it pure — one takes a dally, the next a a hard-tie, the next an anchor. . . ."

54

"Yeah, that Harry Jackson album I got,[52] he calls 'em wrappies."

"Probably because he's a Wyoming cowboy from Chicago, and in Wyoming they use words less influenced by the Spanish, more by the French. They say ravine, not arroyo — rope or lariat, not seago or reata — mountain, not sierra — coosie, not cocinero — beans instead of frijoles. . . ."

"I don't call 'em frijoles neither, calls 'em whistle berries or deceitful beans because they talk behind your back. But you're right about that; up north they say 'the horse cold-jaw'd and the steer coolied.' They're dally men up there too. Here we dally because we've a lot of men from California and Mexico. Mexicans always dally. An ol' boy was out huntin' strays one day, when here come this steer over the ridge with the most beautiful reata hangin' on his horn. Ol' boy says, 'Bygum, I've always wanted a reata, here's where I git me one!' He lopes over to the steer and is just about to five-finger the reata when here comes a Mexican down the other end of the twine takin' up his dallies."

The painting grins back a duplicate of the one spreading over Gail's freckled features. Phippen's painting of *The Sierry Petes* is about as close to reality as one can get when the subject is mythical and he's required to dream up a cowboy's devil.[53] The evil, hairy satyr is half man and half steer, and redder than long-handles at sunset. Sandy Bob has the makin's drooping off his bottom lip, a loop over the Devil's horns and smoke rising off the saddle horn from his dallies. He's mighty tippy in the rig, but not about to fall. Buster Jig (Gail), the heeler, leans way out of his saddle, mouth open and hollering, his reata has been flung into a morning glory (the name of a loop that's built to open when it gets there) and is about to take itself up around the devil's hind feet. The look in Buster's bleary eye says, "I gotcha!"

"Where'd you ever get a name like Buster Jig? You must have danced a lot."

"Heh," he chuckles. "No, that ain't the reason. My dad had the old mercantile store here and his initials were J. I. On the store front those letters were jammed up close so it looked like JIG, and when I was a button, o' course, they called me Buster — but hell, they use every name invented but Sandy Bob and Buster Jig in the song."

The old patch-faced cowboy listens peaceable to all botched and garbled versions until we come across one Peter LaFarge (now deceased)[54] and here I think he's going to throw a wall-eyed fit because Pete not only claims authorship of *Sierry Petes,* but other well-known classics that were written before the kid was born.

Gail says the first encounter with the thieving of his song happened back in 1931 when the old pirate Powder River Jack Lee took it, along with Curley Fletcher's *Strawberry Roan,* put them in a songbook and claimed them for his own.[55]

"That dude come swingin' into Phoenix thirty years ago packin' a steel guitar and a hula skirt fer his wife, Kitty. They found rather sorry reception for that sorta music on the radio, so he bought hisself a fancy cowboy outfit, loaded him and Kitty down with belt buckles 'n boots, and began singin' every cow song he could wrap his tonsils around. Curley and me got pretty damn sore about his liftin' our songs without so much as a by-your-leave, but when we got together to see what we could do about it, we found our only recourse was to sue him.

Hell, the ol' bastard didn't own the clothes he stood in, and of course neither of us wanted Kitty."

THE DUDE WRANGLER*

I'll tell you of a sad, sad, story,
Of how a cowboy fell from grace.
Now really this is something awful,
There never was so sad a case.

One time I had myself a pardner,
I never knowed one half so good;
We throwed our outfits in together,
And lived the way that cowboys should.

He savvied all about wild cattle,
And he was handy with a rope,
For a gentle well-reined pony,
Just give me one that he had broke.

He never owned no clothes but Levis,
He wore them until they was slick,
And he never wore no great big Stetson,
'Cause where we rode the brush was thick.

He never had no time for women,
So bashful and so shy was he.
Besides he knowed that they was poison,
And so he always let them be.

Well, he went to work on distant ranges;
I did not see him for a year.
But then I had no cause to worry,
For I knowed that some day he'd appear.

One day I rode in from the mountains,
A-feelin' good and steppin' light,
Fer I had just sold all my yearlin's,
And the price was out of sight.

But soon I seen a sight so awful,
It caused my joy to fade away.
It filled my very soul with sorrow
I never will forget that day.

For down the street there come a-walkin'
My oldtime pardner as of yore,
Although I know you will not believe me,
Let me tell you what he wore.

He had his boots outside his britches;
They was made of leather green and red,

56

His shirt was of a dozen colors,
Loud enough to wake the dead.

Around his neck he had a 'kerchief,
Knotted through a silver ring;
I swear to Gawd he had a wrist-watch,
Who ever heard of such a thing.

Sez I, "Old scout now what's the trouble?
You must have et some loco weed,
If you will tell me how to help you,
I'll git you anything you need."

Well he looked at me for half a minute,
And then he begin to bawl;
He sez, "Bear with me while I tell you
What made me take this awful fall.

"It was a woman from Chicago
Who put the Injun sign on me;
She told me that I was romantic,
And just as handsome as could be."

Sez he, "I'm 'fraid that there ain't nothin'
That you can do to save my hide,
I'm wranglin' dudes instead of cattle,
I'm what they call a first-class guide.

"Oh, I saddles up their pump-tailed ponies,
I fix their stirrups for them too.
I boost them up into their saddles,
They give me tips when I am through.

"It's just like horses eatin' loco.
You can not quit it if you try.
I'll go on wranglin' dudes forever,
Until the day that I shall die."

So I drawed my gun and throwed it on him,
I had to turn my face away.
I shot him squarely through the middle,
And where he fell I left him lay.

I shorely hated for to do it,
For things that'd done you cain't recall,
But when a cowboy turns dude wrangler,
He ain't no good no more at all.

Curley Fletcher, one of the most popular cowboy song writers and composers of western verse from Gail's era,[56] had over half of his songs stolen before he got wise to copyrighting. And I happen to know that Gail, as of this writing, hasn't been half compensated by Folkways Records for all the times they've taken *Sierry Petes*. They have known about his copyright and renewal since I told them in 1960. It wasn't the cowboy ethic to think in terms of profit for his verse. The songs could be sung on the range for years before a cowhand might wake up, and jingle into town to brand his brainchild. Gail has allowed many persons to use his songs for nothing more than acknowledgment to the author, but fur flies when someone burns another brand on them.

Things settled back to a walk for Gail and his old Devil that summer of 1960. He didn't shake out any more rustlers and I didn't hear from him until fall, after I'd returned East for the last time. Before Christmas, I sent him a copy of Alan Lomax's new book *Folk Songs of North America*,[57] which contained a new printing of *Sierry Petes* with no credit, plus rust on the knife — inferred plagiarism. Then I sat back and waited for the shit to hit the fan!

> *Tying a Knot in the Devil's Tail* . . . is a ballad from the dude ranch period and the sort of haywire song the guide serves up to his Eastern charges around some nice, comfortable campfire in the mountains. A ranch poet, desperate to find something to match the tourists' idea of the wild and woolly West, remade the Charles Badger Clark poem, which began . . . "Way high up in the Mokiones . . ."

(Which beginning is not the Badger Clark poem, but the corruption of same called *High Chin Bob*. Clark knew how to spell Mogollon.) Meanwhile I wrote Alan, tried to tell him what was coming, sent him the correct *Sierry Pete* lyrics and background, and protested that in no way did it resemble Clark's poem. To call it a "remake" was stretching the point even further — they resemble each other not at all (one's about a lion, the other, a devil) outside the first line, which begins a score of western poems. The only similarity is in the music, another working of *Pollywolly Doodle*, and even that is not identical because of a three-line rhyme in the chorus. Some cowfolk sing all three, some only two. (So far as I knew then, the lone cowpoke hadn't been uncovered who first decided to sing *The Glory Trail* to that tune, or for that matter, which song was set first, though Clark's poem was first printed in 1915.)

THE GLORY TRAIL*

'Way high up the Mogollons,
    Among the mountain tops,
A lion cleaned a yearlin's bones
    And licked his thankful chops.
When on the picture who should ride,
    A-trippin' down a slope,
But High-Chin Bob, with sinful pride
    And a mav'rick hungry rope.

"Oh, glory be to me," says he,
    "And fame's unfadin' flowers!
All meddlin' hands are far away;
    I ride my good top-hawse today

And I'm top-rope of the Lazy-J —
    Hi! kitty cat, you're ours!"

That lion licked his paw so brown
    And dreamed soft dreams of veal —
And then the circlin' loop sung down
    And roped him 'round his meal.
He yowled quick fury to the world
    Till all the hills yelled back;
The top-hawse gave a snort and whirled
    And Bob caught up the slack.

    "Oh glory be to me," laughs he.
        "We hit the glory trail.
No human man as I have read
Dast loop a ragin' lion's head,
Nor ever haws could drag one dead
    Until we told the tale."

'Way high up the Mogollons
    That top-hawse done his best,
Through whippin' brush and rattlin' stones.
    From canyon-floor to crest.
But ever when Bob turned and hoped
    A limp remains to find.
A red-eyed lion, belly roped
    But healthy, loped behind.

    "Oh, glory be to me," grunts he.
        "This glory trail is rough,
Yet even till the Judgment Morn
I'll keep this dally 'round the horn,
For never any hero born
        Could stoop to holler: ' 'Nuff!' "

Three suns had rode their circle home
    Beyond the desert's rim,
And turned their star-herds loose to roam
    The ranges high and dim;
Yet up and down and 'round and 'cross
    Bob pounded, weak and wan,
For pride still glued him to his hawse
    And glory drove him on.

    "Oh glory be to me," sighs he.
        "He cain't be drug to death,
But now I know beyond a doubt
Them heroes I have read about
Was only fools that stuck it out
    To end of mortal breath."

'Way high up the Mogollons
    A prospect man did swear
That moon dreams melted down his bones
    And hoisted up his hair;
A ribby cow-hawse thundered by,
    A lion trailed along,
A rider, ga'nt but chin on high,
    Yelled out a crazy song.

    "Oh, glory be to me!" cried he,
        "And to my noble noose!
    Oh, stranger, tell my pards below
    I took a rampin' dream in tow,
    And if I never lay him low,
        I'll never turn him loose!"

A week or so later came Alan's answer:

I enjoyed your letter and look forward to hearing from Gail Gardner. It's going to take a long time to convince me that the Sandy Bob poem is not a rewrite from Charles Badger Clark's *High Chin Bob*. . . . It's hardly likely that two cowboy poets would have picked this rather unusual theme and treated it in such a similar way completely independently of each other. Literary history contains very few cases. I'm also not convinced Gail's text is the parent of the one we printed. Anyway, if he writes me I'll certainly give him co-credit in the next edition of *Folk Songs of North America*. Thank you for telling me about this.

                                          Sincerely yours,
                                          Alan[58]

"Hot cowpies!" I says to myself. "You gonna find out who is the parent all right, boy!" And I wondered if Alan had read Badger Clark's foreword in the 1952 edition of *Sun and Saddle Leather*, where he expresses some surprise at the Lomax family trait:

The Glory Trail is a versatile kid and seems equally easy with cowpuncher and intelligentsia. He even developed a sort of dual personality a few years ago when he turned up among New Mexican cowboys as a song under the name of *High Chin Bob*, and John Lomax, meeting him under those circumstances, put him into *Poetry*, as an "indigenous Western folksong, *author unknown*," which jolted his fond father for a moment.

Alan's statement, "It's hardly likely that two cowboy poets would have picked this rather unusual theme," is naive considering the number of them who've gravitated to this sort of fantasy. It would be more accurate to say that any cowboy who ever rounded up wild brush cattle could convince himself he'd latched onto a bear, a lion, the devil, a wildcat, or the whole City of Hell, to say nothing of the top screw. Hairtrigger Newt is the sort of character — also lion conscious — that I've heard cowboys sing of since I was a potty case.

HAIR TRIGGER NEWT*

As I was a-roundin' Scorpion Butte
On a routine cattle inspection
Who should I meet but Hairtrigger Newt
A-ridin' Hell-bent-for-election.

The lion he rode was a-havin' fits
And kickin' up plenty of dirt,
Newt used a Bowie knife for a bit
And a rattlesnake for a quirt.

The wildcat he carried under his arm
Chewed the loose end of a rein,
A gila monster for a charm,
Tied on with a barbwire chain.

A six-shooter cocked in his right hand;
I thought the dern fool would crack 'er
But all he done was to spit in my eye
With a pound of chawin' terbacker.

I asked him where he was headin' for
What his hurry was all about.
He said, "A tough guy just hit town
And he done chased me out!"

To the contrary, literary history is full of such similarities. Loneliness and isolation draw imagery from the same allegorical pipe, simultaneously and independent of one another, in all parts of the world. Emerson reminds us: "There is one mind common to all individual man. Nature is a mutable cloud which is always and never the same. She casts the same thought into troops of forms, as a poet makes twenty fables with one moral."[59] In cowboy lingo these fables are called "big windies."

Having sent Gail the letter, I could smell hair burning two thousand miles away from the powder keg. When she blew it was a dilly!

Dear Sir:
 I refer to one of my poems printed in your recent book, inaccurately, without permission, and without credit to the author. Since most of my writing is done for fun rather than profit, I have paid little attention, but now, when you make the libelous insinuation that I have plagiarized from the work of Mr. Badger Clark, I make vigorous protest. . . . I have ample proof of my authorship and a very little research on your part would have led you eventually to the Library of Congress and the copyright entry Class AA, No. 192120. I won't bore you with how and why I wrote the poem, be it sufficient to say when I wrote it in 1917, I had not seen the work of Badger Clark.
 Professional singers of cowboy songs and editors have much in common, neither knows which end of a horse the hay goes in or which end of a cow gets up first. . . .

If and when you reprint your book, I do not request, I *insist* that: (1) you leave it out entirely, or (2) you print it correctly as it was written with due credit to the author and without that slanderous and smart-aleck reference to plagiarism. And let's have no loose talk about co-authors, the poem is mine and *mine alone*.

Yours very truly,
Gail I. Gardner[60]

Gail sent me the following from Alan's answer to him a couple of weeks later:

2/22/61

I will correct the note in the book and properly credit you for the song at the first opportunity. I certainly sympathize with the problems you've had with the whole thing.

Alan[61]

How difficult for researchers like Alan and myself to maintain a perfect score!

This book, too, will be open to the Double O — the many hours spent in the Library of Congress are often not enough. What I hope will help me in that event, is the bond of friendship I have with these wonderful men. And should it happen, accidentally, that we slight someone in the first edition, we will have the opportunity to repay them in the second.

> Singers, they of the open land;
> The timbered peak and the desert sand,
> Peril and joy of the hardy quest,
> Trail and pack of the unspoiled West;
> Though crowded back to the lone, last range,
> Their dream survives that will never change.[62]

In a more ethereal sense, Gail's songs don't belong to him anymore. As we talk away the morning in the old Mount Vernon house and he sings for me, I can see them as much more than something fun to listen to. His songs are a symbol of personal and territorial freedom, things we creatures enjoy less and less with the passing years. In spirit they belong to everyone who loves the legend, are as rooted in it as if they'd been planted with the cactus and the cedars.

I believe they are far more than regional songs. Akin to the Child Ballads of England, they'll be handed down, ad infinitum. We must admit that ranches and cowboys, as we know them, are going. Ranches are the space we choke to death by selling to developers who choke us to death; cowboys are the anti-toxin for our pace-dizziness, reminding us of past freedoms and a severed part-nership with the earth. These songs of our over-ridden West will rise from the Collective Unconscious when we are jam-packed cheek-to-jowl in the all-too-near — rise to recall that soothing expanse and leave us with the same vague kinship we touch on when we stand looking out to sea.

With his cracked and ragged voice, Gail Gardner brings us the vividness of the world he lived in: stretching out steers, hunkering over campfires, crashing through brush on fiddle-footed horses, watering at stock tanks, trailing in to the home corral, sore and tired after a day of wrestling muley cows, or up to some cowboy devilment with tongue in cheek.

First ya ring the bell,* and then ya ask for Anna,
    Then ya put a nickle in the Bell Piana.
Down comes Anna in a silk Kee-mona,
    All dressed up in perfume and kee-lona.
Then ya pay two dollars for the music that ya hear.
    Then ya pay two dollars for a lousy bottle of beer,
And then ya pay two dollars for a coupla weeks of fear,
    Down the line . . . down the line.

You go to the Doctor, still thinkin' of your Anna
    To see what's the matter with your ol' banana.
He sez, "Young feller, there ain't no cause t' fear;
    Ya got a simple case of the gonorrhear!"
Then ya pay twenty dollars for your first examination,
    Then ya pay thirty dollars for a course of cauterization,
Then ya pay ninety dollars for complete emancipation,
    Down the line . . . down the line.

And the dream that was walkin'
    And the dream that was talkin'
        And the heaven in my arms was you
Good Evening Fray-ends!

THINK YOU CAN SPARE YOURSELF a lot of mental pain and anguish, lady," said Bill Mekeel's voice over the Ameche. "I flew over what the topo maps call Dolores Spring Ranch yesterday and there's nothing there but a ranch house, a big pile of sawmill wood, a corral, and some feeble cottonwoods."

"How d'you know the ranch is the site of the town?"

"What else would it be?"

"A ranch!"

"Dammit, Katie, I've got treetops up my *como se llama* from eyeballing the bugs on the ground. Somebody's done what I said a while back — bulldozed the place."

"Dammit yourself, Willie. When a whole historical town gets bulldozed somebody at the Historical Society is going to get wind of it, and nobody has."

Silence. Then some mumbles about private property.

"Mr. Rogers' letter said a movie short was taken at the site so there had to be something there to film."

"*Had* to. Right. He didn't say *when* they filmed it," reminded Bill.

"He also said, 'well known cattle drive point'. Surely some old cattlemen in the valley would have an inkling where it is. Wish I were there to help you, but Gail and I are in the middle of a good bunch of talk and tomorrow he's taking me out to meet Billy and Betty Simon at their Horse Camp."

"We know from all the correspondence you left here, that it was known as a mining town — gold. The fact that the cowboys stopped to water cattle is romantic but secondary, Katie."

"Since when is water secondary in the Southwest?"

"They probably went there more for the booze than the water anyway. If it was up here in the mountains it was a helluva long way to drive cows from the Galisteo in the valley."

"Yeah! *'Nearly allus half a day to water.'* Did you see any sign of the Old Placer diggings? They're supposed to be at the mouth of Cunningham Canyon, which is supposed to be 'at the almost deserted little town of Old Dolores.' That's what the USGS Professional Paper, 1910, say."

"Sure I saw them, they're all over the side of the mountain, but *there aren't any buildings around them,* I keep trying to tell you. That was 1910, this is 1960. . . . or hadn't you heard?"

"And the twenty-stamp mill on up the canyon. Ferkrissake, how can you lose a twenty-stamp mill?"

"Bulldozers, Tinkerbell!"

"Aw come on, Willie, be a good boy and go over to the museum library and see if Mrs. Medearis has unearthed any photographs yet."

He sighed resignedly. "Okay, boss, but I wish you'd write to Mr. Rogers and find out where he was sitting when he wrote that little ditty . . . b'fore I burn up five hundred dollars worth of petrol guessing."

Well, Mekeel was right about one thing. The town certainly didn't *start* as a watering place for cattle, though it may have ended that way when the gold was gone.

It all began in 1828 when a Sonoran herding cattle in the mountains stumbled over a rock in an arroyo, a rock that resembled the gold ore of his native state. He had it assayed in Santa Fe that fall and found it rich with gold particles. Then began the rush to the Ortiz range to placer its gold. But the vein in a stratum of rock on the property of José Francisco Ortız and Ignacio Cano was not petitioned for and granted until December of 1833. This was the Dolores mine, and was approximately a mile up canyon from where the town was later built, with *the whole wide world before us.* In the Mexican governor's Letter Book,[63] I had found notation of a claim established for the "Old Placers, downstream of Dolores." The names *Real de Dolores,* or *The Placers* were used in records concurrently, as if they were the same place. There are the Old Placers and the New Placers. Maybe there was an Old Dolores and a *Real de Dolores.* Grants and claims have changed hands and names over the years, but if over two hundred people (some records say two thousand!) lived there during the gold days, well, hell, it's even hard for a bulldozer to get rid of a whole town.

That's what I kept telling myself. And Mekeel.

"That's about the best cowboy song I've ever heard, Papoose." Gail is at the wheel driving us to Bill and Betty's Horse Camp. I have just sung *Old Dolores* for him. "Why, it's just loaded with the kind of pictures that please a cowpoke's mind."

"Did *you* ever hear of a cowboy who was a dean of law, or vice-versa?"

"Can't say I have; you mean it wasn't written by a cowboy?"

"Well, I haven't got it quite figured out yet, Gail, but it sure looks like the town has tried to get up and walk away since 1912 when this man wrote about it."

Settling back for a long drive into cattle country, I watch the wind tickle new green grass into dancing fits and seconds later flatten it down against last winter's sod with a sudden spatter of raindrops. May is going out like a lion, pussyfooting one minute, snorting in bad-tempered fits the next.

In about ten minutes we are at the gate.

Never thought about a horse camp being in suburbia, but here it is. Ten acres cut off from sight of the other houses by immense granite boulders and a thick stand of piñon and juniper. Billy is in the corral working a cutting horse, dust flying under the colt's feet as he spins on a dime. He trains horses for working cowboys, for country gentlemen as show horses, for children, and for ladies who want to trot the bridle path to lose some of the sit-down flab. "A deal," Billy reflects, "that mostly turns into an ass and saddle fight."

Nearing seventy, he sits the horse like a chunk of bronze, molded to the mass as part of the rigging, moving in rhythmic response with butter-smooth ease. (At eighty-three he still does!) I suspect he can cool an angelfood cake without its collapsing while the horse spins, weaves and twists beneath him, reined or unreined, trotting or at a dead run. Yet, when he climbs down to greet us, he says nothing about what makes a horse do such impossible things; he praises the horse.

"Lookit them beautiful britches on him, Gail, that's one of the prettiest sights you'll ever see."

Inside, on the north wall of what they call "the shack," hang thirty or so bridles and hackamores specially designed and executed by Billy for the kind of training he does. Gentle bits, bits without bits, halters, martingales, leather bits, even something with a pool ball that rolls up and down the horse's throat, making him flex his head from the pole (upper part of the neck) instead of the withers.

"I figured this gadget out to use on a show horse, or pleasure horse; keeps his neck and head high — that gentle pressure on his adam's apple — every time he wants to drop his head. Now I wouldn't use that if I was training a cutting horse because you want him to flex from the withers, so's his head goes down eye to eye with the cattle. Well, I try to study each horse that I get as an individual, sort of diagnose each horse's disposition, and if he doesn't like one kind of hackamore I put on him, why, I work around until I find another. It isn't what *I* like, it's what the *horse* likes. But any guy who thinks he knows all about training horses is goin' backwards. Horses is all I know, but I'll never know it all."

"You make them look pretty smart, Billy."

"Some are and some aren't. Jack Cooper used t'say that my ol' horse, Settin' Hen, was such a good cutting horse she could cut the stink out of a skunk."

Betty interrupts to ask him to tell me George Cox's cutting horse story.

"Ol' George, he was mighty proud of this horse, and one mornin' when he was cookin' breakfast, he happened to look out the window, saw the horse lookin' down at the ground, eye-ballin' something on the right, then he'd move a foot and swing his head over to the left and look down over there. George thought he'd spotted a rattlesnake or something and he didn't want him to get bit, so he goes out t' see what it's all about. Come to find there was this anthill where the horse was standin' and he was cuttin' out one pissant, the next two down the hole, one pissant out, two down the hole."

> It happened on this roundup that two Kansas City guys
> Was out to buy some cattle, and it sure did bug their eyes
> To see ol' Jeff on Shucker siftin' out them Bar U cows
> With calves that needed brandin'. Finely one of them allows
> He sure just doesn't savvy how Jeff sorts 'em out so fast.
> "Well, now, it ain't *my* doin's," Jeff explains at last.
> "I jest go 'long for ballast and I never lift a hand;
> For Shuck knows all the earmarks and can read the dimmest brand!
> An' if you don't believe it, boys, I'll bet a hat, by heck,
> He'll cut the proper cattle with the reins loose on his neck!"

> "We never *seen* you use the reins — that much we must admit —
> But s'pose you take his bridle off and see what brand he'll git!"
> Ol' Jeff shucked Shucker's bridle off and throwed it on the ground,
> Then rode him right back in the herd and started scoutin' round.
> It didn't take a jiffy until here comes Shuck again,
> A-shovin' out a Bar U cow. The dudes believed it then,
> And paid their bet, and went back home a-tellin' all who'd heed,
> How them there Pecos cowboys learnt their horses how to read.

> It gives ol' Jeff a chuckle when he tells about it yet —
> The easy way he fooled them dudes to win his little bet.
> "O' course ol' Shucker couldn't read no earmarks nor no brand,
> But when he'd find a Bar U cow, I made him understand
> By jest a gentle pressure of my knees or of my spur.
> That's how he'd know which one to cut, and take right after her.
> Them fellers thought ol' Shuck could read — but here's the funny
>   part:
> Sometimes I wonder if he cain't! For boys, that pony's smart!" [64]

Billy is handsome, lean and small boned with light blue quartzite eyes; a cowboy who might have posed for Remington or Russell as the flinty, hard-butt little bronc rider who leaves the saddle only when the saddle leaves the horse. His voice is so soft and drawley it's hard to imagine him yelling curses at wild stock in rodeo rings, bulldogging, or crashing through junipers looking for mavericks. Yet, all these things have been in his life, plus singing to a few dudes now and then. He is one of the very few cowboys who was able to make the transition from just plain cowpunching to the art of training horses.

The coffeepot is on; Betty pours us a cup and I wander about the room looking at trophies, ribbons, awards and pictures that decorate the walls and bookcases. Years of rodeoing hang there; winnings for themselves, their horses, headlines for Billy the bronc buster, for Betty the clown, with her famous cutting horse, The Spaniard. She's taller than Billy, statuesque is a better word, a smiling, silver-haired woman, in no way horsey looking, though one has the inclination to call her a thoroughbred. She paints, draws, writes poetry and reads avidly, is risible and brimming with energy. The two are billed as "the only act of its kind in North America." When I ask specifically what the act consists of, they haul out the scrapbooks. There is a picture of Betty in gingham blouse, bib overalls and a goofy hat, perched on a wildly leaning horse, her arms waving, mouth open — the horse is working without bit or bridle.

"Did ol' Tot Young ever tell you what made him so broke?" asks Billy.

"Oh, I dunno," answers Gail. "He prob'ly did."

"He told me, he says, 'What made me broke was houses and lots.' I says, 'How come?' and he says, 'Whore houses and lots of whiskey.' "

"That was prohibition time, of course," Gail looks up at me, "and all that stuff would just knock your hair stiff!"

I ask if that was the kind he poured down the Moonshine Steer?

"Naw, we didn't really do that. We thought about it though," and his little eyetooth twinkles.

"That fool, Tot," Billy continues, "he come to the dance all done up in frog-eyed shoes 'n stuff, and some woman come up and asked if he'd dance with her. He said, 'No, I ain't got but one good dance left in me, and I'm savin' that."

"And he said he didn't git t' dance with anybody but the featherlegs and the drags," recalls Gail.

"And them old smooth-mouthed biddies," Billy nods, smiling. "Him and another cowboy was working up in Wyoming one season, and it was colder 'n a stepmother's heart. Finally he had to throw in his rope. He told his pardner, 'I'm gonna leave this light-bread eatin', tea-drinkin', snow-flyin', sonofabitchin' country, and get back to Arizona!' "

"Katie, I'll tell ya a story on me, just to show you I'm not afraid to. This fella I knew wanted t' match me at calf ropin', and I used t' go lookin' for that kinda stuff, so I said, 'I'll match you for three hundred dollars.' 'All right,' he says — he had a cotton farm down in the valley — 'I'll bet you a bale of cotton.' So we did, and I beat him two or three tenths of a second. He said, 'when you git time, come down and pick up that bale.' I figured t'sell it, see, and get my money. Well, I went down there a week or so later t' git it and he points over and says, 'Well, there it is, out there in the field, you'll have to pick it.' Guess what? I still got a bale of cotton comin'."

> "Big windies," if you'd like to know, are tales us
>   cowboys spin
> To kinder kill the lonesomeness when night comes
>   closin' in:
> About the mighty Pecos Bill, with cyclones in his
>   loop;
> About the wring-tailed wowser and the barbwire-tailed
>   kadoop.

68

In fact the so-called "Windy" of the well known
    cow range stamp,
Ain't nothin' but us cowpokes huntin' grizzly bears —
    in camp! [65]

I'd heard from Gail that Billy's name was really See-moan, French deriva-
tion, not Sigh-mun, the way everyone pronounces it, but like Gail with *cow-
pyrography*, he just gave up when none of the cowboys ever said it right.

"Where were you born, Billy?"

"Mount Airy, Pennsylvania, but my grandfather was born in Bordeaux,
France. My mother's name was Murdoch — Scottish. My grandmother was an
old bitch and I was glad when she died. She'd get me trapped behind the stove,
shake her ol' hairy fist at me and call me a limb-o'-satan."

"What's a limb-o'-satan?"

"Damned if I know, but I was *it*. She scared the hell out of me. You know
older folks very often don't know what sort of impression they make, what a
kid will remember all his life. I had an uncle one time, and I was very fond of
him; he was sort of the black sheep of the family — and he died. Everybody got
ready to go to the cemetery that day he was buried — it was just about a mile
from our house — and all they had was a little old carriage and the hearse, and
there wasn't room to take me. Well, after they all pulled away from the house I
put on my little blue coat with brass buttons — I was about eight, I think — and
my old Civil War cap that I had, and I cut across the field in the snow to the
cemetery and hid in the bushes until the ceremony was all over and everybody
left. Then I broke off a pine bough and went over and put it on his grave as
my contribution, because I really did like Uncle Joe. I'll never forget that cold,
snowy day. I can see it plain, right now."

The sun has no real fire today, but the wind and showers seem to have
passed. We all go outside to see if we can't give spring a little boost by admir-
ing its shine while sitting on a bench in one of Betty's many charming grottos
drinking beer. I've come to hear *Spanish is the Loving Tongue* sung by the
man who put it to music some fifty, or more, years ago. My curiosity has been
considerably aroused. The melody I've always heard and sung is far too sophisticated to be the work of someone like Billy Simon. I'm even more convinced
of this now that I've seen and talked with him, but am prepared to keep my
mouth shut about it unless he offers some explanation of where he got the tune.

From somewhere his guitar appears.

"Lord, I can't play that thing no more. I got arthritis in m' hands so bad my
fingers won't stick on the strings."

"Try," I say. "Otherwise how am I going to hear the right version."

"Right? I dunno if it's *right*, it's the way I sing it."

A BORDER AFFAIR*
(*Spanish is the Loving Tongue*)

Spanish is the lovin' tongue,
    Soft as music, light as spray.

'Twas a girl I learnt it from,
  Livin' down Sonora way.
I don't look much like a lover,
Yet I say her love words over
  Often when I'm all alone —
  "Mi amor, mi corazon."

Nights when she knew where I'd ride
  She would listen for my spurs,
Fling the big door open wide,
  Raise them laughin' eyes of hers.
And my heart would nigh stop beatin'
When I'd hear her tender greetin',
  Whispered soft for me alone
  "Mi amor! Mi corazon!"

Moonlight in the patio,
  Old Senora noddin' near,
Me and Juana talkin' low
  So the Madre couldn't hear —
How those hours would go a-flyin'!
And too soon I'd hear her sighin'
  In her little sorry tone —
  "Adios, mi corazon!"

But one time I had to fly
  For a foolish gamblin' fight,
And we said a swift goodbye
  In that black, unlucky night.
When I'd loosed her arms from clingin'
With her words the hoofs kep' ringin'
  As I galloped north alone —
  "Adios, mi corazon!"

Never seen her since that night,
  I kain't cross the Line, you know.
She was Mex and I was white;
  Like as not it's better so.
Yet I've always sort of missed her
Since that last wild night I kissed her,
  Left her heart and lost my own —
  "Adios, mi corazon!"

A simple, three-chord melody, no fancy minors, no bridge after the first four lines (where all the others versions change melodic line), only the same melody repeated again, all through the song. Any cowboy could sing it, hum it, play it and pass it on in one night's learning. It is Billy's tune all right — before the non-cowboys got wind of it.

I don't suppose Clark expected his poem would go the "art song" route to be sung as that quaint and sentimental selection toward the end of Lawrence Tibbett–Grace Moore–Jan Peerce concerts, or that it would turn up in many vocal solo music books labeled, "Folk Song, arranged by ———," but it did. In all likelihood one of those "arranged by's" is where the complicated part sprouted. Richard Dyer-Bennett's version is like that. I wrote several times asking if he'd written it but never got an answer. Certainly those ribbons-'n-bows arrangements don't fit Wild Bill's, though they all basically use his original melody.

"Where did you find the tune, Billy?"

"Where'd I *find* it?"

"I mean, how come — what happened? What prompted you to write a melody for this particular song?"

"I was workin' for the Hays Cattle Company way the hell out on a line camp a hundred miles from nowhere. The only sign that humans had even *seen* the country was a little spur railroad line. The train come along once every coupla weeks — didn't stop, y' understand, but every now and then somebody'd throw a book or a magazine to me on the way. One of those books was Badger Clark's *Sun and Saddle Leather*, and I liked the poem *The Border Affair;* late models call it *Spanish is the Lovin' Tongue*. Well, I pounded a lot of leather on that job — had a lot of time to think up a tune so's I could sing it, and I finally fooled around until I got me one that suited me pretty good; the words seemed to git married with the music."

"Got it while you were riding the horse, didn't you?"

"Oh yeah. Then I'd come back to camp and wait till the moon come up and sing it with my guitar. When I came back to civilization I dude wrangled at Castle Hot Springs a couple of seasons,[66] and I'd sing it for those people."

"And other cowboys and dude singers probably picked it up from you there."

"Prob'ly. Put Gail's old *Sierry Petes* to music and sang it down there too."

I play the version of *Spanish is the Lovin' Tongue* that I have always sung, with all its fancy trimmings, and ask him, "How ya like that chord?"

"Oh, that's great!"

"But *you* didn't write it."

"No, I didn't write that. . . . I didn't write nothin'. I just fooled around till I found a tune."

"Bet you never dashed down to the copyright office and put a brand on it, did you?"

"No, I never did that either."

I smile at Gail who shakes his head, "Don't matter if you do or if you don't, they rustles it off anyway. The only people I ever gave permission to record *Sierry Petes* were George German and George Gillespie. The rest of them sheepherders I didn't give permission to do anything!"

The more garbled the versions, musically and lyrically, the higher the proof of the composition's popularity. Billy doesn't care what happens to his tunes; he only made them for his amusement. If he'd wanted to put any sort of stamp on them he would have had to make arrangements with the poets to copyright a musical version of their work. Billy had enough respect for Clark's and Gail's poems to leave them as they were, yet, on the other hand, he has never sung

Curley Fletcher's version of *Strawberry Roan;* he found a later version which tickled his funnybone more. Sometime during the thirties, at the annual "house warming" affair thrown by Porter's Saddlery in Phoenix for their regular customers and cowboys, he heard a fellow named Tex France sing what follows, so he uses Curley's tune, but never his words.

NEW VERSION *of* THE OLD STRAWBERRY ROAN *

Now you have all heard of that Strawberry Roan,
That famous old bronc, and the boys he has thrown.
Let me tell you a tale that will make your head swim,
How a blame country girl took that all out of him.
His fame is broadcasted until she got upset,
I know I can ride him and straight up, I'll bet.
So she bid farewell to the old folks at home,
And lit out to find that old Strawberry Roan.

Oh, that Strawberry Roan, Oh, that Strawberry Roan,
I'll find him, I'll ride him, I'll break his old heart,
I'll pound on his lattice work right from the start,
On the ribs of that Strawberry Roan.

Well she found that old horse at a big rodeo,
I'm telling you, boys, it was half of the show.
He came out of the chute a-buckin' straight up,
Making kangaroo jumps, and he wouldn't let up
Till she crawls right on him, and bit his crop ear
Right then and there they left this old sphere,
But the girl's settin' pretty and seemed right at home
As she spurred the full length of that Strawberry Roan.

Oh, that Strawberry Roan, Oh, that Strawberry Roan,
He can't jump a lick, he's puddin' to ride,
She is making lace curtains out of his old hide,
The hide of that Strawberry Roan.

Now while he's a-buckin' she jumps to the ground,
Then back in the saddle with one single bound,
She's makin' a monkey of old Roany's hide,
Says she'd like to have him for her kid sis to ride.
She 'lows that her grandma could ride him to town,
Take a settin' of eggs to the old widder Brown.
Now a man that can't ride him should never compete,
But go back to his home ranch and start herdin' sheep!

Oh, that Strawberry Roan, Oh, that Strawberry Roan,
There was never a Cowboy that couldn't be throwed,
And never a Bronc that couldn't be rode,
Including that Strawberry Roan.

Now this old outlaw is hitched to a cart
A Chink huckster bought him, and he works right smart,
He peddles onions, and string beans and peas.
Old Roany's plumb gentle, and sprung at the knees.
As he patiently waits at some lady's back door,
You can see on his left hip that old forty-four.
So cowboys, beware before it's too late,
Or like Roany you'll be waitin' at some lady's gate.

Oh, that Strawberry Roan, Oh, that Strawberry Roan,
Like salty young cowboys he roamed far and wide,
But now he's a-waitin' while women decide,
He's a busted old Strawberry Roan.

I'm sure there are those who hate to see Old Roany's career end in this manner, but if they'd been smashed, banged and "throwed" from the hurricane deck of as many wild broncs as Billy Simon has, well. . . .

"Billy, have you set music to any more poems beside Gail's song and *The Border Affair?*"

"Hmmm. Yeah, I think there were some others. In that same book there was one I liked a lot; used an old tune like I used for *Sierry Petes*, but had to change it a little. Can't remember what it was called."

Betty remembers, "The one about the lion."

"Oh yeah, *The Glory Trail*. Cowboys who sang it called it *High Chin Bob*,[67] I think."

"Mother's folks! Us types have been lookin' all over hell for the cowpoke who . . . why didn't you tell me that before?"

"You never asked me."

"When did you do it?"

"Oh, I dunno, 'bout the same time as *The Border Affair* — when was that?" he asks Betty.

"When you worked for the Hays Cattle Company."

"Hell, I worked for them a number of years, off, and then on, before and after the war. So it was sometime between 1915 and 1920, thereabouts. But you know, someone else could have made a tune to that song too. I wasn't the only cowboy ridin' around exercising m' tonsils and actin' smartassed."

"Can you sing it for me, or hum the tune?"

"I can only hum in French, and you wouldn't understand it," he said. But I did. It's a French version of *Pollywolly Doodle*.

In spring of 1970 when we came to film Gail and Billy for *The Last Wagon* series, we got some more talk going and turned up another song I had failed to *ask* him about. I had heard it in southern Arizona only once, and by one person. The memories of Shorty Mac flooded back to mind. His wonderful way of smiling through half a mouthful of teeth, the way he hitched his pants, or unhitched them, the way he spat on target and grabbed hair when he mounted.

"Shorts, d'you grab a woman like that when you mount her," I asked.

"If I'uz t'show you how I grabbed a woman, it'd curl yer nectie, Buttonhole.

73

You ask lotta pointed questions fer a little squeezer don't know sheep shit from Arbuckle's coffee!"

"Well, I was just wonderin' if you hurt her as much as you do Monkeyface."

"Lissen, goddamit, that's what shag manes is for, t'mount when you got yer hands and mouth fulla ropes and other things — and it don't hurt the horse neither, he ain't got no feelin' up there. As regards your other fresh remark, I got a reputation as a wolf and I got t'keep 'er. (That was why he asked every woman he met to marry him). When I wife one, I stays with'er a reasonable time, till she puts me on nickles 'n dimes, then I dissolve with her, cause I'm just like an ol' hen — I don't like the nest I ain't a-gonna lay in it. Want t' see me really make tracks, jest show me one's that's about to calf out! They gits turrable grabby when they needs a father for it. 'Bout the onliest thing a feller kin do when one of them gits a-holt on him is to make a run fer the Grand Canyon and bullfrog off the side!" And in that context he sang:

JOSE CUERVO*

jose cuervo, mitey ranchur,
    owner uv a large estate,
spoke untwo hiz doter saying,
    "time haz come fur thee to mate.
si, my doter, pick thou wizeley
    father fur thy child to be
who in hiz turn wil inherut
    awl this hear estate frum me."

said she, "father, i kno no wun
    fur whom i wud give a dam —
most the gin-hounds in the village
    on a friday eat uv ham.
& the rest uv them, my father,
    are about az dumb az hell."
sed he, "thou hast spoken hiyu —
    wurry not fur awl is wel.

i shal send out invetashuns
    to awl grate men uv the land;
bid them to my hacienda,
    hear two woo thee fur thy hand.
& we shall make dem rite merrey;
    feasts fur them i wil prepare —
hootch we shall hav uv a-plentey —
    venisun & meet uv bear."

rode the peons on jackassez
    out a-roundin up the buntch,
biding grandes to a partey
    whare they wud be surved free luntch . . .
cum a-troopin awl the nobuls —
    drunken-pieyed to the gills —

cum the cusses from the desurt;
　　　cum they frum the raggud hills.

Then old jose slung a dinnur
　　　that wud giv a banquet shame;
gave them mutch uv hot tamales,
　　　mutch tequilla & wild game.
went he milling round the tabuls
　　　saying awl wuz hiyu-well,
shakeing hands & pattin' shouldurs
　　　while the grandes ate like hell.

& at last the feast wuz over —
　　　nun the nobuls cud eat mour —
grabbin' hats and cotes and pistuls
　　　awl uv them milled out the dore.
"But my doter —" yelled old jose
　　　as they sasheyed down the street.
"damn yer doter!" yelled the grandes —
　　　"We cum hear to drink & eat."

The frivolous spring wind races through the Horse Camp grotto. Sounds of
closing zippers punctuate its susurrus passing in the pines and we walk down
a path that might, in earlier days, have led to the granite formation rising above
a city's haze — Thumb Butte. To the left of the path I see a platform high on
the boulders; steps leading up have been built of rocks and hewn from the
granite. "What's that for, Billy? D'you have square dances up there?"

"No," he answers with a little smile, "the reason I put this platform up here
— c'mon, I'll show you." I follow his agile gait between rocks and gnarled oak
branches to the top. "For one thing, it gives a terrific view in every direction.
You can see the Frisco Peaks, which are about 110 miles away, a good portion
of Lonesome Valley; you can see Thumb Butte, Mingus and the Bradshaw
Mountains, but the main reason . . ." he turns and looks past me, his gaze
thoughtful and faraway, "I'm not a person that goes to church, but I have a
feeling when I come up here that it's sort of like a big church and I'm often
reminded of a few words that starts out . . .

Oh, Lord, I've never lived where churches grow.
　　　I love creation better as it stood
That day You finished it so long ago
　　　And looked upon Your work and called it good.
I know that others find You in the light
　　　That's sifted down through tinted window panes,
And yet I seem to feel You near tonight
　　　In this dim, quiet starlight on the plains.

. . . and those lines sort of fill my soul when I come up here — it's my church.
That's the way I feel about it."

Here is the rest of *A Cowboy's Prayer* *:

75

I thank You, Lord, that I am placed so well,
    That You have made my freedom so complete;
That I'm no slave of whistle, clock or bell,
    Nor weak-eyed prisoner of wall and street.
Just let me live my life as I've begun
    And give me work that's open to the sky;
Make me a pardner of the wind and sun,
    And I won't ask a life that's soft or high.

Let me be easy on the man that's down;
    Let me be square and generous with all.
I'm careless sometimes, Lord, when I'm in town,
    But never let 'em say I'm mean or small!
Make me as big and open as the plains,
    As honest as the hawse between my knees,
Clean as the wind that blows behind the rains,
    Free as the hawk that circles down the breeze!

Forgive me, Lord, if sometimes I forget.
    You know about the reasons that are hid.
You understand the things that gall and fret;
    You know me better than my mother did.
Just keep an eye on all that's done and said
    And right me, sometimes, when I turn aside,
And guide me on the long, dim trail ahead
    That stretches upward toward the Great Divide.

Billy Simon died of cancer October 25, 1976, one month before this book went to press. But he left his boots for me to walk in — a loving thought, though I could never fill them.

BEFORE BLACK CANYON HIGHWAY was built, the big step from northern Arizona to the Great Sonoran Desert (averaging 4,000 feet) was over Yarnell Hill, or off the Mogollon Rim into Tonto Basin, or down the Coronado Trail. From certain places on the step, which roughly cuts the state in two, one can see deep into southern Arizona. People used to mountain and eastern greenery find this southern half barren, hot, dry and unattractive. If not that, they find a world different from what the word "desert" brings to mind.

Traveling south from Prescott down the Black Canyon in early June, we see deep arroyos lying dry and patient with hot, sparkling sands in their bottoms; their names far more appealing than their appearances: Squaw Creek, Skunk Creek, Dead Man Wash and Agua Fria (mostly it is *Caliente*). Signs point to tantalizing places like Horse Thief Basin, Skull Valley and Bloody Basin; names from an age past.

On this morning white puffs are afloat in a soft blue sky, but let a little rain fall and suddenly the stage is set for *Die Valkyrie!* I've literally been washed from these mesas when lightning split through clouds that look heavy enough to knock off the peaks. Black rock blotted up the light as sudden violent winds whipped through the pass, thrashing mud, more rocks and rain against the windshield with such force that wipers couldn't clear the view. Traffic stood still. Dislodged boulders crashed down the cuts. Below, the dry and thirsty desert awaited a pittance which might not be sucked up by the arroyos. With not so much as a telltale raindrop these floods flash down the slickrock, announcing their advance with ominous hiss and rumble. Rolling before them a licking tongue of scum, foam and debris, from a few inches to several feet high, they rise like hasty pudding, then fall to nothing before reaching the arid plain below.

A few of these mutable arroyos have a felonious history.

"Hell of a place to have your Cadillac stick!" Shorty Mac hollered as he and Buck drove the six steers through the sand and up the other side of the embankment. I waited under a scrawny tree out of the blistering sun until they got the bunch together. One of the steers had made a run for it down the wash. Buck ran the stray into the dusty two-track road where he joined the rest.

"There she is, settin' in the shade pickin' her nose, as usual," he thumbed at me as he passed, "Mac, would you mind tellin' me why we bring her along to interfere with our teamwork?"

"She laughs at our stories and she makes better sandwiches than you do," he answered. "Remember when that Hollywood ding-a-ling got his Cad stuck down there?" He tossed his head back in the direction of the arroyo.

"No," said Buck with a pasted-on grin, "Be sure to tell me about it."

"I wuz doin' some horse ridin' fer Warner Brothers out here several years ago — 'bout when them new automatic shifts came in general use — and I made the mistake of accepting a ride to town in this dude's car. Well, we crossed back there, and runnin' true to form fer them types, the ol' boy got stuck. Then, instead of takin' my sage advice, letting air out of the tires and sticking rocks and brush under the wheels, he tries his fancy new shift for'erd and back a few times and buries 'er. Well, the pore dumb bastard lets her idle for a minute, and it's of a sudden I hears this ominous rumble that ain't got nothin' t'do with motor cars. Being all too familiar with the Arizona aphorism, He-Who-Sit-In-Dry-Wash-Get-Wet, I departs that chariot like a fart in a windstorm, while the rest of them sports sets there a-bellerin' at each other, 'Cram it in reverse, Charlie! . . . Floorboard the sonofabitch! . . . What the hell's that noi——— *Jesus Christ!*' They looks up and sees this wall of mud, cactus and fenceposts a'comin' down on 'em like Noah's flood. Well, that Cad empties quicker'n an ol' man's purse at a peepshow, and them old boys clamored up the bank barely in time t' save their suedes."

Shorty Mac jettisoned a stream of tobacco juice at a big beetle ten feet off the side of the road and hit dead on target, rolling him end over end in a ball of wet, sticky sand. "I went down below here couple days later when they finally disinterred the car. Ya' know, it looked jest like a kid's toy after he'd throwed a mad and stomped it in the mud."

> To barter the sting of the mountain wind for the
>   choking fog and smoke?
> To barter the song of the mountain stream for the
>   babble of city folk?
> To lose my grip on the god I know and fumble among
>   the creeds?
> Oh rocks and pines of the high, far hills,
>   Hear the lisp of the valley reeds! [68]

Off the Big Jump I drive beside the dry Agua Fria River, moving in and out of cloud shadows. Warm, dry air rises from the Sonoran Desert, and in a notch of one of the canyons I catch a glimpse of chartreuse carpeting on the desert floor. Saguaro cacti are in bloom, foolishly crowned with waxy white blossoms. Space. Miles of uninterrupted distance fold around me like rich silk as the horizon stretches; familiar smells and visions trail past the open window. . . .

Palo Verde in the spring . . . a damp riverbed in evening . . . the new, tinny smell of sweaty children playing beside an irrigation ditch . . . a lathered horse, a puma, a mule deer in musk, and under all, the sharp, almost medicinal smell of greasewood mixed with damp caliche dust. Swimming the icy spring floods of Sabino Creek . . . climbing trails to Tanque Verde, Seven Falls and Mt. Lemmon, or driving the old control road up the back way, loaded with steaks and beer for a weekend on the mountain . . . horses snorting, cattle squalling, birdcalls muffled in the dust, a lone coyote's shrill yelp, and under all, the soundtrack of voices harmonizing, in the car, on the horses, along the trails, under bridges, beside campfires, and even in our bedrolls . . .

ROUNDUP LULLABY*

Desert blue and silver in the still moonshine
    Coyote yappin' lazy on the hill,
Sleepy winks of lightnin' down the far sky line.
    Time for millin' cattle to be still.

    So — o, now, the lightnin's far away,
        The coyote's nothing skeery;
        He's singin' to his dearie —
    Hee-ya, tammalalleday!
        Settle down, you cattle, till the mornin'.

Nothin' out the hazy range that you folks need,
    Nothin' we kin see to take your eye.
Yet we got to watch you or you'd all stampede,
    Plungin' down some 'royo bank to die.

    So — o, now, for still the shadows stay;
        The moon is slow and steady;
    The sun comes when he's ready.
    Hee-ya, tammalalleday!
        No use runnin' out to meet the mornin'.

Cows and men are foolish when the light grows dim,
    Dreamin' of a land too far to see.
There, you dream, is wavin' grass and streams that brim
    And it often seems the same to me.

    So — o, now, for dreams they never pay.
        The dust it keeps us blinkin'
        We're seven miles from drinkin'
    Hee-ya, tammalalleday!
        But we got to stand it till the mornin'.

Mostly it's a moonlight world our trail winds through.
    Kain't see much beyond our saddle horns.
Always far away is misty silver-blue;
    Always underfoot it's rocks and thorns.

So — o, now. It must be this away —
The lonesome owl a-callin'
    The mournful coyote squallin'
Hee-ya, tammalalleday!
    Mocking-birds don't sing until the mornin'.

Always seein' 'wayoff dreams of silver-blue;
    Always feelin' thorns that stab and sting.
Yet stampedin' never made a dream come true,
    So I ride around myself and sing.

So — o, now, a man has got to stay,
    A-likin' or a-hatin'
    But workin' on and waitin'.
Hee-ya, tammalalleday!
    All of us are waitin' for the mornin'.

The sky is no longer blue.

In place of high altitude clarity, an opaque yellow hangs over Phoenix. A metallic taste spreads over the roof of my mouth, becoming the more unsavory as we descend the tomb-like cement freeway that cuts through and around the city. The air stays pretty much the property of the mining industry all the way to Tucson.

But cowboys still gather at spring roundup, going from ranch to ranch, helping cut, brand, and separate stock and drive it from dry desert to mountains of a summer range. And though jeeps run chuck now instead of wagons and dynamite makes water holes, old timers on faraway ranches will tell you "it ain't changed much," until they try shopping in the city for a side of bacon, then all hell breaks loose. "Couldn't git none in that goddam super markit 'thout she's all cut up in little bitty ribbons!"

The desert wears her spring crown, the gift of a good wet year. The coyotes who come to drink at my mother's pool are glossy and fat. Peanuts, the little chipmunk, wearing a new battle scar over his left eye, enters the house, scampers to the big chair and takes peanuts from my hand. I visit the old cowboys, write some letters, and hear from Mr. Rogers.

Dear Katie Lee,

I am slow in answering your letter for several reasons — one being that I have so little to say.

With regards to Old Dolores. I have been looking for old notebooks which I do not find here and which I am sure are either back in the Yale Library, the Congressional Library, or with the Colorado Historical Society, here in Denver. Not finding them, I have tried to recall something of that time, but many years have passed and one's memory plays tricks. My son, Hamilton, recently took a trip to that area and was successful, I think, finding the old site. I am afraid it will be a disappointment to you, as he told me the place had fallen in very bad repair and there was little or nothing left.

Now, as respects the locale of Old Dolores. When I was there, somewhere about 1912, there was a little plaza surrounded with adobe one-story houses with a pool in the center of the square, almost deserted. There was a store where we bought cheap beer and cheese. There were a lot of willows and trees around the pool, which was fed by a trickle that splashed from the mountains behind. It had been a mining town for lodes on the Ortiz mountains which we did not visit. The owner told me that the watering place had been used in the 1870s by cattle herders driving north to the railends from Texas and was a favorite cowboy resort for the herders. He told some yarns of shooting frays and a posse incident looking for cattle thieves. There was, he said, a famous Mexican guitar player who was crippled by a horse fall and begged contributions in a tin cup on the plaza . . . all this was said fifty years or more ago and dealt with events forty years earlier. I cannot remember the detail. One of our motor drivers we brought had a guitar and sang *La Paloma* while we had a Harvey House lunch in the shade. The view was spread out before us — a view over this country where anybody can own a whole mountain but nobody can afford a water supply.

Come and see us when you are nearby. I am sorry to be so unhelpful.

J.G.R.

Georgetown, Colorado [69]

Tucson, Arizona

Dear Willie:

Enclosed you will find a copy of James Grafton Rogers' letter. *Now* try and tell me that cowboys stopping to water cattle at Old Dolores is a romantic, but *secondary* fact! And yippee! Cattle thieves! . . . shooting frays! . . . and guitar players! A whole plaza with one-story adobe houses around it all gone? The pool? The spring from the mountain behind gone? Nutz! Maybe you can't see it from the air, but if you spot any faint trails or roads heading in that direction mark them on the topo map for me. When I get there in the fall, I'll by God find Old Dolores!

Love and kisses,
"Tinkerbell" [70]

Museum of New Mexico Library
Santa Fe
Box 1727

Dear Miss Lee:

We have delayed answering your letter awaiting a conference with Mr. Bill Mekeel. Mr. Mekeel was sure he could locate Dolores, New Mexico on the topography map you left with us. We are not too sure that we can, but lest he be long delayed in coming we will give our interpretation and send his when we receive it.

On page 164 of the United States Geological Survey *Professional Papers* no. 68 published by the Government Printing Office in 1910, Dolores is shown as being 2 miles north and one mile east of Lone Mountain. The Cunningham Mine is shown just south of Dolores. Our guess is that the

Cunningham Mine and the Universal Mine (on your topography map) is the same mine. Sierra del Oro translates "mountain of gold." The old map does show Dolores south but very little, if any, east of Cerrillos.

When Mr. Mekeel comes we will ask him to make a definite mark on your map showing Dolores.

Very truly yours,
(Mrs.) Elma A. Medearis
Assistant Librarian [71]

June
Santa Fe
Dear Tinkerbell:

You're quite a case! Ignoring completely the important parts of Rogers' letter, i.e., the place fallen in very bad repair, little or nothing left, all this 90 years ago, you still have a picture of the plaza with all its trimmings just like it was then. Need I tell you that once in a while it rains in the Ortiz mountains, like a *lot*, and adobe doesn't stand up very well in rain. Furthermore, baby, springs *do* dry up!

But anyhow, I went to see Mrs. Medearis at the Museum Library. No pictures have turned up in her files, but she is checking the Historical Society and random sources . . . etc. . . . Mekeel[72]

Museum of New Mexico Library
Santa Fe,
Box 1727
Dear Miss Lee:

Your most charming friend, Mr. Mekeel came in Wednesday and spotted Dolores, New Mexico on your map. He says he will be able to get an aerial map that gives a larger scale view of the town. This he will do and bring to us and we will send it to you. He is most interested and helpful. When he gets a day for his own use he wants to drive down to Dolores and see it from the ground. He plans to photograph the site. He tells me that the miners lived in the village and that the mines were in the vicinity, but the town and the mine were not in juxtaposition.

Very truly yours,
(Mrs.) Elma A. Medearis
Assistant Librarian[73]

No, no, no, Mrs. Medearis, that's not the way it works. *You* are supposed to tell *Mekeel* where Old Dolores is because he doesn't know either! The small tangle has become a snarl which is working its way toward a jumble of knots.

I reach James Grafton Rogers on the phone.

A soft, kindly voice with an inflection of humor and humility answers: "Oh, you're the girl who is looking for the Old Dolores of my song, is that right?" Affirmation. "Well, you're quite a way from it; didn't the operator say this call is from Tucson?"

"Yes, Mr. Rogers. I plan to return to Santa Fe in the fall and search the place out, but right now I have the Museum, the Historical Society, the Folk

Art Museum, and several acquaintances trying to pinpoint the site. I'm wondering if you can give me any clues? One friend is even searching for it by air."

"Why, I would think it might be very difficult to see from the air. As I remember there were many trees around, and it is quite high up on the side of the mountain. The view from there was magnificent!"

"Have you any idea how far it is from Santa Fe?"

"Oh, my, I doubt if I can help you there. We went over in these big old cars from Santa Fe, crossed rivers and streams, and wound around through and up the hills and mountains. It took us all day; we didn't reach Santa Fe until after dark — I'd say it was thirty or forty miles anyway."

"I see . . . do you remember if there was a sawmill close by?"

"No, no, I don't. There were some stone houses along the stream and in the gulch that approached the old town, and our guide informed us that many more such buildings were on up the canyon about a mile above the plaza."

"*Stone* buildings?"

"Yes, quite substantial — some were partly fallen, of course, but several were still standing, roofs caved in and the like."

"There's a place on the topography maps called Dolores Spring Ranch; it's near where Dolores could have been. Do you know if that's the town site?"

"No, Katie Lee, I don't, but you contact my son, Hamilton, he might know. Or perhaps write to the ranch and ask them what they know of the place."

"Say, I'll do that. Thank you so much, Mr. Rogers. I'll be in Denver by the end of the summer and I'll bring my guitar and tape recorder so you can sing *Old Dolores* for me."

"Oh, I don't sing very well, I'd rather hear you sing it. By the way, did you get my little package? I've sent you the *Golden Treasury Song Book* that has the other verse written by George A. H. Fraser."

"No, it hasn't come yet. Has *he* ever been to Old Dolores?"

"Oh, I think not. He just liked the song. George was an old friend; he told me one time, 'Jim, you've left something out of that song — all those houses down there near Santa Fe have chili peppers hanging from the beams drying in the sun. You should put that in the song.' I said, 'Well, George, I'm through with the song, why don't you write a verse about it,' so he did."

"I think you've written the greatest cowboy song of all time, Mr. Rogers, but I must admit you don't sound like one."

"No," he laughed, "I'm not much of a cowboy, and it has been many years since I've been on a horse. Right now I'm digging at Colorado geography and trying to finish a book on mountain natural history, but you call when you get this way and we'll spend some time together. I'm very interested in what you're doing."

Chapter 8

JUNE HAS SLIPPED BY, July has come, and every day great thunderheads pile higher and whiter over the Catalinas — mountains of my name — while the heat presses down until finally they rupture and a heavy, thumping pulse of rain gushes through the desert's veins from mountain crest to Sea of Cortez. I saddle a horse, kidney pack my bedroll and slicker, stick some apples in the saddlebags and head out for Buck's.

> A man for himself and all humankind; where the
>   winds no leash have known,
> And the soul is king of itself again, up there
>   with the stars, alone . . .
> Saddle and rifle, spur and rope, and the smell of
>   sage in the rain,
> As down the canyon the pintos lope and spread to
>   the shadowed plain. . . .[74]

Buck Watson lives alone near the top of the mountain in a cabin he built from old mine shacks that were abandoned in the thirties.[75] He makes all the money he needs at two part-time jobs; some of the year he prospects and mines, the remainder, he acts as a sort of line-camp cowboy. He is paid by several ranchers who lease National Forest grazing land to keep an eye on their beeves, check waterholes and wells, and in the fall, bring the strays down to their respective brands. These are his jobs *now;* some of his past occupations have been right colorful — boatman, professional hunter, game warden, mucker, truck-driver, guide, trick roper, circus barker, mechanic, border patrolman and ranch foreman — but what tops this list is the meaningful word, loner. Buck is a loner.

MY HOMESTEAD*

I built me a homestead way out on a desert
A great sandy desert
And I didn't know why.
And when it was finished I sat on my doorstep
And stared at my desert
And stared at my sky.

There I watched and I waited to find what I'd come for,
To end all my seekin'
To peacefully die.
When from out of my desert I heard me the answer
The soft-spoken answer
I could not deny.

From the wind in the sagebrush I felt the caresses
Of soft tousled tresses
That told me no lie.
And I felt the great warmth of a soft, sandy bosom,
A great naked bosom,
That pressed to the sky.

For the desert's a woman, all copper and golden
All warm and beholdin'
And true as the sky.
And each night with the sunset she creeps to my doorstep
And enters my homestead
And there we two lie.

His cabin is a cache of books and maps, arrowheads, rocks and tools; his mind a store of geology, poetry, music, songs, philosophy and history. He likes to think, putter, and be alone. Just as much he enjoys physical labor to keep his strong, muscular body fit and his libido under control. He looks at women like he would a pan of jumping beans, amused by their gyrations, temporarily fascinated, and finally bored.

Our lives are hid, our trails are strange;
    We're scattered through the West
In canyon cool, on blistered range
    Or windy mountain crest.
Wherever Nature drops her ears
    And bares her claws to scratch,
From Yuma to the north frontiers,
    You'll likely find the bach'
        You will
    The shy and sober bach'!

85

Our days are sun and storm and mist,
    The same as any life
Except that in our trouble list
    We never count a wife.
Each has a reason why he's lone,
    But he keeps it 'neath his hat
Or, if he's got to tell some one,
    Confides it to his cat,
      He does,
    Just tells it to his cat.[76]

The ride up to his place is near twenty miles of trail over desert floor to foothills, up rocky canyons, across streams, through ten or more stock gates, into manzanita and scrub oak, over Cow Head Saddle, and down a way to the little spring. There, in a rock armchair, bolted to, relaxed against and hung over the seat like a Salvador Dali clock, is Buck's castle. One arm of the chair consists of a corral, outhouse, feed-and-tack shed and a cluster of trees. The other protects a three-room structure with screened porch; kitchen-livingroom built out to the cliff's edge, overlooking the city — bedroom and porch toward the back. An ingenious water tank made from an old boiler caps a natural abutment above the bedroom where a spring trickles down. Heated by the sun, this water runs a warm bath on cool evenings. Come winter, I take mine in the kitchen sink.

Walkin' John, Buck's horse, is not in the corral, and the usual note he leaves for strangers is tacked to the door: BACK AT SUNDOWN. But Horny and Priss, the desert canaries (burros) are hobbled in the yard, so I know he'll be back tonight.

I unsaddle, unbolt the door and go in.

Cool and clean as a plate. It smells like juniper, leather, and Buck. My immediate attention fastens on an old fashioned bow-tie strung between two kitchen beams. Pinned to this bit of dilapidated elegance with clothespins are chunks of dark venison jerky. A drop of saliva hits the floor before I can get a strip of it to my mouth. The black bow-tie is one of the West's asterisks, virtually forgotten. I've found these relics in old Colorado mining camps, in ghost towns, in isolated placer diggings along the Colorado river, in abandoned trunks, and once in an old mine shaft. At the turn of the century cowboys wore them to work in, with vest and shirt, as pictures indicate — a strand of that mid-western noose he tried so hard to escape, perhaps.

I wander about looking at Buck's latest improvements — little labor-saving devices he thinks up in his spare time — such as his mousetrap; a tiny derringer, of which he says, "No traps to bait, no rats to pitch, just blow a hole in the sonofabitch!" In the outhouse is a Rube Goldberg thing of springs, wires, strings and a can that dumps lime into the hole *after* you get up. I sincerely hope so!

Quarter of an hour before sundown I hear a horse on the trail. As he passes the corner of the tack shed I say from its shadow, "You're early."

"Kitty! Goddam!"

He throws a leg over the dally horn, leaps down and grabs me off the ground. "There's gonna be a face-lickin' in camp tonight, shore," he says. "Yah-hoo!"

As I slide down his front we hook belts, resting eye to eye, looking long and deep, remembering each other again. Words are for people who can't read sign.

I cannot recall how far back, or where, I first saw Buck. When I was in my teens it seemed he sort of grew out of a rib of Shorty Mac McGinnis — except he was a better looking man — when I got to knowing what "better-looking" was. They were alike in their manner of speaking and moving. They were both cowboys. They both played cowboy songs, but only Shorty Mac sang. In the back right pocket of every pair of Buck's jeans there was, and is still, a hole, patched or wearing, where his latest harmonica has or will fall through.

Unlike other cowboys, Buck most always has a deep tan above the waist from riding shirtless. Hair and brows of wheat gold contrast the lean, tanned face where sun wrinkles etch his forehead and make a trimming for his china blue eyes. Wind and sun have eroded him beyond his years, but in another way the great outdoors has preserved him. There's a little kid behind his smile, a coltishness in his gait, power in the lean muscles of his arms and legs. Beneath his changing moods and the secrets in his gaze there is warmth and gentleness.

Nor do I remember how it came to pass one starry night in my twenties, that Buck warmed up in that stock tank I finally got him into, instead of cooling down. Luckily, by then I knew the rules, so neither one of us got grabby. We were able to enjoy each other's thoughts, each other's songs, and for short and vivid periods, each other's company. It is much easier to accomplish a goal when you've been sent out into the world with a slap on the butt and words like: "I'll miss your bright eyes and sweet smile, n' all that crap, but keep yer tail up, Kitty. Go give 'em hell! And . . . well, look me up when you come back . . . *if* you do."

THE TRAIL HERDING SONG*

Oh, your backs they are weak
And your legs they ain't strong
Don't be skeered little dogies
We'll git there 'fore long.
From dawn until midnight
We strike down the trail
Just ya foller yer leaders
And hold up yer tail.

> Ki-yi-yip! Git along . . . git along.
> Ki-yi-yippie, ki-yay . . . ki-yay!

Though we foller a trail
That sometimes kain't be found
Just like that ol' river
That runs underground,
We'll pick it up further

Somewhere in the land
Where the cactus and mesquite
Stand thick in the sand.

Oh, we ain't found a blade of grass
Here 'neath the sky.
And we ain't found a river
That hasn't run dry.
But there's sure water somewhere
And grass growin' too,
So just keep yer tails up,
Don't ya never git blue.

Now I ain't seen m' gurl
Since the last of July
Her little hand wavin'
Against the red sky.
The soft evenin' breeze
Was a-blowin' her hair
Don't ya make no fuss, dogies
We gotta git there!

Ki-yi-yip! Git along . . . git along.
Ki-yi-yippie, ki-yay . . . ki-yay!

"Thought you was back east in the grime pots with all them dudes rattlin' up tunes," says Buck.

"You did not. Mom told you I was coming last time you were in town."

"Yeah, I kinda figured you'd be along one of these days. What took ya so long?" He gives me a quizzical look, pleats his forehead and narrows the electric blue eyes down to slits. "Your mom says you're writin' a book. What about?"

"The disappearance of guys like you, Goodlookin." He always glances back of him when I call him that, pretending to look for whomever I must be talking to.

"Hell, I ain't going to disappear. B'sides, you better keep me out of it or I'll sue your pants off – if you happen to have any on at the time." Grabbing me by the seat of my jeans, he marches me toward the cabin, then, tugging to a halt, he says, seriously, "How long will you stay?"

"Couple days maybe . . . if we can go to the top."

"We can." His eyes move down my frame to the boots and back, slowly, like he's checking for mange or something.

"What'sa matter?" I growl.

"Just lookin' t' see if you still fit in the sink."

While Buck gets dinner I take a warm tank shower, splash in the cold spring, find a clean shirt in his closet and go stand in the kitchen doorway to watch the colors fade. Down the western horizon, reflected light of a sun already set makes an orange layer-cake of the haze over the valley. The spring gurgles over its rocky bottom and stars turn on in the deepening blue. Horny and Priss tune their bagpipes and a soft breeze stirs the trees.

BLAM!

I leap straight in the air, cover my head and fall out the door. "Jesus! What's that?"

My host pads barefoot to the stove. "Biscuits are ready," he states matter-of-factly. "Fixed up a timer on m'oven door. Great, eh?"

Cautiously, I poke my head inside. "Oh, *colossal* . . . if you don't die of shock before you get something to eat!"

> We're young or old or slow or fast,
>   But plumb versatyle.
> The mighty bach' that fires the blast
>   Kin serve up beans in style.
> The bach' that ropes the plungin' cows
>   Kin mix the biscuits true —
> We earn our grub by drippin' brows
>   And cook it by 'em too,
>   We do,
>   We cook it by 'em too.[77]

Our breeze shifts down canyon, ruffles the coal oil lantern and brings down a smell of pine from the crest. Buck puts the dishes in the sink, runs water to soak them, takes his knife and whittling stick and walks outside. I follow him to the stout rail fence where he sits and I lean, looking at the lattice work of Tucson's lights blinking far away. The breeze makes little wailing sounds in the rocks and an occasional whittle-chip falls in my hair. A three-quarter moon splashes silver in the yard. The whittling stops. His head tilts down into cupped hands and from the reedy depths of his harmonica Buck pulls a tremulous tune:

WARING OF SONORA TOWN*

> The heat acrost the desert was a-swimmin' in the sun,
>   When Waring of Sonora-town
>   Jim Waring of Sonora-town,
> From Salvador come ridin' down, a-rollin' of his gun.
>
> He was singin' low an' easy to his pony's steady feet,
>   But his eye was live an' driftin'
>   Round the scenery an' siftin'
> All the crawlin' shadows shiftin' in the tremblin'
>   grey mesquite.
>
> Eyes was watchin' from a hollow where an outlaw Cholo lay:
>   Two black, snaky eyes, a-yearnin'
>   For Jim's hoss to make the turnin',
> Then — to loose a bullet burnin' through his back —
>   the Cholo way.
>
> Jim Waring's gaze, a-rovin' free an' easy as he rode,
>   Settled quick — without him seemin'
>   To get wise an' quit his dreamin' —
> On a shiny ring a-gleamin' where no ring had ever glowed.

But the lightnin' don't give warnin' — just a lick, an'
    she is through.
Waring set his gun to smokin'
Playful-like — like he was jokin',
An' — a Cholo lay a-chokin', an' a buzzard cut the blue.

It is a familiar tune, one that I wrote for Mr. Knibbs's poem in the late forties. Shorty Mac used to recite it for us, as he did many of Knibbs's poems, but I wanted to sing it and I wanted to hear Buck play it. So it happened that I set *The Rustler, Waring of Sonora Town, Boomer Johnson* and *Walkin' John*, altering some of the verses in the process to shorten them and get the best meat — something I probably wouldn't do now that I don't have to sing them for nightclub audiences. Without ever hearing *Walkin' John* sung, (up to that time) the melody I invented came so close to that sung by the Arizona cowboys as to raise my hair! (More from that allegorical pipe that Alan Lomax has no faith in — yet all musicians know there is no such thing as an original melody). The version that follows is exactly as Henry Herbert Knibbs wrote it — my version is printed with the music.

WALKIN' JOHN*

Walkin' John was a big rope-hoss, from over Morongo
    way;
When you laid your twine on a ragin' steer, old John
    was there to stay.
So long as your rope was stout enough and your
    terrapin shell stayed on.
Dally-welte, or hard-and-fast, it was all the same
    to John.

When a slick-eared calf would curl his tail, decidin'
    he couldn't wait,
Old John, forgettin' the scenery, would hit an amazin'
    gait;
He'd bust through them murderin' cholla spikes, not
    losin' an inch of stride,
And mebbe you wished you was home in bed — but
    pardner, he made you ride!

Yes, John was willin' and stout and strong, sure-
    footed and Spanish broke,
But I'm a-tellin' the wonderin' world for once, he
    sure did enjoy his joke;
Whenever the mornin' sun came up he would bog his
    head clear down,
Till your chaps was flappin' like angel wings and
    your hat was a floatin' crown.

That was your breakfast, regular, and mebbe you
    fell or stuck.

At throwin' a whing-ding, John was there a-teachin'
the world to buck.
But after he got it off his chest and the world come
back in sight,
He'd steady down like an eight-day clock when its
innards is oiled and right.

We give him the name of Walkin' John, once durin'
the round-up time,
Way back in the days when beef was beef and John
he was in his prime;
Bob was limpin' and Frank was sore and Homer he
wouldn't talk,
When somebody says, 'he's Walkin' John — he's makin'
so many walk.'

But shucks! He was sold to a livery that was willin'
to take the chance
Of John becomin' a gentleman — not scared of them
English pants.
And mebbe the sight of them toy balloons that is wore
on the tourist's legs
Got John a-guessin'; from that time on he went like
he walked on eggs.

As smooth as soup — till a tourist guy, bogged down
in a pair of chaps,
The rest of his ignorance plumb disguised in the
rest of his rig — perhaps,
Come flounderin' up to the livery and asked for to
see the boss:
But Norman he savvied his number right and give him
a gentle hoss.

Yes, Walkin' John, who had never pitched for a year
come the first of June.
But I'm tellin' the knock-kneed universe he sure
recollected soon!
Somebody whanged the breakfast gong, though we'd all
done had our meat,
And John he started to bust in two, with his fiddle
between his feet.

That dude spread out like a sailin' bat, went floppin'
acrost the sky;
He weren't dressed up for to aviate, but, sister, he
sure could fly!
We picked him out of a cholla bush, and some of his
clothes stayed on;

91

We felt of his spokes, and wired his folks. It was
    all the same to John.

I wish now that I had paid more attention to the songs that are inherently
mine. I surely heard enough of them when I was younger, but I thought "cowboy songs" were corny and that *Riding Down The Canyon, Tumbling Tumbleweeds,* and *Cattle Call* (all songs from motion pictures of that time) were the
be-all and end-all. What I was hearing was the last gasp of the true western
folk song and the beginning of what Buck calls "that poor and separated piss
— Country-Western — which is neither of either . . . the yodel being about as
native to the true cowboy song as tits on a boar." (Another example in this
spurious category is *The Western Plains*). It wasn't until Buck began talking
about the old songs, dropping hints about who wrote them, when and why, that
I became the least interested. He'd tell me stories about some of the writers and
the next thing I knew I was scouring the western history and poetry section of
libraries in every city I played. From 1950 to 1965 that was a bunch of libraries!
He had a thing about Henry Herbert Knibbs's poems — even named his horse
after one of them — and was always on the prowl for HHK's books, (which are
scarcer than fish feathers) so I was mighty pleased to write from Kansas City
that I'd found one of our favorite songs (which we sang under the title *Jake
and Roany*) to be *The Bosky Steer* written by Knibbs. Unfortunately we never
uncovered the tunesmith for it, nor the original composer of *Walkin' John.*

THE BOSKY STEER*

Jake and Roany was a-chousin' along,
    And Jake was a'singin' what he called a song,
When up from a waller what should appear,
    But a moss-horned maverick, a bosky steer.

Jake he started with his hat pulled down,
    Built a blocker that would snare a town;
That steer he headed for the settin' sun,
    And believe me, neighbor, he could hump and run!

Roany he follered his pardner's deal,
    — Two old waddies that could head and heel —
Both of 'em ridin' for the Chicken Coop,
    With a red-hot iron and a hungry loop.

The sun was a-shinin' in ole Jake's eyes,
    And he wasn't just lookin' for no real surprise,
When the steer gave a wiggle like his dress was tight,
    Busted through a juniper and dropped from sight.

Jake and his pony did the figure eight,
    But Jake did his addin' just a mite too late;
He left that saddle, and a-seein' red,
    He lit in the gravel of a river bed.

Now Roany's hoss was a good hoss, too,
    But he didn't understand just why Jake flew,
So he humped and started for the cavviard,
    And left Roany settin' where the ground was hard.

Jake was lookin' at a swelled-up thumb,
    And he says, "I reckon we was goin' some!'
When Roany hollers, 'Git a-movin' quick,
    Or you're sure goin' to tangle with that maverick!'

Roany clumb a-straddle of the juniper tree.
    "Ain't no more room up here,' yells he.
So Jake he figured for hisself to save,
    By backin' in the openin' of a cut-bank cave.

The steer he prodded with his head one side,
    But he couldn't quite make it to old Jake's hide;
Kep' snortin' and pawin' and prodin' stout,
    But every time he quit, why, Jake come out.

'You ole fool!' yips Roany, 'Keep back out of sight!
    You act like you're *hankerin'* to make him fight!'
Then Jake he hollers kind fierce and queer:
    'Back, hell, nothin'! There's a bear in here!'

Knibbs was not a fake who wrote vicarious rot behind a desk; he went to live his dream. Born a Canadian, he learned in his youth to love wild country, to forage from it, to canoe its white water and understand the tricks of survival. For years he drudged away at a stenography job, then when he was nearly thirty-five, he and his wife took off with his pittance of a savings for Harvard, where they enrolled in English literature courses. All the savings were gone when they finished, except enough to buy a canoe and camping equipment for a winter hole-up in the Canadian wilderness. There he collected atmosphere for his first novel (he wrote a dozen or more — the best selling one, *Overland Red*). In 1911 the two of them built a little ranch at the foot of the Sierras, in California, where he learned to rope, and ride a cow pony. Knibbs stayed to become an American citizen, to write five books of poetry and many stories — a literary man, to be sure, but of the caliber of Charles Badger Clark, and one who knew the feel of a good horse beneath him. Cowboys recognizing him as one of their own kind, so honored him by singing his poems. I suspect many have been 'set' again and again by lonesome herdsmen, long forgotten, in places once so wild and woolly, now so tame and shaved.

    What you want to happen in these vignettes usually does, but whether your expectations are realized or not, you are titillated by the artistry of the poet's method, his manipulation of words.

BOOMER JOHNSON*

Now Mr. Boomer Johnson was a gettin' old in spots,
    But you don't expect a bad-man to go wrastlin'
        pans and pots;

But he'd done his share of killin' and his draw
    was gettin' slow,
So he quits a-punchin' cattle and he takes to
    punchin' dough.

Our foreman up and hires him, figurin' age had
    rode him tame,
But a snake don't get no sweeter just by changin'
    of its name.
Well, Old Boomer knowed his business — he could
    cook to make you smile,
But say, he wrangled fodder in a most peculiar
    style.

He never used no matches — left 'em layin' on the
    shelf,
Just some kerosene and cussin' and the kindlin'
    lit itself.
And, pardner, I'm allowin' it would give a man a jolt,
To see him stir *frijoles* with the barrel of his Colt.

Now killin' folks and cookin' ain't so awful far
    apart;
That must 'a' been why Boomer kept a-practicin'
    his art;
With the front sight of his pistol he would cut a
    pie-lid slick,
And he'd crimp her with the muzzle for to make the
    edges stick.

He built his doughnuts solid, and it sure would curl
    your hair,
To see him plug a doughnut as he tossed it in the
    air.
He bored the holes plumb center every time his
    pistol spoke,
Till the can was full of doughnuts and the shack was
    full of smoke.

We-all was gettin' jumpy — but he couldn't understand
Why his shootin' made us nervous when his cookin'
    was so grand.
He kept right on performin', and it weren't no big
    surprise,
When he took to markin' tombstones on the covers of
    his pies.

They didn't taste no better and they didn't taste no
    worse,

But a-settin' at the table was like ridin' in a
    hearse;
You didn't do no talkin' and you took just what you
    got,
So we et till we was foundered just to keep from
    gettin' shot.

Us at breakfast one bright mornin', I was feelin'
    kind of low,
When Old Boomer passed the doughnuts and I tells
    him plenty, 'No!'
All I takes this trip is coffee, for my stomach is
    a wreck,'
I could see the itch for killin' swell the wattles
    on his neck.

Scorn his grub? He strings some doughnuts on the
    muzzle of his gun,
And he shoves her in my gizzard and he says, 'You're
    takin' one!'
He was set to start a graveyard, but for once he
    was mistook;
Me not wantin' any doughnuts, I just up and salts
    the cook.

Did they fire him? Listen, pardner, there was
    nothin' left to fire.
Just a row of smilin' faces and another cook to
    hire.
If he joined some other outfit and is cookin' —
    what I mean,
It's where they ain't no matches and they don't
    need kerosene.

The sycamores have stopped their chatter at Buck's cliff-hanging castle and
only the sound of a trickling spring punctuates the stillness when he stops playing and raps the harmonica on his knee.

"What's the latest word on our favorite song? Have you found Dolores
yet? Been there?" he asks.

"You'd get a telegram clear up here if I had. I'm moving in though, slow
but sure. Willie Mekeel is still beating bushes, and I wrote to the owner of the
Dolores Spring Ranch. Asked him if his place was the site of the old town, and
if so, did he know who'd torn the buildings down, and how long ago. He answered and said he *thought* the ranch was the site and that the one building
standing, the ranch house itself, had been a general store of the mine's office
and assaying building — he wasn't sure. He told me it was like that when he
purchased the property a few years ago and he didn't knock anything down.
But he referred me to a Mr. Parks whom he thought had owned it before him;

I've got Parks' answer in my pocket. You got eyes like a nit on a gnat's nut, you can probably read it in this light."

Carlsbad, New Mexico
Pine Springs Route

Dear Katie Lee:

In reply to yours of June 10th. Yes, I owned Dolores ranch at one time. We did not destroy the old structures on the ranch.

A Mr. Sweeten, of Cerrillos, has lived in that area for years so we are told. I feel sure he could tell you when and by whom the buildings were torn down.

Sorry I can't give you all the desired information. Trusting I've been some help.

Yours very truly,
Lester A. Parks.

P.S. The Protestant Cemetery is due east of the house, I understand the Catholic Cemetery was bulldozed off.

Mr. Sweeten's mother was cook for the old mines years ago when they were in operation.[78]

"Hmmm . . . wonder how you bulldoze a cemetery off? As a gleaner, you ain't gleanin' much from this guy — what about Mr. Sweeten."

"That name rang a bell — something Ortiz-y-Davis said when Bill and I were in Galisteo — he'd mentioned a Mr. Clarence Sweet who lived in Albuquerque. I phoned Frank to see if they mightn't be the same person and he said, yes, that Sweet had left Cerrillos some time ago. He gave me the address and I wrote Sweet the same letter I wrote Robertson and Parks — all of them were asked for old pictures, drawings, photos of the place. Nothing. That was three weeks ago — haven't heard a word from Mr. Sweet."

"Knowing you," Buck says, tooting on the willow whistle he has finished whittling and handing it to me, "you probably used your best Arizona vernacular — 'which one of you son's a-bitches knocked down the town of Old Dolores.'"

"I did not! I can be very charming and persuasive to people who . . ."

"A side of you I'm not too familiar with." He picks up the harmonica again and plays a few bars of Old Dolores, but is smiling behind the notes too much to continue.

"Okay, smartass, I was saving the best 'till last. Now I don't think I'll sing you the new verse I found."

"That would only bear out my theory that you have a mean streak in you long as a din-owzer's tail." Reaching over, he takes the back of my neck in his big hand and pulls me toward him, "I can always wring it out of you."

All the strings of peppers hung
On the 'dobes in the sun,
Blazin' red as some young puncher's new bandana,
And the scented smoke that came
From the piñon wood aflame
Smelt like incense to Our Lady of Mañana;

The scarlet lips, the clinkin' chips!
The drinks Ramon poured for us!
But the friendly lights are dark,
And the coyote's lonesome bark
Is the only music now in Old Dolores.*

"My . . . my . . . now ain't that fine," Buck sighs. "How'd you find it?"

"Written by *another* lawyer, a friend of Mr. Rogers'."

"I thought he was a cowboy."

"No, I told you he *ought* to be a cowboy — anybody writes songs like that has no business being *other than* a cowboy, right?"

"Right."

Buck lops a finger in my shirt neck and starts toward the cabin. "C'mon, shortpants, take off my shirt and let's hit the feathers — if we're goin' to the top tomorrow we have to get the dawn up early."

"Why can't we sleep out here, Buck, don't want to spend any nights under a roof until I have to — especially any Arizona nights."

"You can spend a whole month of weeks out here if ya want to, as my special guest."

"To find you gone after the third or fourth day."

We like to breathe unbranded air,
    Be free of foot and mind,
And go or stay, or sing or swear,
    Whichever we're inclined.
An appetite, a conscience clear,
    A pipe that's rich and old
Are loves that always bless and cheer
    And never cry nor scold,
        They don't.
    They never cry nor scold.

Old Adam bached some ages back
    And smoked his pipe so free,
A-loafin' in a palm-leaf shack
    Beneath a mango tree.
He'd best have stuck to bachin' ways,
    And scripture proves the same,
For Adam's only happy days
    Was 'fore the woman came,
        They was
    All 'fore the woman came.[79]

BUCK RIDES AHEAD, taking out a hand ax now and again to wing a branch that intrudes on the trail. He rides shirtless, his shoulders in a permanent slump, a little shaded hollow in his sternum, body loose, head moving as if set in a gimbal ring.

The mountains of my name are cast in purple shadow. A sultriness hangs in the air. Above a sea of scorched sand, heat waves ripple the city. I take off Buck's shirt, shove one end of it through a belt loop, watching the figure in front of me.

A maverick, self-cut from the herd, a man molded by his surroundings; tough, stubborn, resolute, non-combative, but not at all passive. A sensitive man, and sad as a girdled tree. One day this trail will be a road and he'll dismount to pick up the first beer can. Next day, he'll pack up and move on.

Where do old cowboys go?

THE LAST WAGON*

Someday when the bobwire flings its bands,
Like a fisherman's net on the last rangelands,
The last roundup wagon will roll its way
To the last bedground at the end of day.
　　Lord, don't let me live to see.

The last remuda will jingle in
To the last corral, while the nightbirds sing.
The last cookin' fire will flicker bright
By the dwarfed mesquite on that roundup night.
　　Lord, where will that bedground be?

98

And then in the morning from tarp and tent
The roundup crew on their work intent,
Will answer the call of their Wagon Boss;
On the dew-wet range their circles cross.
    Lord, where will those circles end?

The drives will come from flat and hill,
And the cattle bawl while the irons grow chill,
And silent men watch their last herd go,
While notched in the hills the sun sinks low.
    Lord, how will you make amends?

Last roundup wagon, last wagon boss.
How will you measure the thing that's lost?
What will live on the grass-grown range?
All will be lost and what will be gained?
    Lord, how will you comfort me?

The trail steepens and switches back on itself as we move up into what used to be, and what I hope is still, lion country. Flanking the up-side of the trail are immense out-croppings of jagged granite and down below the clotted brush and tumbled rock of a natural watershed. Hasn't really changed in twenty years, by the look of it. During the war when I was taking flying lessons, I'd buzz these mountains every afternoon. On the highest rocks, lolling in the sun, would be a pride of six to eight sleek lions. Pumas, they're called in these parts. At first, they streaked for shelter like coffee-colored liquid pouring down the cracks, then they seemed to get used to the noise and would stay, looking up at me with their long tails twitching. Our reason for going to the top today is to see them again. Maybe.

Buck and I make sparks on the subject of bounty. Buck kills for more than just food, whereas, my desire to shoot everything that moved ceased at the age of twenty-five, when I put a two-hundred pound buck in my *open* sights and couldn't pull the trigger. I saw him suddenly in a new light; he was more beautiful than any reason I had for killing him. Since Buck is one who upsets the deer-lion ecology by doing away with too many lions, I'm glad he's pestered out of house and home by a multitude of deer stealing his horse and burro grub.

> Ye speed the sting of the spreading slug, giving
>   your lust a name;
> Sport! to shatter the bouyant life, to sever the
>   silver thread!
> Then ye stand with a gun in hand grinning your
>   pictured shame;
> "See at my feet the mighty thing that I, yea,
>   that *I* struck dead!" [80]

From his buddy, Mr. Knibbs.

We've climbed a couple thousand feet, slowly. It is nearing lunchtime, and hot, but now rain is falling under boiling cumulus high above the Santa Catalina range — maybe the heat will break today and spill a storm on us. The trail splits around Man Head, going to a spring near the head of Madrona Canyon. Around a buttress of rock the bay and I come upon a small hidden valley, see Walkin' John ground reined to a patch of grass and Buck beside the stream catching a cool drink. "This 'ere's the real thing," he smiles up at me, "unlike the kind that comes channeled, tanked, piped and polluted, reservoired, salinized and screened, filtered and fluoridated, chlorinated and aerated — direct to YOU! Want some watercress? Some up there under the trees."

"Sure, wait a second," I tell him, sliding off my horse and grabbing hair the way Shorty Mac used to. "Help me get my boots off."

"Why don't'cha ride barefoot, shortpants, then we won't have t'go through this every time."

"Quit naggin' and pull." He bends, facing the stream, reaching between his legs for my boot. "You should get *in* that lovely water and cool off."

"My skin's delicate as a baby's — can't afford to git it all cracked and roughed-up like yours. Gimme your other foot."

Trust in a man is a beautiful thing.

As my foot slides from the boot I give a gentle push and he falls headlong for the stream, but not before a reptile-like strike at my foot and a circus performer's grip on the ankle. We hit the drink together!

I could drown down here. It's hard to laugh underwater.

Surfacing, I hear him sputter, "You black-hearted little bitch! You haven't changed a goddam bit!" He stands hip deep, glowering.

"You smell better already, Goodlookin'."

From the saddlebags comes jerky and buttered sourdough, which we jam full of nippy cress. Buck waters the horses. We lie down on the water-carved rocks, eat apples and let our clothes dry. Tapping water from his harmonica, he then plays a few tentative chords to see if the notes are still damp.

"I figured why you like outlaw songs so much," he scowls, "You're the prize of the pickin's."

" 'N' what are you?"

"Why I am the sweetest tempered little angelchild that . . ."

"Play!"

THE ARIZONA KILLER*
I killed a man in Dallas,
And another in Cheyenne,
But when I killed the man in Tombstone
I overplayed my hand.
I rode all night for Tucson
To rob the Robles Mine,
And I left old Arizona
With a posse right behind.

I rode across the border
And there it did not fail
The men that was a follerin' me
They soon did lose my trail,
They lost my trail.

They galloped back to Tucson
To get the Cavalry,
While I stayed on in Mexico
Enjoying liberty.
　　　Ayi-ha! Enjoyed my liberty!

I promised my Rosita
A pretty dress of blue
She said, "You'd go and get it
If you really loved me true,
　　　Did love me true."

So I went back to the border
Just to get that gal a dress
I killed a man in Guaymas,
And two in Nogales —
　　　Killed two in Nogales.

But the posse was a waitin'
To get me on the trail,
Now in Tombstone I'm a layin'
In the Cochise County jail —
　　　The Cochise County jail.

They're gonna hang me in the mornin',
A'fore this night is done.
They're gonna hang me in the mornin,'
And I'll never see the sun.
I want to warn you fellers,
And tell you one by one,
What makes a gallows rope to swing —
A woman . . . and a gun!

"Kitty, how's our lady *Lasca* doing?"

"She was a smash in New York. When I figured how to use her in that padded cell, The Blue Angel. Downstairs At The Upstairs this winter I found she fit beautifully late in the show — you could hear a pin drop." [81]

Buck rolls over on his stomach. "Sandburg was right then, after all. That's nice."

"Yup."

Hollywood, Circa 1950. Working with Gordon MacRae on NBC's Railroad Hour — summer series.

They wanted to do obscure western stories in ballad form. (Radio, remember.) I thought of this great old epic poem that Shorty Mac (with Buck behind him on harmonica) used to say aloud and that I had cut and put to music. The story is about an American cowboy who falls in love with a Mexican Senorita, down along the Rio Grande. I showed at the writer's conference table, then Lawrence and Lee,[82] with the poem's ten long stanzas cut to a short seven.

They would have preferred three. The producer was so hot to do it that he abandoned the whole idea in favor of western (?) *Casey At The Bat.*

All, well, nothing wasted. I knew I had a good audience oriented song. Shortly after, I ran into Carl Sandburg and sang it for him. I won't forget his kind words:

"Katie, you have revived one of the great western poems. Keep singing it. Folks don't listen to 'recitation' like they did when I was younger, but they *do* listen to ballads. This is a classic!"

Or Woody Guthrie's from:

Haggerty House
932½ Lucile Ave.
Los Angeles 26, California
Aprils 26th try —
hard year of 19.50

". . . but when you as a folk spokestress get up and stand up or keep your seat and sit down and tell them it's that way, well, then, then you make their eye to see how it is, and you make their inner ear to hear it like it is, and of course they clap hands and whoople and holler and beller and rave and rankle and bang and clatter for you to come back, see, and stick around for a long time to heal their hurts by telling them how it looks to you." [83]

Or Eddie Albert's reaction, sitting at the bar of the house on Amalfie Drive:
"My god, what a song!"
"It was a *better* poem."
"I could do it in my nightclub act with a guitar background."
He did, and does.

In order for me to sing it properly I had to get involved — the kind of involvement like *Old Dolores* — when-where-why-what-who? It was the only western ballad that I didn't sing with a quasi western accent; they all call for it, but *Lasca* had a mildly rose-scented breath about her, hardly Texan in character. It fascinated me — Buck also. She started us on the prowl for her creator.

Most printings of it appear with the name, Frank Desprez, which is unusual for a poem old enough to have been in my parents' rhetoric books, printed again in anthologies and cast adrift among the cowboys. He was Mexican, or perhaps French? People my age had never heard of the poem, much less the man, nor did the Library of Congress do me any favors when I went there looking for his background. But an anthology printed in London lit up the fact that Texas-printed versions deleted the first six lines of the poem, and seven more in the middle, which gave the only clues about the author. These had been left out to suggest that the poem was made in Texas by Texans. It wasn't. The poem began:

> It's all very well to write reviews,
> And carry umbrellas, and keep dry shoes,
> And say what everyone's saying here,
> And wear what everyone else must wear;
> But to-night I'm sick of the whole affair.

Finally there was a rhyme for the line which always appeared as the first in American printed versions: "I want free life, and I want fresh air." And in the middle:

> Why did I leave the fresh and free,
> That suited her and suited me:
> Listen awhile, and you will see;
> But this be sure — in earth or air,
> God and God's laws are everywhere,
> And Nemesis comes with a foot as fleet
> On the Texas trail as in *Regent Street*. (Italics mine)

Regent Street, Texas?

The anthology also revealed that Desprez was born in Bristol, England, February 9, 1853, and died in London, November 22, 1916. Neither French nor Spanish, he was of Norman extraction. This the Library of Congress coughed up. No more.

Buck wrote telling me to get in touch with J. Frank Dobie of the Texas Folklore Society, which I did. He was kind enough to send the name of a lady professor at Baylor University in Waco, a Miss Mable Major. I'm indebted to her for the rest of the story. A few of my early speculations turned out to be fact: That he wasn't a Texan, that he *was* a skilled professional writer who had *been* to Texas. From her article in the *Southwest Review*, Autumn, 1951, the following:

She found his birthplace the same way I did and sent everyone there named Desprez a letter asking information of Frank, the writer of the poem, *Lasca*. She was fortunate enough to turn up the brother, A. H. Desprez of Trowbridge, Wiltshire, England, whose letter revealed, among other things, that: "Frank was the eldest child of the late Charles Desprez (a jeweler). He was one of seven sons and four daughters. Upon leaving school he was apprenticed to do copper plate engraving. At the conclusion of his apprenticeship, finding that the constant use of a magnifying glass for his work had affected the sight of one eye, he decided to give it up . . . and go abroad.

"Of his life in Texas I know nothing, but understand he was out there about three years occupied on a cattle ranch in the days when cattle were herded on horses and not in Ford cars. When he returned to this country, . . . he found employment on a Bath newspaper as reporter and finally found his way to London. He secured the position as secretary to D'Oyly Cart, the founder of the Savoy Theatre and Hotel, and a great and lasting friendship sprang up between them.

"As regards *Lasca*, this was first published in Temple Bar, (no, it was first published in *London Society*, "A Monthly Magazine of Light and Amusing Literature for the Hours of Relaxation," November, 1882.) which had previously published two or three poems written by my brother before he went to Texas. Whether it is based on an actual experience of the writer's I do not know."

The rest of the letter need not concern us here, except to note that Frank Desprez was a drama critic for a theatrical newspaper, *The Era*, finally editor of same; that he wrote "curtain raisers" for operettas; that he wrote sometimes under the penname of Frank Soulbien, a family surname; that in silent movie days the story of *Lasca* was filmed in the U.S. with dubious results, especially the stampede where "the cattle never got going faster than a trot in spite of every inducement from behind," and that it has been recited at least twice on records by popular actors of that day. Miss Major thinks Desprez must have been in Texas circa 1874-75, and that he'd gone up the Chisholm Trail on drives in order to know what *a sapling pine that grows on the edge of a Kansas bluff* looked like. She received a picture from the brother that showed Frank as a middle-aged man with a monocle and a waxed mustache!

Now that I envision him with "a leetle glass clamped in his starboard optic",[84] I'm somewhat inclined to go along with the Texans — but not altogether. I find the incongruities one of the poem's major charms, that and its style, written in the age of sentimentality's floral language.

LASCA

It's all very well to write reviews,
And carry umbrellas, and keep dry shoes,
And say what everyone's saying here,
And wear what everyone else must wear;
But to-night I'm sick of the whole affair,
I want free life, and I want fresh air;
And I sigh for the canter after the cattle,
The crack of the whips like shots in battle,
The melee of horns and hoofs and heads
That wars and wrangles and scatters and spreads;
The green beneath, and the blue above,
The dash and danger, and life and love —
    And Lasca!

Lasca used to ride
On a mouse-gray mustang close to my side,
With blue *serape* and bright-belled spur;
I laughed with joy as I looked at her!
Little she knew of books or of creeds;
An *Ave Maria* sufficed her needs;
Little she cared, save to be by my side,
To ride with me, and ever to ride,
From San Saba's shore to Lavaca's tide.
She was as bold as the billows that beat,
She was as wild as the breezes that blow,
From her little head to her little feet,
She was swayed in her suppleness to and fro
By each gust of passion; a sapling pine,
That grows on the edge of a Kansas bluff,
And wars with the wind when the weather is rough
Is like this Lasca, this love of mine.

She would hunger that I might eat,
Would take the bitter and leave me the sweet;
But once, when I made her jealous for fun,
At something I'd whispered, or looked, or done,
One Sunday, in San Antonio,
To a glorious girl on the Alamo,
She drew from her garter a dear little dagger,
And — sting of a wasp — it made me stagger!
An inch to the left, or an inch to the right,
And I shouldn't be maundering here tonight,
But she sobbed, and sobbing, so swiftly bound
Her torn *rebosa* about the wound,
That I quite forgave her. Scratches don't count
    In Texas, down by the Rio Grande.

Her eye was brown — a deep, deep brown;
Her hair was darker than her eye;
And something in her smile and frown,
Curled crimson lip and instep high,
Showed that there ran in each blue vein,
Mixed with the milder Aztec strain,
The vigorous vintage of Old Spain.
She was alive in every limb,
With feeling to the finger-tips;
And when the sun is like a fire,
And sky one shining, soft sapphire,
One does not drink in little sips.

Why did I leave the fresh and the free,
That suited her and suited me?
Listen awhile, and you will see;
But this to be sure — in earth or air,
God and God's laws are everywhere,
And Nemesis comes with a foot as fleet
On the Texas trail as in Regent Street.

The air was heavy, the night was hot,
I sat by her side and forgot — forgot
The herd that were taking their rest,
Forgot that the air was close oppressed,
That the Texas norther comes sudden and soon,
In the dead of the night, or the blaze of noon;
That once let the herd at its breath take fright,
Nothing on earth can stop their flight;
And woe to the rider, and woe to the steed,
Who falls in front of their mad stampede!

Was that thunder: No, by the Lord!
I sprang to my saddle without a word.

One foot on mine, and she clung behind.[85]
Away! on a hot chase down the wind!
But never was fox-hunt half so hard,
And never was steed so little spared;
For we rode for our lives. You shall hear how we fared
    In Texas, down by the Rio Grande.

The mustang flew, and we urged him on;
There was one chance left, and you have but one —
Halt! jump to the ground, and shoot your horse;
Crouch under his carcass, and take your chance;
And if the steers in their frantic course
Don't batter you both to pieces at once,
You may thank your star; if not, good-bye
To the quickening kiss and the long-drawn sigh,
And the open air and the open sky,
    In Texas, down by the Rio Grande.

The cattle gained on us, and, just as I felt
For my old six-shooter behind in my belt,
Down came the mustang, and down came we,
Clinging together, and — what was the rest?
A body that spread itself on my breast,
Two arms that shielded my dizzy head,
Two lips that hard on my lips were pressed;
Then came thunder in my ears,
As over us surged the sea of steers,
Blows that beat blood into my eyes;
And when I could rise —
    Lasca was dead!

I gouged out a grave a few feet deep,
And there in Earth's arms I laid her to sleep;
And there she is lying, and no one knows;
And the summer shines, and the winter snows;
For many a day the flowers have spread
A pall of petals over her head;
And the little gray hawk hangs aloft in the air,
And the sly coyote trots here and there,
And the black-snake glides and glitters and slides
Into the rift of a cotton-wood tree;
And the buzzard sails on,
And comes and is gone,
Stately and still, like a ship at sea;
And I wonder why I do not care
For the things that are, like the things that were.
Does half my heart lie buried there
    In Texas, down by the Rio Grande?[86]

When presenting the sung version, I speak the last verse as Desprez wrote it, and also the first five lines; the "cutting" is as follows:

LASCA* (The Song)

I long for the canter after cattle,
The crack of the whips, like shots in battle
The mellay of the horns and hooves and heads,
The free life, the fresh air, and starlit beds,
The green beneath, and the blue above,
And dash and danger and life and love —
    And Lasca.

All day my dark-eyed Lasca used to ride
On a spooky little mustang by my side,
With a red and blue *serape*, and bright-belled spur;
Oh, I laughed with joy as I looked at her!
Beauty she was, empassioned and sweet;
She was bold, and as wild as the winds that fleet —
    My Lasca.

One Sunday, down in San Antonio
I kissed a blue-eyed girl, just for the show
Ah, but Lasca from her garter drew a dagger,
And — sting of a wasp — she made me stagger
Then from her waist she ripped her sash
And sobbing, and sobbing, she bound the gash —
    Oh, Lasca!

The desert air was damp, the night was hot
My head lay in her lap and I forgot —
Forgot the Texas norther comes sudden and soon
In the dead of the night, or the blaze of noon,
And woe to the rider and woe to the steed
That falls in front of their mad stampede
    In Texas — down by the Rio Grande.

We sprang into one saddle, she behind;
Away the mustang flew, on down the wind,
Racing for the lead before the cattle gained
But the load was too heavy and down we came,
Clinging together, and what was the rest? —
A body that spread itself o'er my breast —
    'T'was Lasca.

Two arms that shielded close my dizzy head,
Two lips that hard against my lips were wed.
And then a rage of thunder burst in my ears,
As over us surged a wild sea of steers;
Blows that beat blood down into my eyes,

And when at last I could start to rise —
Lasca was dead!

I gouged a little grave a few feet deep,
Down in the arms of Earth, laid her to sleep.
And there she lies so quiet, and no one knows;
And the summer shines, and the winter snows.
And it's no wonder I do not care
For half of my heart lies buried there —
With Lasca — down by the Rio Grande.

Buck and I ride out of the small valley and up into the pines, wind-trained and low, like the protective wings of a great teal-blue bird hovering over its brood. Crags appear from the soil in monumental upthrust, stratification vertical, covered with lichen.

At a miner's old cabin hidden in the trees, we stop to check the locks, nail up a couple of loose boards and clean out a spring. For many years it has acted as a line shack, where Buck keeps feed for the horses and stray cattle, also a few supplies for himself if ever he's caught at the top when it snows.

Beyond the outer trees the land drops away, east, to the San Pedro Valley and Little Dragoon Mountains; south to Ft. Huachuca and Tombstone. Books written about Tombstone and the goin's-on there toward the last of the Nineteenth Century could make another mountain. Seemed a kind of sticky-flypaper place that attracted every gunman in Western history, most of whom died with their boots on. But one who did not.

Johnny Ringo (of the Ringold family of Kentucky bluebloods, grandson of Colonel Coleman Younger, close friend of the Clantons and McLowerys, and buddy-buddy to Buckskin Frank Leslie) was a cool and deadly killer. When *his* turn came, no one seemed to know who shot him. Oh, there was speculation that it could have been Wyatt Earp, because Ringo had been in Tucson with Charlie Stillwell when Stillwell killed Wyatt's brother Morgan — but Ringo was found one day in West Turkey Creek of the Chiricahua mountains, sitting at the base of a giant oak with a bullet through his skull. His horse, money, coat and boots were gone. The horse was found in a draw with the boots tied to the saddle — so says one version.[87] Another states that his boots were found beside him and his feet wrapped in rags, because the boots were new and too small for him.[88]

But it wasn't Ringo's dying with his boots off that interested me, as much as his classic Western Badman appearance. He was handsome, very tall, loved good books and culture, often went to church in Tombstone (all the stock contradictions), was a ladies' man and wore ladies' garters on his sleeves, wore matched ivory-handled Colts on two separate gun belts, and drank whiskey like Doc Holiday, by the tumblerfull.[89] The song *My Love Is A Rider* (rumored to have been written by another outlaw, female, Belle Starr, but more likely written by a hundred cowboys, being a long root of cowboy pornography) fits Ringo's personality just fine. My part in this holdup is adding a chorus using Ringo's name, and composing a melody to suit it — though in reality he had nothing to do with the song.[90] It has since become "authenticated", meaning that a great many folk-singers think it is an early version. Buck is still sore at me for screwing up the record. I hereby set it straight.

Johnny Ringo*

My love is a rider, wild horses he breaks;
He promised to quit it all, just for my sake;
He sold off his saddle, his spurs, and his rope —
There'll be no more ridin', and that's what I hope.

Chorus:
> Ting-a-ling-o, Johnny Ringo
> Let's sing, oh, yes, by Jingo
> Ting-a-ling-o, Johnny Ringo
> Let's sing, oh, yes, by Jingo.

The first time I saw him was early last spring
A ridin' a bronco, a high-headed thing,
One foot he tied up and the saddle throwed on
With a jump and a holler, he's mounted and gone!

My love's got a gun, now he's gone to the bad.
This makes Uncle Sammy feel pretty damn sad.
He gave me some presents, among them a ring.
What I gave in return was a far better thing!

Now all of you girlies, wherever you ride,
Beware of my cowboy who swings the rawhide;
He'll court you, he'll love you, he'll leave you and go
A ridin' the trail on his buckin' bronco.

Riding out from the cabin, the wind, tempered for the moment, hisses like a snake in the stunted pines. It is now late afternoon. The storm over the mountains of my name has followed the ridges, jumped Reddington Pass and is crawling toward us along the tops of the Rincons.

The wind cools.

At the base of a large outcropping Buck reins up. "If we stay with the wind head-on like this and try for that break between the two rocks, instead of going around in back of them, we might see the cats before they smell us — if it's not their day off." He reaches in the saddlebag, pulls out his .38 and begins strapping it on his hip.

"Dammit, Buck, don't you dare!"

"S'posin' they're hungry," he says innocently.

I glare at him until he grins and returns the gun to his saddlebag. Taking a tight rein on the horses, we spur them through the undergrowth until we're near the top of the rocks where the lions used to sun themselves; then, slowly, quietly we inch forward to a place where we can see the tops.

Their day off.

"Maybe tonight," Buck says.

We throw the tarp about a hundred feet from the big rocks and make camp, while the old sun takes its plunge in a deep purple sea, splashing rays of red-orange above the waves. Wind dies to a whisper.

After venison steaks Buck relaxes against a tree playing Bob Nolan tunes while I wash dishes. I pour his fifth cup of coffee, lie down, watching his face in the fire-light — eyes closed, forehead wrinkled in ecstatic pain.

> Shall I leave the hills, the high, far hills
>   That shadow the morning plain?
> Shall I leave the desert sand and sage that gleams
>   in the winter rain?
> Shall I leave the ragged bridle-trail to ride in
>   the city street —
> To snatch a song from the printed word,
> Or sit at a master's feet?[91]

"Buck, where'll you go this time when they build a road in?"

He makes a lonesome train whistle sound. "Oh, Mexico, South America, Australia, maybe."

"How's about takin' me along?"

"How's about . . . *what did you say!*" He slaps spit from the harmonica hard into his hand. "You crazy, or something?"

"No, I'm fed up with smokey, noisy, nightclubs. I'm ready to do something different."

"Listen, you got to go out there and spread sweetness and light, like Mr. Sandburg, and Woody, Shorty Mac and the rest have told you. . . ."

"Shorty Mac's dead. So are Sandburg and Guthrie."

"You're not!" he hollers, then adds, very off-hand, "B'sides, married men make the worst sort of husbands," and begins to play again.

"Who said anything about marrying," I declare, indignantly, "I've *been* there already!"

"You've also been in the big city too long; I ain't that civilized — I got some right ol' fashioned principles."

"Marrying you'd be like tacking to the tail end of a bomb — never know when you'd go off."

"An' marryin' *you'd* be like livin' with a centipede in a doughnut — wouldn't be no place to go without stumblin' over *your* feet!"

A game we play . . . or is it?

> Our hopes were ours — and by no other heard;
>   Our joys were rugged and our quarrels swift;
> Sunk in conclusive action — or a word
>   And set adrift.
>
> And that was when the West was in its dawn:
>   And that was when the range was far and free:
> The trails are overgrown, the boys are gone
>   Who rode with me.[92]

A mad wind sweeps through camp, slugging our bedroll, whipping dead ashes in our faces. We bolt upright, eyes wide, senses tuned to catastrophe. Blue light opens the night with a flood of arc-lights from all directions. The sky crashes down in thunderbolt after bolt, holding the night open. In the sudden blue brilliance of the minute we see one lone, mottled creature drinking from the pothold, his scraggly fur looking as though it were eaten by mange. He raises his head, looks at us, drooling water that catches a stream of rainbow colors. Then he bares his teeth in a sneer and lumbers away.

Rain spatters down.

THE SOUTH COAST*

My name is Lonjano de Castro,
My father was a Spanish grandee;
But I won my wife in a card game
To hell with those lords o'er the sea.

In my youth I had a Monterey homestead,
Creeks, valley, and mountains all mine;
I built me a snug little shanty
And roofed it and floored it with pine.

I had a bronco, a buckskin —
Like a bird he flew over the trail.
When I rode him out forty miles every Friday
To get me some grub and my mail.

Chorus:
But the Monterey Coast; wild and lonely —
You might win in a game at Jolon,
But the lion still rules the barranca
And a man there is always alone.

I sat in a card game at Jolon;
I played with a man there named Juan.
And after I'd won all his money
He said, "Your homestead 'gainst my daughter, Dawn."

I turned up the ace, I had won her!
My heart which was down at my feet
Jumped up to my throat in a hurry;
Like a young summer field, she was sweet.

He opened the door to the kitchen;
He called the girl in with a curse;
"Take her, God-damn her, you won her!
She's yours now, for better or worse!"

Chorus:
Her arms had to tighten around me
As we rode up the hills from the south,

But no word did I get from her that day
Nor a kiss from her pretty red mouth.

We got to my cabin at twilight
The stars twinkled over the coast
She soon loved the orchard, the valley
But I knew she loved me the most.

That was a glad happy winter;
I carved on a cradle of pine.
By a fire in that snug little shanty
I sang with that gay wife of mine . . .

Chapter 10

Chorus:
But the Monterey Coast; wild and lonely —
You might win in a game at Jolon,
But the lion still rules the barranca
And a man there is always alone.

But then, I got hurt in a landslide
Crushed hip and twice-broken bone;
She saddled up Buck just like lightning,
And rode out through the night to Jolon.

A lion screamed in the barranca;
Buck bolted and fell on a slide.
My young wife lay dead in the moonlight;
My heart died that night with my bride.

They buried her out in the orchard.
They carried me out to Jolon.
I lost my Chiquita, my niña;
I'm an old, broken man, all alone.

The cabin still stands on the hillside,
Its doors open wide to the rain;
But the cradle and my heart are empty,
And I never can go there again.

Chorus: (as sung today)
Oh, the South Coast is a wild coast, and lonely —
You might win in a game at Jolon.
But the lion still rules the barranca
And a man there is always alone.

Harrydick Ross is of silver mane, voice soft like wind in willows. For all I know he may be impetuous or emotionally unstable, but his eyes tell me that he is intuitive and wise, as well as kind and thoughtful. He is a sculptor and looks to belong to the place he lives: face tanned and strongly lined, body lean, resilient. Harrydick is all that's left of direct contact with *The South Coast* song, he being the widower (twice removed) of its author, Shanagolden Ross, or Lillian Bos-Ross, depending on how well you knew her.

The nights are many and indelible that I have shared with Harrydick (and wives) since the death of Shanagolden in 1960; and a man *is* wise who does not live alone in Big Sur if he misses at all the nearness, the voice or the love of another human being.

To take permanent, solo residence there a person must have great inner strength and stability; otherwise, he is likely to become one of El Sur Grande's many casualties. A moody and mysterious place that works on the human soul and mind. Feral forces of nature are "heavy" in Big Sur with weeks of constant fog, when one feels sealed inside a steamed glass jar that muffles all sounds, even the pounding surf; heavier still when the torrential rains of December lock him in his cabin with a mudslide, forcing a long journey on foot for provisions and every object is dripping wet and slippery to the touch; nothing lighter when the flogging Pacific winds rip the tops off breakers, sending long sheets of needles against the cliffs and houses; or less heavy when vertical canyons funnel these winds screaming (not howling or moaning, but *screaming*) through the tops of the Coast Redwoods to further torture the cypress and tatter the madrona and bay laurel on the crests.

Then day will dawn on a William Tell morning, crystal clear, wafting soft, sweet smells, colors shocking in their intensity, sky blue all the way to China, the sea docile, inviting, kissing the shore with soft murmurs, almost as if it said, "I'm sorry." A truly kaleidoscope place that sends writers in search of new ways to do it justice.

No one has succeeded better at this portrayal than Robinson Jeffers, who unfortunately didn't write songs — nor did Shanagolden Ross, really; she wrote a poem.[93] But she called it *The Coast Ballad,* so she must have had in mind the very real possibility that it would be sung, even though she never wrote a melody for it.

I never knew Shanagolden Bos-Ross (Harrydick was living alone when I first met him; later he married Eve Miller, an ex-wife of Henry Miller, who had been his neighbor on Partington Ridge for many years — then Eve died in 1967) but I do know that Shanagolden came to the South Coast in the twenties with Harrydick and they built their own house on Partington Ridge where I have sat by candle and firelight singing songs with Harrydick and Eve while fog swirled and billowed from the sea's cauldron. It was there he told me:

"The song was written in 1926 when Lillian and I were camped at Big Creek. This was long before the road came in and the country was served by a narrow trail. High above us on the mountain was a deserted cabin with a forgotten orchard and around this she wrote the ballad."

"But what of De Castro," I asked, "Did he once live up there? Castro Canyon is a long way from Big Creek."

"No, Castro Canyon has nothing to do with the ballad, she used the names on the land, that's all."

"Really? What about the cradle in the last verse — the verse I've never heard anyone else sing."

"The cradle was there in the ruins. I think it's what fired her imagination to write the ballad in the first place, and you're not the only one who sings it as written, Sam Eskin does.[94] He wrote the melody that's sung now."

"Well, I don't really, Harrydick, I've changed something. The line 'crushed hi — ip and twice broken bone' is awkward as hell to sing — doesn't scan — and I use 'was crushed by a hundred-weight stone.' Of course we all sing the 'South Coast' not the 'Monterey'."

He smiled and tipped a glass of red wine to his lips, then as if thinking aloud said, slowly, "I always feel a folk song must grow, and that it only grows and changes through the singers . . . I know nothing of scanning, but I'm sure no one in Big Sur in 1870 would have used the words 'hundred-weight'."

"Did you and Shanagolden ever sing it?"

"We used cobbled-up versions of several Spanish-American ballads before Sam set it. But the strangest version I've ever heard was from a young folk singer who learned it in South Carolina; he made it sound almost medieval."

In case somebody is wondering why this song, with its obvious style and sophistication and the change in locale from the arid Southwest to the Pacific coastlands, should be included here, the answer is obvious. Big Sur was cattle and sheep country, still is, and cattle ranches and ranchmen are part of the culture and heritage of those vast, tawny, trail-marked mountains. Looking up or down one wonders how a cow manages to keep foothold on them, much less find forage. And though the song was not written by any cowboy, it was by one who knew them, lived there, and was most certainly a westerner. And, as stated earlier, it's one of the *best* western songs I know written in the folk tradition.

While we are still, more or less, with that Golden Age of songs, I want to talk about another that I consider a real classic. (I've already used it in the text — page 98). Along with the Knibbs and Badger Clark era there were many good 'unsung' poems, poems not set to tunes until many years later. Such a song is *The Last Wagon*. As the cowhand saw his range shrinking, this sort of poem expressed his loss, probably first appearing in the poetry section of a pulp magazine. The melody for it, written by an ex-cowhand, makes one of those "perfect weddings" that Billy Simon spoke about; one enhances the other, giving us a song of fine quality. It is the title of the TV film series based on this book.

Slim Critchlow, of Oakland, California, is the composer, and a sweeter-voiced cowboy never wiggled a tonsil. He has the sort of voice I'm sure Easterners thought all cowboys had — a lyrical, night-herding, true-note, story-telling voice — plus the manner to go with it: soft-spoken, open and friendly. A gentle fella. Slim was, until settling in California, an outdoor man; a cowboy in Idaho, a deputy sheriff in Salt Lake County, a park ranger in Bryce and Zion National Parks, and finally corraled indoors, a radio singer. Further, he was a friend and gatherer-of-songs for John A. Lomax back in the 30's. (Lomax was then collecting for the Archive of American Folk Songs, Library of Congress, I believe). When someone found out how good Slim is, and that he is a traditional singer, the like not easily rounded up these days, he was put back in circulation with requests to sing at folk festivals and civic clubs and on university and college campuses.

I met him as the "self-appointed guardian" of another song I was running down at the time, one written by a friend of his, and he wasn't about to cough it up for just anybody — wanted to know how-why-where it was going to be sung, a syndrome known to me as Old-Doloresitis.

From letters he sounded like my kind of guy, so I spun the tires out to Oakland the summer of 1965 and looked him up. I had learned *The Trusty Lariat*, the song for which Slim had appointed himself guardian, from a fellow folk-singer while working a coffee house gig in Oklahoma City. The song had turned the bend away from the golden age and was looking back with tongue-in-cheek at the poor unemployed rope-slinger. Slim had written:

> For some reason I can't help but feel a bit sad that my old and faithful friend is now in the hands of the professional singers. I've heard what some of them can do to a good song. The next time I see (the gent who sang it for me) I think I'll lift his hair with a dull knife. Of course, I've borrowed one or two songs in my day, and forgotten to return them, so I guess I shouldn't complain too loudly. . . .[95]

Haywire Mac (Harry K. McClintock) wrote it using a mild manipulation of the tune *East Bound Train* which is natural enough, because the kind of songs Mac's fame rode on were mostly railroad-hobo songs. Though he left footprints on many trails — was cowboy, railroad man, hard-rock miner, author and singer — his compositions and his years on San Francisco's KFRC are what most people remember. He was the creator of *Fireman Save My Child, Hallelujah, I'm a Bum, When It's Time To Shear the Sheep* (I'm Coming Ba-a-a-ack to You). Slim sent me a Xerox copy of *The Trusty Lariat* from *Mac's Songs of the Road and Range*, copyright 1932 by Harry K. McClintock and Sterling Sherwin, published by Southern Music Publishing Co., New York, with this note:

> This Sherwin fellow seems to have made quite a thing in those days of collaborating with a lot of the country singers and bringing out these song books, getting his name on the copyright as co-author and probably as co-owner of any loot that might be realized. Somewhat in the way Alan Lomax got his name prominently displayed on his father's enlarged "Cowboy Songs". Mr. Lomax didn't like that a little bit.

Mac wrote the song much earlier than the 1932 copyright date, somewhere around 1926, I'd guess. He put out a Victor record of it in an abbreviated form several years before the songbook came out. Well, Mac's "out there in the marble orchard where the tombstones are in bloom," as he put it, so he couldn't care less what happens to his song. But I do . . . treat it kindly and it'll never let you down . . . Mac died in 1957 in San Francisco, with just a handful of folks at the service to see him on his way. Somebody should have been there to sing "The Cowboy's Lament."[96]

If any of you can't recall what I said back there at the front of the book about the Irish cowboy, you might want to finger back and take a little refresher, since this song is making light of that historical movement. Hanging it all in reverse, Mac envisions the fenced-in, fenced-out plowed-under cowboy deserting his ol' broom tail hoss for the iron hoss . . . once again. At least across the tracks there were no fences. Oh yes — and he took with him his

Trusty Lariat*

Through the high Sierra mountains,
Came an Es-pee passenger train.
The hoboes tried to ride her,
But found it all in vain.
The conductor took the tickets
And counted every soul.
The engineer looked straight ahead
And the fireman shoveled coal.

> The fireman was a cowboy
> But do not think it strange
> He could make more money shov'ling coal
> Than ridin' on the range.

But though he was a fireman
And though he had to sweat,
He still remained a western guy,
And kept his lariat.

Oh the train was way behind time,
And the passengers were all wild.
When on the tracks a sudden,
There strolled a little child.
Her golden hair in ringlets
Was a hangin' down her back.
She little knew her danger great,
As she strolled along the track.

> "My Gawd", the hog-head shouted
> As he slammed on all the brakes,
> "I'll never stop this train in time
> Cause I ain't got what it takes.

117

Oh heaven help that wee tot!"
He cried in accents wild.
"Can nothing stop this Es-pee train,
And save that little child!"

Then up sprang the cowboy fireman
And a gallant lad was he,
"I'll save that tiny baby
If I wreck the whole Es-pee!"
Then he climbed out on the running board,
With tears his eyes were wet
And in his hand our hero brave
Had his trusty lariat.

    He quickly dropped a fast loop
    Round a pole beside the track
    Then tied the other end of it
    Around the big smoke stack.

He jerked that train right off the rails
And caused an awful wreck
And our hero lay there in the ditch
The engine on his neck.

    Oh, we will all remember
    That forty-fifth of May
    For there were so many brave hearts
    All filled with fear that day.

They buried that poor fireman
Where the prairie winds blow wild.
He killed two hundred passengers,
But thank Gawd! he saved the child!

    It doesn't take a great deal of analysis to conclude that the best songs were written by men who were poets first, cowboys second. A once-or-twice-inspired cowpoke who had never put pen to paper except to answer his mother's letter rarely came up with a lasting piece. We see the proof of this in poets like Badger Clark, Henry Herbert Knibbs, Frank Desprez, Gail I. Gardner and Curley Fletcher. People with imagination are in command only when they have the gift of expression, and in nearly every case the lasting songs have been written by those who had a talent for writing, along with throwing a rope.

The Critchlow house was open to me whenever I could get there. Eff, his wife, being one of the best chuck-line cooks on the trail, I went often and kept in touch by letter otherwise. In 1969 when I knew the film series was going to be started and told him I wanted to use his "Wagon" for the title piece, he was happy for us both:

I guess we've both been living right lately . . . After considerable pro-ing and con-ing I've decided to copyright the tune to "The Last Wagon" — what the hell — something for my posterity! I'll do it myself and *not* through any music company, so subject to that, go ahead and use it if you want to . . . Arhoolie (recording company) is putting out my first, and only, LP in about a couple of months, made up from 60 or so songs Barry Olivier has taped over a period of several years[97] . . . the opus will be called "The Crooked Trail to Holbrook" and "The Last Wagon" will be included. Hope you make it out here in August, or whenever. Give me a call and we'll try to cook up something. Kindest regards, Slim.[98]

In November I made a trip to Big Sur and flew to San Francisco, planning to spend a night with the Critchlows. I called, fairly bursting with all the plans and news of the up-coming film series, and Eff answered:

"Oh, Katie . . ." she hesitated. "I tried to reach you. Slim died of a heart attack on October 31st."

I went to see her, was given the new Arhoolie album which he had missed by a couple of weeks, listened, and had a good cry.

> Men in the rough — sons of prairie and mountain —
> Ready in everything, save to deceive;
> Friendship with them is a never-sealed fountain;
> And death cannot sever the bonds that they weave.[99]

Back at the ranch.

A dry and thirsty desert gulps the drenching July rains like something thirst-crazed, spilling more than it drinks. As showers ramble from one side of town to another, so quickly that most of the time the sun is shining where it's raining, arroyos flood and shift their beds, tugging out mesquite, changing roads. The mountains of my name are dressed in deep purple with skirts of light green over their foothills, and a pale chartreuse fuzz sprouts amid the gravels on the valley floor. Dripping cholla needles stand sparkling in yellow light against a backdrop of smokey blue, and the sweetest smell of all to desert dwellers, wet greasewood (creosote bush) plays on the winds. The road to the house must be rebuilt and scraped before I can take to the highway to meet Gail Gardner again in Prescott. He has rounded up a northern Arizona rancher who still runs cattle and sings about it. I'll just have time to run up there before my gig at the coffee house in Phoenix opens on the first of August.

Fixing up my desert cooling system, which is to stand under the garden hose with all my clothes on, I squish onto my coolseat and take dirt roads to the Oracle highway. Near Oracle Junction I steer clear of a dude on horseback, bouncing around in his saddle like a ball in a runaway wagon, and sensing that something eventful is about to take place, I slow to a creep.

The guy is decked out in the kind of duds I thought went out with the thirties — all black and white and jangly-spurred like Bat Masterson, topping a palomino mare who knows more about where she's going (and probably where she's been) than the dude. Jerking her head for more rein, forging and trotting sideways, she is seriously thinking about getting rid of the thing on her back.

The poor jasper looks about as sure of himself as someone trying to fry eggs on a spit, and sure enough, in due time, the mare spots a ditch, edges toward it, pops him in the air, and stacks him neat as cordwood down in the tumbleweeds.

THE LAVENDER COWBOY*

He was only a lavender cowboy,
The hairs on his chest were two . . .
He wished to follow the heroes
Who fight as he-men do.

Yet he was inwardly troubled
By a dream that gave him no rest;
When he read of heroes in action,
He wanted more hair on his chest.

Herpicide, many hair-tonics
Were rubbed in morning and night
Still, when he looked in the mirror
No new hair grew in sight.

He battled for "Red Nell's" honor
Then cleaned out a hold-up nest,
And he died with his six-guns smokin . . .
But only two hairs on his chest.

Harold Hersey, who wrote that poem, must have known it would make a great song for dude ranching. He was once editor of *Ace High* and *Cowboy Stories* magazines — the ones that found their way regularly into the ranch bunkhouses, stimulating the cowboys' memories of adventure and derring-do in the manner that *True* and *Saga* now aid the fantasies of men who herd desks all day and play patio chef on weekends.

Shorty Mac hated those magazines, or said he did, though I suspect that he hid a few of them out under his favorite boulder to be scorned and sneered (or leered) over when time got slack on his hands; claimed he knew better and truer stories than they could ever dream up and didn't need that "chawed 'n' gergitated stuff to remind him how the West never was." His stories, some of them, weren't all that old — "Me 'n' the boys keep up with modern times. Why, hell, I even went to Las Vegas a few years back. . . ." One afternoon out by the tanks he was telling Buck:

"We had a fella in the Curly Q outfit was so goddam shy he couldn't look up at the sky without blushin'. He kep things private to himself, but a course we ragged him every chanct we got, nevertheless. Tonsil was his name — Hoppy Tonsil — Tenskill really, but hell, with a name like that he never had a show t' keep it. Got the name Hoppy fer bein' so lax as t' not shake out his boots one mornin' — you know how centipedes is about dark, stinkin' places. . . ."

Buck took out the makins and started rolling one, "C'mon, McGinnis, I'm a good listener, but Jesus Christ, get on with the story — I've heard it b'fore anyway."

"*I* haven't, lippy," I said. "Why don't you just stick that rope in your mouth and ride off into the sunset?"

"Sooo-woosh! Slobber me timbers! Ain't *she* feelin' oatsy this morning." Buck flicked his match at me and Shorty Mac went on.

"Well, ol' Hoppy shore pulled a slick'n on us. Saved all his pay fer months, and b'fore any of us got wind of it he was off t'git spliced and spend his honeymoon in Las Vegas. We was disgruntled we didn't git a chance t'kid him some or give him a proper send-off. He ain't no more'n gone when the boss lets it out, so a couple us boys takes off and follers him t' see where he's gonna wind up — mebbe we kin pester him a little. Well, he goes to one of them motels on the outskirts of Vegas, cause he ain't rich by no means, and he walks up t' the desk with his little filly t'ask fer a room. We come in another door and stands outta sight over by the magazines, but we kin *hear* what he's sayin' cause the clerk is one a them smart-alecky dudes who's all the time passin' crocodile glances at Hoppy's new ball and chain, an' every time he says something the clerk makes him repeat it louder and louder till he's damn near bellerin. '*I says I wants a room fer me an' m' wife!*' — an' he's so goddam red his head looks like a pimple about t' bust outta his collar. Then this slinky-eyed bastard says, 'Would you like a bridal suite?' lookin' at the filly, sly ya know. . . ." Shorty Mac paused and glanced knowingly at Buck.

Buck was a good listener.

"So, Hoppy's about to answer this monkey, whereupon *she* leans herself over the counter right into his face and says, louder 'n hell, '*I don't need no bridle, and don't you call me sweet — I'll jist hang onto him by the ears till I gets used to it!*' "

Shorts gathered up his reins and left me laughing so hard I near fell off my horse.

"See?" he slings over his shoulder at Buck. "That's why I put up with her — knows when t' laugh. You, ya stony old sonofabitch, jest set there like a wart on a toad, garglin' smoke rings. (Buck smiled because he couldn't help it). Let's go! I'm hungry as a possum eatin' candy off a hairbrush."

It's hard for me to remember anyone in a lifetime I ever thought funnier than Shorty Mac. Every now and then Buck could inch into his domain, but never with the off-hand, classic style that Shorts came by so naturally. One of my earliest memories was when he was borrowed for roundup from another ranch, Bellota, maybe, or the Taylor place, I forget, but after supper he sat hunkered down on his boots by the corral, under his old beat-up, sweat-stained hat, playing guitar and singing wonderful and interesting songs, especially appealing to teenagers:

> Last night I got laid on the prairie
> As I nestled down deep in the burrs
> I wondered why this here young cowboy
> Had failed to remove his spurs
>
> Roll on . . . roll on . . .
> Roll on, handsome cowboy, roll on.

... or some of those enticing verses of *My Love Is A Rider* (alias *Johnny Ringo*) which might cause the reader to think that Shorty Mac was a different sort of fellow than he really was, if I included them — he'd never have sung them for me if I hadn't worried him to death. And he sang me a lesson in frontier geology that has always tickled my fancy.

> The miners came in '49
> The whores in '51
> They rolled about the barroom floor
> And begot . . . the native son.

But when he sang *Little Joe The Wrangler's Sister Nell* there wasn't an eye that was dry. All my life I'd heard and sung Thorp's original, *Little Joe, The Wrangler*,[100] but when Shorts brought this one in, I had to allow it was even sadder.

Little Joe the Wrangler's Sister Nell*

She rode up to the wagon as the sun was goin' down,
A slender little figure dressed in grey.
We asked her to get down awhile and pull up to the fire
And red hot chuck would soon be on the way.

An old slouch hat with a hole on top was perched upon her head,
She'd a pair of rawhide chaps, well greased and worn,
And an old twin rig all scratched and scarred from workin' in
    the brush,
And a slick mague tied to her saddle horn.

She said she'd rode from Llano, four hundred miles away,
Her pony was so tired he wouldn't go;
She asked if she could stay a day and kinda rest him up,
Then maybe she could find her brother Joe.

We could see that she'd been cryin', her little face was sad,
When she talked her upper lip it trembled so;
She was the livin' image, we all saw at a glance
Of our little lost horse herder, Wrangler Joe.

We asked where Joe was ridin', if she knew the outfit's brand.
"Yes, his letter said it was the Circle Bar;
It was mailed from Amarillo about four months ago
From a trail herd headed north to Cinnabar."

I looks at Jim, he looks at Tom, then Tom looks back at me.
There was something in our hearts we couldn't speak;
She said that she got worried when she never heared no more
And things at home got tougher every week.

"You see, my mother died," she said, "when Joe and I was born,
Joe and I was twins," her story ran.
"Then dad he ups and marries and gets another wife
And then it was our troubles all began."

"She beat us and abused us, and she starved us most the time,
Cause she never had no children of her own;
Nothin' Joe or I could do would ever be just right.
Then Joe pulled out and leaved me all alone."

I give the kid my bedroll and I bunks in with Jim
We planned and schemed and talked the whole night through
As to which of us would tell her the way that Joe was killed
And break the news as gently as we knew.

"I'll wrangle in the mornin', boys," she says as she turns in.
"I'll have the horses at the wagon 'fore it's day."
As the mornin' star was risin' I saw the kid roll out,
Saddle up the grey night horse and ride away.

Soon we heared the horses comin', a-headin' into camp;
'Twern't daylight but we plainly heared the bell,
And then someone a cryin' a-comin' on behind,
It was Little Joe the Wrangler's sister Nell.

We couldn't quite console her, she'd seen the horses' brand
As she drove 'em from the river bank below.
From the look upon our faces she seemed to realize
That she ne'er again would see her brother Joe.

And McGinnis could get mad, real mad, about some things. The more
ranches that turned to duding, the more Shorty Mac cussed his Irish up. He'd
come near upping his beans in the same order they went down when he'd see
a bunch of peach-faced, gabardine-frontier-pantsy grasshoppers that called
themselves cowboys, bunched up at the bar making steamy-eyes at the girls.

"Goddamit," he'd sputter, "don——— don't them fools know that cowboys is
skeered of wimmen! Mind ya, shortpants, stay away from them kind, they're
about as sightly as turds in a punchbowl!"

He'd had a taste of the trail, like his father before him, knew the caliber of
the tough, gritty men who'd ridden it, knew they weren't leaky-mouthed, or
lazy, and didn't have time for much of anything except the working of cattle.
He saw all that change, saw the land fill up with strangers "who didn't have the
sense God give a cow — come t' this country t' git outta the cold, then plug
themselves into cold-air systems all day and night and stay outta the sun!"

Funniest song I ever heard came from the funniest man; but before Shorty
Mac died he was singing it out of the other corner of his mouth as "ten thousand
goddam people, or fences, or freeways, politicians, whatever." Arizona was selling her land cheap. Her cowboys, she was *giving* away.

TEN THOUSAND GODDAM CATTLE*
Ten thousand goddam cattle,
A-roamin' far and wide
Shore wisht I had my sweetie here
A-layin' by my side,
A-layin' by my side.

M' gal, she up and left me,
I spect she's gone to stay.
She lit outta here a runnin'
With a sonofabitch from Io-way.
With a sonofabitch from Io-way.

I'm a lone man, a real lone man.

He wasn't tall ner handsome,
Jist an ornery lookin' cur,
Shucks, I dunno what she seen in him,
Or what he seen in her-r-r,
Or what he seen in her.

They took my pinto pony,
And they took my six-weeks pay;
The only thang they left here fer me
Was this damn gee-tar to play
This damn gee-tar to play.

I'm a lone man, a real lone man.

She never wrote no letter,
She never sent one line,
T' tell me whar the hell she put
Them French postcards of mine,
Them French postcards of mine.

Ten thousand goddam cattle
They kin rot fer all of me,
Unless 'n I finds me a purtier gal
T' ease my misery-y-y
T' ease my misery.

I'm a lone man, a real lone man
DEAD BROKE!

Shorty Mac McGinnis died in 1951, ending eighty years of pounding leather, swearing, loving, singing, hating dudes and fences. He never quit the horse — rode right on into the other life without stopping for hay.

When my old soul hunts range and rest
    Beyond the last divide,
Just plant me in some stretch of West
    That's sunny, lone and wide.
Let cattle rub my tombstone down
    And coyotes mourn their kin,
Let hawses paw and tromp the moun'
    But don't you fence it in!

Oh it's squeak! squeak! squeak!
     And they pen the land with wire.
They figure fence and copper cents
     Where we laughed around the fire.
Their house has locks on every door;
     Their land is in a crate.
These ain't the plains of God no more,
     They're only real estate.[101]

THE DAY I RETURNED from Buck's place and found no letter from Mr. I. C. Sweet re *Old Dolores,* I got on the telephone and asked information if there was a listing for him in Albuquerque.

A very nice lady with a very old voice answered:

"Ye-e-es," she said, thinly and slowly, "I have a letter by someone named Lee, but Mr. Sweet is deceased. However, his sister taught school at Dolores and she would be the one to talk to. Bell Sweet is her name — I'll give you her address if you can wait a minute."

I asked her about directions to Dolores when she came back to the phone, telling her I'd be there at the end of next month to see if I could locate the place. (Of course I could write to the owner again and ask him the way to his ranch, but he hadn't been *positive* that it was the site of the old town. Perhaps Bell Sweet would know more.)

"Well, it's up in the Ortiz Mountains near Santa Fe."

"Yes, I know that, but do you know where the road is that leads up to the townsite?"

"I believe it is near the coal camp of Madrid." *Mad*rid, she pronounced it.

"Which way? North or south?"

Long pause. "Uphill."

That wasn't very clear to me, but I figured when I got to the spot I'd know it, so I thanked her and tried to get in touch with Miss Bell Sweet. There was no phone for her. I wrote my usual pleasant, inquisitive letter — not the one Buck accused me of sending — giving a return address in Phoenix where I would be playing the month of August. After that I was to appear at the Exodus in Denver, and thought there would be time to go by way of Santa Fe from Phoenix, slip into Dolores and, after seven years of guessing, be able to take Mr. Rogers a picture of how she looked today . . . when at last I made the trip to Georgetown to see how *he* looked. That would wrap it up. Once and for all I'd know exactly what I'd been singing about.

By this time, Sam and I had introduced some minor changes in the song.

I didn't like "long seegars" which I had changed to "sweet guitars" — you especially don't like them if you sing in nightclubs — nor did we go around singing "greaser girls" in those days; the radio and TV people wouldn't let us. But I've reinstated the latter because I like my songs to hang true, and without the "greaser girls" line, the second one following makes no sense; i.e., "But I guess most *any* girl gives a feller's head a whirl", meaning that a greaser girl was better than no girl at all. That was certainly the cowboy's social code in those days.

Many things I love about singing Old Dolores, but must admit that part of its great appeal is its one-upsmanship. None of my contemporaries (Burl Ives, Pete Seegar, Cisco Houston, Josh White, Woody Guthrie, Harry Belafonte) had heard it until I sang it for them — without exception they agreed it was one of the great finds. I think it's what caused Burl (one of my first idols, later turned friend and mentor) to lay a nice ego-building line on me. When asked about cowboy songs and singers he would say, "The best cowboy singer I know is a girl . . . Katie Lee." I asked him one time if he didn't want to record it, he liked it that much, and his answer was, "No, Kathryn, that song belongs to you, you should be the one to record it."

Well, I've never had that opportunity. Record companies aren't onto girls singing cowboy songs. Won't sell. During my Hollywood years there were several opportunities to jazz it up and get it pressed, but even if I could have gotten permission from Rogers, I wouldn't have been party to the "bulldozing." Old Dolores' ghosts would surely have returned to haunt me!

> The soft wind sways the whispering grass,
> The sun sinks low o'er the Western pass;
> As a coyote mingles his dismal howl,
> With the sad sweet note of a lone hoot owl.
> A hawk soars lazily up on high,
> A speck of black in a crimson sky,
> And you would this spot so sweet, so grand,
> Might remain untarnished by human hand.
>
> But e'en this spot shall see the day
> When it will fall the easy prey
> Of lust and greed, and in the place
> Where yon pine sways in supple grace,
> An axe-scarred stump will stand, instead,
> Bowing in shame its branchless head,
> And down the rivers will float the spoils,
> All helpless victims to human toils.[102]

July rains have brought everything to life again in the range country of northern Arizona, as Gail Gardner and I drive north from Prescott, turning off on the road to Perkinsville. The sky is a big blue hanging lake over Chino Valley, with a few cirrus clouds stringing across it from the north. Off to the southeast a shower scouts the ridges, dropping a piece of purple gauze over Mingus Mountain . . . for the moment. All the rest is space, red earth and grass. Coming up along our gravel road is a windmill turning arbitrarily with the breeze, the stock tank beneath it like a ring set with turquoise.

"Just like she was fifty years ago," Gail says — and pointing to where a cowboy herds four yearlings toward the tank — "that too."

"We on the Perkins' spread yet?" I question.

"Oh yeah, have been for about ten miles."

"Wonder how many head they run."

"Oh, Christ, you don't never ask a cattleman *that!* In the old days he couldn't tell you, these days he won't."

We rattle across half a dozen cattle guards, trailing a cloud of dust, and as we near the foothills, drop down along the Verde River toward Benny Perkins' ranch house. The acrid smell of cattle mingles with sage and hay on the bottom-land where cattle graze against the new green. "Had one helluva drouth here in 1903," recalls the old one-eyed cowboy, "all the cattle drifted down to the only source of water and grazed 'er plumb out. It's only the last few years the grass has come back to full growth. Hello there, Marion! Where's Ben, down t' the house?"

We've pulled alongside a holding pen where three cowboys are having a smoke and looking over some stock. They are Benny's brothers, Marion, Dave and Tom. This was a busier place a couple of months ago during spring roundup when the yearling heifers were separated in a cross-fence, the rest of the stock driven down from forest land to the summer range grass, the sore, sick and stringy put in pastures where they could be tended, wells and water-holes checked, windmills repaired, salt licks replenished, horses shod, the vet kept busy inoculating, and the branding and cutting done. If I'd come then, I'd have seen these men only in a cloud of dust, and Ben with no time to take his old guitar across his knee.

A tire iron whangs a steel rim near the house and the boys say, "Chow! C'mon."

It is easy to tell a working ranch from one that's playing at it. The floor isn't scrubbed and polished, the screens, windows and doors probably need repair, and the yard isn't raked, because the house gets little attention before the cows. Women spend a good deal of time in the kitchen, or helping with the stock, washing, looking after kids, running errands. Children, if they're big enough, are also working stock, gardening, irrigating, helping bust horses and what not, but likely they aren't cleaning house. Tomorrow five to ten cowboys will be trailing through it anyway.

Ben's grandfather, M. A. Perkins, drove cattle into the area in 1900 — a contemporary of Shorty Mac's Pa. He had three sons that were Gail's age, only one left now is Benny's father, Old Nick, in his early nineties. A really tough old bird. Nick's voice is a kind of gravelly gargle, like water running over a grate, his walk is permanently bent to fit the saddle he still climbs into every morning (with the aid of one of the boys) gets off at dinner, back on until sundown, then down for supper and bed. His eyes are little blue beads in a fiery face — a fightin' Irish face. In his own words he tells about coming to settle the Chino and Verde Valleys:

"I been here an awful long time. I've seen a lotta stuff. We come here in

November, 1900 . . . main ranch was up there 't Chino Valley — called it Dobe Ranch. I had *worlds* of cattle there . . . wasn't no such thing as Perkinsville then. From Big Chino wash, the ranch extended over to Sycamore Canyon, (Dave runs his cattle over there now, other side the Verde narrows) up to Seligman, and beyond."

I ask him if the family planned to raise cattle when they first came here, which must have been when he was near nineteen.

"Why shore, been in it all our lives. Cattle you see here today is sired by the stock we drove and shipped from Fort Davis, Texas — 1500 of 'em. Shipped 'em by train to San Marcial, down below Albuquerque, then we drove 'em over to Luna Valley, 'bout forty miles the other side of Springerville. Luna Valley had a little old place had good grass. Kep 'em there a year, drove 'em over a trail here t' this ranch."

"Did you lose many?"

"Not many, lost some over in those alkali flats near Winslow, but we got 'em here! Had some drouths that wiped out some — *bad* one in 1903, an' one year we fed 800 cows up here in the feed pen — but the grass come back real good in 1905 . . . with the help of my wife, we built up a good stock. She's a wonderful girl, just dropped right into my business and she shore pulled me by. Taught school for fifty dollars a month. We'd buy a few cattle with the money and I made good with 'em."

With a stroke of luck like four *big* sons to keep the ranch going over the years, Old Nick has managed to hang on through just about everything, including the Forest Service, on whose land they have grazing permits.

After too much to eat, some beer, and getting to know everybody, we adjourn to the front room where the guitars are. There's a rustle of wind in the big cottonwoods, a horse neighs, and Benny starts a favorite old song:

FLYIN' U TWISTER*
(*Bad Brahma Bull*)

I was snappin' out bronks for the old Flyin' U,
At forty a month a plumb good buck-er-oo,
When the boss comes around and he sez say my lad,
You look pretty good ridin horses thats bad,
Now you see I ain't got no more outlaws to break,
But I'll buy you a ticket and give you a stake,
At ridin them bad ones well you ain't so slow,
And you might do some good at the big Ro-de-o.

Chorus:
Lay off of hard liquor and don't you get full
And think you kin tame that there bad brahma bull,
Go right down and choose him and when you get through,
Just tell them you learned on the old Flyin' U.

So I wraps up my riggin and starts raisin dust,
I'm huntin that show and that brahma to bust,

So I enters that contest and pays entrance fee,
And tells them to look at the champion, that's me.
Well they looks me all over and thinks that I'm full,
So they offers a seat on that bad brahma bull,
Sez I, good enough cause I ain't here to brag,
But I come a long way just to gentle that stag.

Chorus:
You claim he's a bad one I guess he may be,
He looks like a sucklin' or weaner to me,
Go bring on your long-horn you never had one,
Could set me to guessin' nor bother me none.

So while they're puttin' that bull in the chutes,
I'm strappin' my spurs to the heels of my boots,
I looks that bull over and to my surprise,
It's a foot and a half in between his two eyes.
Right on top of his shoulders, he's got a big hump,
And I cinches my riggin' just back of that lump,
I lights in his middle, and I lets out a scream,
He comes out with a beller, and the rest is a dream.

Chorus:
Well he jumps to the left, but he lands tow'rd the right,
But I ain't no greenhorn, I'm still sittin' tight,
The dust starts to foggin' right out of his skin,
And he's wavin' his horns, right under my chin.

At sunnin' his belly, he couldn't be beat,
He's showin' the buzzards the soles of his feet,
He's a dippin' so low, that my boots fill with dirt,
And he's makin' a whip, of the tail of my shirt,
He's a snappin' the buttons, right off of my clothes,
Just a buckin' and bawlin', and a blowin' his nose,
The crowd was a cheerin' both me and that bull,
But he needed no help, while I had my hands full.

Chorus:
Then he goes to fence-rovin' and weavin' behind,
My head starts to snappin', I sorta went blind,
When he starts in high divin', I lets out a groan,
Next we went up together, but he comes back alone.

Up high I turns over, and below I kin see,
He's a pawin' up dirt, just a waitin' for me,
I kin picture a grave, and a big slab of wood,
Readin' here lays the twister, that thought he was good,
Then I notices somethin', don't seem kin be true,
But the brand on his hip was a big Flyin' U.

When I landed he charged, but I got enough sense,
To outrun that bull to a hole in the fence.

Chorus:
I dives through that hole, and I want you to know,
That I ain't goin' back to no wild west show,
At straddlin' them brahmers you kin bet I'm all through,
And I'm sure-footin' back to the old Flyin' U.

"Al Schauffler,[103] the vet over in Cottonwood — good folk singer, sings the hell outta that song. Guests on our fall roundup love it."

"Guests?" I question.

Gail clears his throat in preparation for a statement of some weight. "Ah — hum . . . the Perkin's got a new thing goin' for them, a manner of making ranching more economically sound — uh — they invites a crop of friends — those who own horses and can sit 'em for at least part of a day — to join them, for a small fee, on their fall roundup. Ben provides the chow, the booze, the cots, and even a little sanitary privvy. . . ."

"Holy cow!" voices my surprise, not to say, dismay.

"We butchers a couple of them too and throws them in with the deal," Ben grins, "but I sing like an ol' shoat caught in a bog — we could add a little class to this thing if you'd come along."

"You sing *right*, Benny Perkins, for the cowboy that you are. When did all the dudin' start on this perfectly respectable cow ranch?"

Ben looks up at Gail under raised brows. "Aw, hell, we don't invite just *anybody*. We're fussy."

The thought occurs to me that after all the Perkins family has pulled through in the past, this ranch needs dudes like Custer needed more Indians! Just the way Benny sings and plays epitomizes the ranch-cowboy-land relationship. With a voice that's a cross between a whine and a gentle moo — part talk, part song — and a guitar that leads or follows as the song tells it, that voice fits this rough, rocky country like horns on a bull.

I hear the words of my eastern friends echoing faintly.

"There's people back East, Benny, who tell me that cattle ranches are as good as gone, that ranching is a dying form of feudalism . . . you aren't about to agree, are you?"

Smiling, he shakes his head. "I think she gets close to *futile*ism sometimes, but she's a long way from dead. I'd like those fellers to tell any rancher hereabouts who pays his cowboys two hundred fifty bucks a month and found, plus all his bunkin' that there's anything feudalistic about it. They'd get laughed right off the back forty!"

"Course they haven't explained to her," puts in Gail, "what the population's goin' to use fer beef when there ain't no more places to raise it."

"Prob'ly raise test-tube cows in antiseptic glass houses with plastic bags tied under their tails so's they won't crap all over their hocks," suggests Benny.

"Not funny," warns Betty. "I saw synthetic bacon in town at the market a few weeks ago."

There was the time a few years later, after we'd become good friends, that

Ben and Betty nearly *did* have to sell off a section or two, in order to keep the rest and continue to raise beef against all odds. Many people don't understand that raising cattle is a labor of love, and not much else. If the rancher was money oriented, as our eastern friends tend to suppose, he would long ago have given up his holdings to the developer, turned back his Forest permits and moved to town, but that's not what it's all about.

> I would have no wall or warder
>   Mar my goodly heritage,
> From the yuccas of the border
>   To the snowy northern sage —
> Glad of every wind that passes
>   Down the mesa and the plain.
> Singing freedom in the grasses
>   And my pony's rippling mane.
>
> My own! my own!
> There is freedom here alone,
>   Under midnight's starry masses
> Or the day king on his throne! [104]

But smaller holdings, and sometimes even big ones, are forced into a selling situation in spite of every thing they try to prevent it. Kids leave the ranch, one of the hierarchy dies, the family falls apart at the seams, there's no one to work stock, prices go up, there's no more money to borrow and food gets scarce. A cowboy's got the Subdivided Blues, and the character of the songs he sings changes.

The Subdivided Cowboy*

> Worked half my life on the old home spread
> Till one cold day my dad, he said,
> "I'm too broke to move and too old to ride
> So we'll sell the cows and subdivide."
>   Well, I just up and quit.
>
> Loaded my pickup with all that I had
> (Most of the stuff belonged to Dad)
> Went lookin' for a roost that I ain't found yet.
> The old home place is a hundred ranchettes.
>   I got the subdivided blues.
>
> Got a job chasin' cows on the Double Cross.
> A couple days later, here comes the boss;
> Said "Son, I'm sorry but here's yore pay.
> We put 'er in escrow yesterday."
>   He'd sold to McCulloch.
>
> On the banks of the Santa Cruz, somebody said,
> I could get two hundred, board and bed.
> The steers was mean and the mesquite thick,

And the owner was good at arithmetic.
    He figgered his capital gains.

Come home from Nogales sort of drunk,
Found an adiós letter on my bunk.
Before I could saddle that tired old Ford
I got a supeenee from the zoning board.
    I thought Gulf American made gasoline.

I heard Apache County still grew cows
And there I'd stick, I made my vows.
Pretty soon the straw boss said to me
"This here's a planned community."
    Ninety-nine dollars down and I only had forty-one.

Cochise, Graham and Gila too —
I looked for jobs and I got a few
But everytime I'd immigrate
They'd sell the place to a syndicate.
    Couldn't even get my socks unpacked.

Wore out twelve tires on my sorry old truck.
Everybody said I was out of luck.
"Them dudes pay cash for this mesquite
So raisin' cows is obsolete."
    Everybody wants a two and one-half acre rancho.

Worked for the Indians quite a spell
Chasin' tribal herds all over hell.
I figgered that I'd not have to roam
But they leased the range for summer homes.
    I oughta been a carpenter.

My dad said "Son, it's shore a pity.
Me and Mom like it here in Sun City.
Why can't you find a place to land?
You'd make some feedlot a first-rate hand."
    That tore it.

My pride was broke and my pickup bent.
And every cent I'd made was spent.
Wickenburg was the end of the rope.
Wranglin' dudes. I'd lost all hope.
    But the dudes weren't bad.

I'd show them pilgrims wild game sign
And serve the beans in the barbecue line.
I'd have stayed, but the owner went
Into buildin' homes for retirement.
    He said it's the comin' thing.

A talking blues was never a cowboy way of singing. Though many of them half talk their songs, theirs isn't anywhere near the blues tradition of the South or dust bowl Midwest. Of course, this is a modern song written in the sixties by a Phoenix newspaper man, still, he knew what he was talking about. If he hadn't, Ben Perkins would never have identified with it or thought it funny when I sang it for him. He thought the author's way of saying it was funny — the contents saddened him. I don't recall an evening, a day, or any sort of meeting with him that he didn't express his reverence for nature's gifts, and the great pleasure it gave him to look at them, ride through them, and know them.

Comes the question I dread asking: "What are the chances of *The Subdivided Cowboy* manifesting itself out here, Benny? I know a lot of greedheads who'd give you a bundle to rework this terrain, dam the Verde, make a nice gooey lake, stick the Leaning Tower of Pisa in it, equip a golf course with moving greens that come to the golfer so he won't have to move from one spot. . . ."

"Whoa now," Ben interrupts, "there are some forces mightier by far — those guys haven't met Nick yet."

"Ho-ho!" Gail sings out, "Old Nick, he's somethin'!"

And hidden in a song that Benny wrote is a story I never really got to the bottom of — somehow, I'd just as soon let it hang there and mystify me. I could ask Dave, or Marion, Betty, or the rest of them, but sometimes a big ranch with four fighting Irish brothers and a piece of the old rock itself, like Nick, goes by some rules that others might not understand. I see that Ben went to the "salt lick" for the sarcasm of his title:

SPECIAL AGING OF FINANCE CONTACTS —
DEEP WATER, ICE AND SNOW*

We had deep water, ice and snow —
A thousand cattle we had to go
To get those cattle to the other side,
You can bet your life we had to ride.

Chorus:
In deep water, ice and snow
With a thousand cattle we had to go.

The railroad was but a mile away —
But some men and horses would die that day.
We held the herd on a ridge close by
As the north wind blew the snow flakes by.

Chorus: (between each verse)

We were all chilled our bodies through —
But from cold or fear no one knew.
We took a smoke and watched it blow —
Then slack your cinch, he have got to go.

I pointed them in — we hit her fast,
But our luck by now was fading fast.

That man was talking from down below —
As my horse and I were next to go.

My horse turned over, I floated free —
The waves so high I couldn't see.
Then my horse swam by, I grabbed his tail
To drag me from this icy hell.

(Talked)
I'll never forget that terrible day,
When strong men cried, and I heard some pray.
We crossed the cattle to the other side,
Just to save a vain man's pride.

The hell I have seen is mighty cold,
The other kind is worse, I'm told,
But I hope when I have to go,
It's not in deep water, ice and snow.

Quite some years passed before I had the opportunity to sit and talk to Nick. By then, I'd moved back to Arizona and saw a good deal more of Ben, Betty and the kids. In the early seventies they made Sycamore Canyon a Wilderness Area — something I was all for, but after I went to the hearings and heard some of the Forest Service's asinine proposals, and the brothers fighting for the water holes and wells *they'd* built, I wasn't so sure. I thought of Gail's song and had a smile for myself.

THE COWMAN'S TROUBLES*

I used to make money a-runnin' wild cattle,
In them good old days 'fore the business went wrong,
When a hot runnin' iron and a good long riata
Was all that was needed to start you along.

I had no bookkeeper to help run my outfit,
I just kept her all in a small tally book;
A Durham tobaccer sack held my spare money,
And I ran my layout all on my own hook.

And no one asked questions concerning my business,
I wouldn't have answered a one anyhow,
I just would have told them to go to the Devil.
But things is quite different with cattlemen now.

With the bankers and lawyers and the forest officials,
The land office men and inspectors as well,
A-ridin the cowman all over the country,
No wonder his business has all gone to Hell.

For nowdays it seems that the whole durn creation
Has got to know everything under the sun,

135

They even keep cases on all of your dogies,
And they tell you the way that your outfit should run.

I went to a banker to borry some money,
When times they was hard and my pockets was low;
He looked over his glasses and he pulled his chin-whiskers,
And these was the things that he wanted to know:

"Who was your father and who was your mother?
And where were you born, and if so tell me why?
How many times have you been in the cooler?
And where do you think you will go when you die?"

"Then we'll mortgage your outfit at eight per cent interest,
I'm sure it's the only thing for you to do.
Go see our lawyer an' for five hundred dollars,
He'll draw up the papers and fix it for you."

There come to my ranch house a young forest ranger,
A slim scissor-bill in some leather puttees;
He had him a hatchet tied into his saddle,
And all that he knowed was the herding of trees.

Well he got out a pencil and seventeen papers,
And spread them all out just as neat as could be.
He then looked as wise as a tree full of barn owls,
And these was the words that this man said to me:

"How many cattle have you on your ranges?
And how many head did you say you had sold?
Let's have your calf-tally with the steers and the heifers.
How many have you eat and how many have you stole?"

When you drive to the railroad to ship out some cattle,
You'll find the inspector a-hanging around;
He'll set on a fence post and chaw your tobaccer,
And these is some laws he is apt to lay down:

"Them critters that's packin' two irons must be vented,
And all of them calves must have mothers," says he.
"The Board down in Phoenix claims all 'orejanas,' "
(But there's a Hell of a lot that they never do see).

Oh the income tax "hombre" will ask you more questions,
The assessor will think up a dozen or two,
Each one of these buzzards cuts into your bank roll,
And soon there is nothing at all left for you.

Now maybe the cowman's reward is in Heaven,
If Heaven is a place where a cowhand could go;
But I'll bet you my saddle that here's what would happen,
There would be forty things that Saint Peter must know.

"Oh, how many angels have you in your chorus?
And how many tunes on your harp can you play?
How many white robes have you got in your war bag?
How many gold streets have you dug up today?"

If there is no other place that is safe for the cowman,
I believe that a journey to Hell would be best,
Where they'd shovel him into the door of the furnace,
And there's where old cowman might get him some rest.

The afternoon at Ben's, with Gail and Betty, takes us into more songs. Interesting to observe the combinations — the very old and respected songs woven in with the newer, handwrit, pseudo ditties like *I'm Saving Up Coupons to Get One of Those,* a corny thing that Benny loves. He'll then do an about-face and sing a sad old beauty like:

EMPTY COT IN THE BUNKHOUSE*

There's an empty cot in the bunkhouse tonight,
There's a Pinto's head hangin' low;
His spurs and chaps hang on the wall,
Limpy's gone where the good cowboys go.
There's a range for every cowboy,
Where the foreman takes care of his own;
There'll be an empty saddle tonight,
But he's happy up there I know.

But he was ridin' the range last Saturday noon,
When a Norther had started to blow;
His head on his chest heading into the West,
He was stopped by a cry soft and low.
There was a crazy young calf had strayed from his ma,
And was lost in the snow and the storm;
He lay in a heap at the end of the draw
Huddled all in a bunch to keep warm.

Limpy hobbled his feet, tossed him over his hoss,
And started again for the shack.
But the wind got cold and the snow piled up,
And poor Limpy strayed from the track.
He arrived at three in the morning
And put the Maverick to bed.
Then he flopped on his bunk, not able to move;
This morning poor Limpy was dead.

There's an empty cot in the bunkhouse tonight,
There's a Pinto's head hangin' low.
His spurs and chaps hang on the wall
Limpy's gone where the good cowboys go.

There's a place for every cowboy
Who has that kind of love,
And someday he'll ride his old Pinto
On that range up there above.

Rightly, those old songs belong to Benny's kind. He grew with them, and if he hadn't been invaded by the so-called "country-western" song on the local juke boxes here in the back country bars, that's probably all he would be singing. They fit his style and carry a lot of meaning for him. But I notice which tradition is the strongest. It comes out in his own compositions like *Deep Water, Ice and Snow* — the heroic story, something that really happened, and laced to a simple, uncomplicated melody.

Two horses need to be trailed over to Dave's part of the Perkins's spread, so Gail and I take the long way back to Prescott and will meet them all for a farewell beer at Paul and Jerry's Bar in Jerome.

I unfasten the stock gates. As indigenous to the West as the Rocky Mountains, these unique contraptions just grew. Usually an assemblage of odd lengths of stout chain, a metal ring, or some heavy bailing or bobwire, and a strong stick or small log about two feet long to snub around the fence post, they will secure a flexible bobwire gate. This equipment is arranged in such an imaginative bunch of "fixes" as become a true art form. The above are standard ingredients, but I've seen them with tire irons, old lug wrenches, lengths of garden hose, pipe, rawhide, bones, horns, railroad spikes, and once a dried and treated bull's penis, strong and stiff as hickory!

Another endemic applies to names on cowboy land which no "Complete Dictionary of Place Names" will ever list for you — likewise maps. Once in a while the original name will remain, such as Tail Springs, but the newcomer won't have the faintest notion of its actual meaning. Shorty Mac told me an old cowpoke was at this little spring one day when an Apache squaw was filling her water jug.

"They gits to talkin' and gigglin', then doin' what comes nacherly, smootchin' and ticklin' each other a bit, then they gits to layin' down and doin' it some more — till the cowboy gits hisself a piece of tail. After that, course he told some of the boys, and instead of going the long way around, sayin', 'over thar at the spring where Toad Yates got hisself some tail,' we jest called 'er Tail Springs."

Squaw Peak was called Squaw Tit; Solomon's Needle was Solomon's Prick. There are so many that if the old boys were ghost-rounded up and led back home, they wouldn't know where they were in the clutter of new prissy names stuck on the land by Victorians.

On a high shoulder of the Perkinsville Road to Jerome, Gail and I stop to look over the Verde Valley. Afternoon sun makes deep shadows down in the river bottom where a slash of rich steel blue reflects off the water. Clouds between us and the San Francisco Peaks are a mass of pink featherboas, dressing up the sky. Mountains and mesas rise, tier upon tier, behind each other to a distant horizon, red Supai sandstone accenting the foreground.

"What a great place to get lost," I exclaim.

"Might still could do 'er," he speculates, "I've rode this country runnin' snuffy cattle through Copper Basin from Granite Mountain to the Hassayampa, and I got lost so durn bad I couldn't put m' hand on my own ass."

Nearing Jerome the earth takes on a hard, red fighting strength — but the fight wasn't good enough. Great openpit wounds bake in the sun, and beneath the bulkhead of the mountain runs an eighty-mile maze of tunnels, they say. Phelps Dodge dug them, built the town over and around them, then closed the copper mine, leaving a ghost city spattered over the sides and trailing down cliffs like the droppings of some great bird. For all that, Jerome is indeed a *real* and historic town. Old leaning, buckling board houses weathered to gold and brown patinas lend a Toonerville Trolley air, while on an upper road hang the stately old mansions — prudes in widow's caps — watching with disdainful dark eyes the sinful goin's-on below.

Along with gates and place names is yet another unerased mark of Western heritage — the cowboy boot.

I look at those distributed the length of the brass rail in the bar. One glance separates the rider from the walker. There are peewees, hightops, and stogies, and from a mother's lap a toy pair of Justins dangle above a spittoon. The tops of all the boots are hidden under frontier pants or jeans, but in cattle-driving days, boots were worn high and *outside* (like Billy Simon does yet), or like the Mexican vaquero boot without buttons up the sides — and they never had designs on them. When the fancy hand-tooled pictures became popular, the boots were shortened to peewees; tooling helped stiffen the leather and kept it from wrinkling above the instep and pant legs were worn outside. This was no great boon to brush riders, since no matter if the boot comes to the crotch, brush is going to get in unless it's filled with pants. Nowadays, if through some unavoidable gymnastic, a young cowboy gets his pants caught inside his boot, his embarrassment, and action to remedy same, is quicker than if you said, "Hey buddy, your fly's open!"

The boot was, and is yet, a cowboy's status symbol. It elevates him above the common folk, even on the ground where he seldom likes to be. As a matter of practicality, it keeps him from slipping through his stirrups and gives him a claw to the ground when he's working cattle off his mount. The boot protects him and because of its thin sole allows his feet empathy with the horse's movements. He will skimp and save on everything but his boots. One hundred chips is nothing to pay for a fine-fitted pair. When his pay was a mere fifty bucks, the boots cost more than a month's salary. He'll wear scuffed boots proudly, but there the line stops. Scuffed, yes; frayed and ragged, no. As Ramon Adams says, ". . . when they's so frazzled that he can't strike a match on 'em without burning his feet, he is considered worthless and without pride."[105]

> The cowboy is as proud a cuss
> As ever you will meet,
> And specially fastidious
> About his dainty feet.

He figgers that they wasn't made
    To walk upon a heap,
Like those of men that wield a spade
    Or herd a bunch of sheep.
That's maybe why the high-heeled boot
    He wears at work or play
Sometimes will cost this proud galoot
    Purt near a whole month's pay.
He'll short himself on trips to town
    And pass up payday pleasure
To lay a wad of money down
    For new boots made-to-measure.
He'll have the tops dolled up a bit,
    With fancy stitchin' in,
But mainly they have got to fit
    His feet as tight as skin.
It's lucky he's a man of brawn,
    Of rawhide strength and muscle,
For pullin' tight boots off and on
    Takes plenty tug and tussle.

"Died with his boots on" is a phrase
    That rings through western hist'ry,
But if you know the cowboy's ways,
    That surely ain't no myst'ry.
They died with boots on, day or night —
    I do not wish to scoff —
Because — sometimes — they were so tight
    They could not git them off![106]

Standard boot top designs have been animals, flowers and most often, butterflies for the tops where the boot takes a fancy dip, fore and aft. There was no attempt at congruity, the tooler just fit together whatever covered the tops most completely! Shorty Mac has come up with my favorite cowboy boot story.[107]

"Ol' Chester trips over his sole one day and near falls in the brandin' fire — thus concludin' it's time to go to town fer a pair of made-to-orders. He probably trips a couple more times goin' from bar to bar b'fore he gits to Porter's Saddlery, and by the time he cracks the door, he's fried to the gizzard and feelin' gritty. They know him purdy good cause he's had his boots made there b'fore, but bein' snuffy like he is, he's gonna tell 'em what he wants, *exactly*. 'Lissen,' he says, 'I want a pair a boots what comes up *high* so's yer pants don't flop outta 'em, n' so's the brush don't git *in*. See? I wants the heel jest so.' And he measures off the height with his thumb butted against his little finger. 'Don't want no red and green stop-light-two-tone-dude-boots, an' I don't want no goddam fancy stitchin' on the laigs neither, ya hear? Don't want no pitchurs of no chipmunks tryin' t' fuck a butterfly!' "

We say our farewells to the Perkins and I crawl under the wheel to drive us back to Prescott over Mingus Mountain. As lights come on in the valley, the Verde River seeks cover between dark folds of earth.

"How long d'you think it'll be, Gail, before the Perkins have to give up?"

"Oh, I don't think that's going to happen soon, not this generation anyhow — I won't have to live to see it."

"What about me?"

"Hope you won't either."

> "Twas good to live when all the sod
>   Without no fence nor fuss,
> Belonged in pardnership to God,
>   The Gover'ment and us.
> With skyline bounds from east to west
>   And room to go and come,
> I loved my fellow man the best
>   When he was scattered some.
>
> Oh, it's squeak! squeak! squeak!
>   Close and closer cramps the wire.
> There's hardly play to back away
>   And call a man a liar.
> Job cussed his birthday, night and morn,
>   In his old land of Uz,
> But I'm just glad I wasn't born
>   No later than I was! [108]

In 1965 Benny Perkins knew he had cancer.

By 1969 I had worked my way back to the home range — moved from Aspen, Colorado to Sedona, Arizona, a growing trailer park about forty miles from Perkinsville. Al Schauffler, the vet-folk-singer, and I had become good friends and we often went to see Ben and Betty for a sing, a tubing through the Verde River narrows from their ranch to Sycamore, or some fancy doin's in Prescott at the Gardners.

Then, one day in June of 1971, I got a call from Al.

"Betty's got Ben out of the hospital, Katie, he's at the ranch. (Betty is an RN.) She says we'd better come out because she thinks Benny wants to see us. He's not lucid much of the time, but he's with the family and comfortable as she can make him."

We went.

Ben lay in a hospital bed in the living room; his three children, Pancho their bronco-buster and top hand, the brothers and Nick came and went from time to time. We drank a lot of beer and sang to him. He smiled and nodded, fading in and out of what we were saying and trying to do for him.

A few months prior he'd told us all that when he signed on the "no breakfast forever list" he didn't want any funeral, no preacher praying over him, just a bunch of his friends getting drunk and singing, telling stories and having fun down by the swimming hole and cottonwoods where he wanted to be laid.

Meanwhile, he was busy living it up, not waiting around for that time.

Three days later Al called again.

"Benny's gone, Katie. Betty wants us to sing at the funeral — Sunday."

"But he said he didn't want . . ."

"I know."

"Damn!"

"The family wants it that way. I've written a little thing for him. You sing whatever you like. I know Ben will be pleased."

I guess everybody in Prescott and the Verde Valley, the whole country around, was out there that day. But the grave wasn't down at the cottonwoods by the swimming hole, it was up on the hill by Nick's house. I sang the thing I adapted from S. Omar Barker's *Adiós* — stressing, I'm afraid with a little malice, the lines "We ain't come slicked up fer a showoff/ We ain't brought no preacher to pray." I got through it somehow, but singing that song is one of the toughest things I've ever had to do. Al didn't fare too well with his either.

ODE TO BEN PERKINS*

Ben Perkins was a cowboy,
Well known for miles around.
He was cut down while in his prime,
His spool is all unwound.

Refrain

And he'll go no more a'ridin,
The cattle for to herd,
He's sung his last brave song for us,
We'll miss his smile and word.

His Grandad founded Perkinsville,
Trailed in from Texas' plains.
His folks were Nick and Evelyn,
Of four boys three remain.

Refrain

So we'll drink a toast to Benny
And to Betty sing this song,
Who stood by him through thick and thin;
We'll miss him now he's gone.

He left his home when but a youth,
For Uncle Sam's Navy,
For him no girl in every port,
But always two or three.

Refrain

And he'll go no more a-roping,
The calves to head and heel,
There's no more jackpots he'll collect,
He got a lousy deal.

One time he came to Cottonwood,
To have some fun he said,
He met and wooed nurse Betty,
And to her he was wed.

Refrain

And he'll go no more sing-songing,
His guitar it is still,
He'll never take another drink,
With friends who love him still.

Now Ben and Betty ran the trailrides,
Into Sycamore,
We'll miss the biscuits Benny baked
That he will bake no more.

Refrain

For he'll go no more to Phoenix
To politic and deal,
He loved to visit with the boys,
He loved to deal and wheel.

Benny, he had feet of clay,
As do we one and all,
But he had wife and kids and friends,
Whose loyalty was tall.

Refrain

But he'll be no more among us,
His race is finally run,
He fought a brave, long five-year fight,
And now his days are done.

He made mistakes as we all have,
We overlook them all,
A personality and friend,
We won't forget at all.

Refrain

This last toast drink to Benny,
We loved him right or wrong,
His life was full while he was here,
We'll miss him now he's gone.

Then we all went down to the swimming hole beside the big cottonwood trees and got roaring, singing, Irish drunk!

Chapter 12

DROVE DOWN to Phoenix, moved in with some friends on the west side of town, pulled my guitar out of the T-Bird's trunk and polished up a few songs I'd need to sing at Portofino's Coffee House in Scottsdale.

Found no letter from Bell Sweet, nor had mine to her been returned. But there was a note from Hamilton Rogers, son of James Grafton, composer of *Old Dolores*. For a lawyer, I'll wager his was the least detailed letter in history.

Hamilton had been to Old Dolores, or thought he had, though he didn't use the name Dolores Ranch, and there was little remaining of the original buildings. Above the townsite in a steep canyon were remnants of several stone constructions, and he thought perhaps that was the actual site, not down below where the cemetery had been, and the sawmill. He'd found a shaft and tunnel, he said, "up there somewhere." No mention of how to get there, or if a road took off from State Highway 14. He'd found more buildings of stone below — below what? — concluded that at one time Old Dolores must have been spread all over the mountainside, and dismissed it with the observation that it "certainly was nothing like what my father saw half a century ago."

By now I had accepted the idea no one was going to take the interest in it that I had — ultimately I'd be the one to find my own clues to its exact whereabouts, and shouldn't concern myself with help from others, even from Bill Mekeel who'd done the most to try and find it so far.

I phoned him in Santa Fe to tell him about Hamilton's note.

"Hi, Tinkerbell, wondered where you were. When're you getting here? I've found your town."

"You haven't!"

"Yup, got in my car and *drove* until I found the son-of-a-gun. It isn't exactly the sort of road for your Bird, but I think you can make it if you're careful."

"Hey, Willie, that's great! It's still there, then."

"Yeah, I think I found the old *cantina* — you know, Ramon's place — sorta caved in on one end, but looks like it could have been the bar all right."

"Terrific!" I cried, so excited I could hardly talk, "I just *knew* it! Oh, Willie, I can't wait to get there!"

"I wondered if you'd fall for that." His voice suddenly dropped to a no-nonsense level. "Now listen, Kate, you've got to quit playing games with yourself."

I was really taken aback; it wasn't like Bill to talk that way. "Why, what d'you mean?" I asked, startled by his sudden switch.

"You know goddam well there couldn't be any *cantina* named Ramon's — that's the verse that Mr. Rogers didn't even write! His lawyer friend wrote it, and his friend had *never been near Old Dolores*. He *invented* Ramon!"

I drew a deep breath to say something catty — nothing came out but, "Oh."

He went on like a father talking to his little girl: "Now I'm not going to tell you anything about it, not even how to get there. You're going to find it for yourself anyway. But if I were you I'd start listening to what nearly everyone so far has tried to tell you, so that you won't be disappointed when you finally stumble on the place."

I was silent, and there were tears in my eyes, of frustration, anger, sadness. I was mad at him for tricking me like that, but it did show me how far gone I was. I managed a weak, "Okay," before I gathered up my defense.

Then calling on the only valid reasoning I had left, I said somewhat shakily, "You forget, Willie, that I haven't seen Mr. Rogers yet. Spending some time talking with him about the place is going to make a difference. Properly stimulated, he'll remember things he's forgotten to tell me. He wrote that song because Old Dolores inspired him — certainly he knows how it looks."

"Looked!"

"All right!" I fairly shouted at him; then more in control, I asked a practical question. "Are you sure you were at Dolores and not some other place?"

"Goddamit, yes."

"Is there enough left to tell that it had a plaza? — that it was a town?"

"Go look for yourself, Tinkerbell."

Before World War II the place where Scottsdale, Arizona, reposes was a chunk of untouched desert with no more than a few *jacales* on it. Then a small shopping center appeared to accommodate the luxury homes beginning to encircle Camelback Mountain — I remember the poodles there were directed to weewee on miniature fire hydrants — but since that time the village has spread like a middle-aged madam without a girdle.

There is a decided difference between an old town like Jerome and one that's built to look old, like Scottsdale. No ancient buildings, no whims of fancy poke the skyline to give that look of careless love; buildings in these instant pseudo-western cities resemble piecrust, and the studious effort toward nineteenth century lettering puts them in a bag with bad movie sets.

It is here during the month of August that I'll be performing at Portofino's Coffee House. Here also, I will find Lawrence "Speed" Richardson, who owns and operates a riding stable out on Mockingbird Lane.

A bit after noon I drive into the stable yard.

A swamp cooler roars from the roof, pulling hot air through wet pads of excelsior; flies buzz close to the screens, horses stomp and nicker in the stalls and there's a strong smell of wet grass and manure rising off the lawn where a squeaky sprinkler turns. Speed, his wife Mary and three little house apes exit the back door to greet me.

Sniffing and looking toward the corrals, I observe, "You don't have to carry that stuff, do you?"

"Not *me!*" His brown eyes squint with a grin. "I'm teachin' m'kids to shovel it. Hell, it's good t'see ya! What'cha been up to?" We walk inside, the kids carrying my guitar. "Now, gaddangit, if you rug rats'll git the hell outta here, we kin git on with this little social gatherin'."

"Aw, daddy, please."

"See what nice manners m' kids have? Just like a bunch of wild mustangs! Go on, git! I like m' coffee strong, m' women weak and m' kids *quiet!*"

Glancing up at Mary who is handing us a beer, I can't see what he likes about her — she's anything but weak — little, maybe, but she's from strong New England stock and certainly no pussyfoot.

Lawrence Richardson was born in Powell, Wyoming, in 1914. His dad, who had the first livery stable in town, allowed as how Speed could quit school when he was sixteen and start chasing broomtails — "since I was spending more time lookin' down the teacher's neck," he says, "than lookin' at my 'rithmetic." After that he fell easily into the related trade of cow punching, peeling broncs, raising horses, being a ranch foreman, learning fancy rope tricks, singing on the radio, and falling so low as to become a dude wrangler — "hated that worse 'n a dose of the crabs!"

Next lowest thing he says he did was go East.

When I ask why, he offers something like, "Listen, gotdamit! . . . a big son-ofabitch says to me, 'Wyomin' ain't big enough fer you an' me both' . . . so I left!"

Punctuating his sentences full of underlined words and laughing as he talks, Speed tells wonderful stories. He's a fine singer too, but won't play his old guitar any more — sings like Gail, a cappella, his curly black hair flopping over his forehead in time with the rhythm, eyes to the floor, concentrating. This cowboy has gotten used to sitting chairs instead of hunkering, but still rests his elbows on his knees when he sings as hunkerers will do, I suppose from a habit acquired around the campfire — same way Shorty Mac would sing. His voice is an outdoor one, loud and clear with a slight twang and a decided western accent.

"Come on, Larry, tell her why you really left Wyoming," prompts his wife.

"Well, we raised horses up there for the Eastern Market — had an outlet in *Maine.* When we shipped the stock one spring I went along to close the *deal,* and I got to listenin' to this ol' boy on the radio — WCOU, Lewiston, Maine. He had a western accent and played and sang western songs. I thought, now *there's* one of m' own *kind.* He kept askin' fer folks t' write in and said he'd answer any questions they had about the West and the songs he played, so I thought, I'm gonna have some *fun* with this ol' bastard and I wrote him a card askin' him a bunch of silly questions like, 'why does a cowboy drink his java from an ol' tin *can,* why don't he git a *cup* same's other people?' Next day when he come on I had m' ear glued to the radio t' see what he was gonna say t' *that.* He sang a song or two; then started readin' cards. When he got t' *mine* he says, 'I ain't shore, but I thank *somebody's* tryin' t' pull my *laig.* Well, I got an answer fer this smart so-n-so *anyhow* — a cowboy drinks his java from an ol' tin *can* b'cause his *cup* is fulla *beans!*' Well, to make a long story dawdle, I go down to see this ol' boy, and one thing leadin' to another, me and him takes off fer points south doin' a little act fer the vaudeville circuit — me twirlin' a rope and doin' tricks and him singin' songs and twangin' his geetar" — he looks over at Mary — "but I figure b'fore I leave I better do a good deed and save *her* pore hide, git her outta that place; she's from Maine, ya know. Hell they're so gotdam tight back there you couldn't drive a flax seed up their ass with a sledge hammer! Well, ya can't keep a family raisin' horses, ya gotta *do* something with 'em, so we decides t' come here where the grass is a little shorter — but greener. We ain't never gonna git rich, but we manage t' keep beer in the icebox." He tips up the can and drains it, stands up and rubs his little round belly. "Hell, it's better 'n workin' fer wages or mendin' fence; all an ol' cowboy wants t' do after he comes in from mendin' fence is get *drunk!*"

My Blue Heaven[*]

This mornin' 'bout three
You shoulda seen me,
Hell, I just couldn't see
My Blue Heaven.

I come through the door,
Fell smacko on the floor;
My wife she got sore
In My Blue Heaven.

> She hit me with a rollin' pin,
> Then swung the broom.
> She hit me where you know damn well
> The roses bloom!

Jist Molly an' me,
An' m' mother-in-law makes three;
They beat the hell outta me
In My Blue Heaven.

The late bloom of vaudeville is where Speed came in — when that garden was in full flower with the parody. He returned from the East with a list of such songs that had nothing to do with cowboys or the West, except that cowboys will sing songs like that when they find them lying around. Cowboys were quick to use vaudeville melodies for their homemade lyrics as they had used minstrel tunes before.

I'll Be With You When the Roses Bloom Again*

I was comin' down the river to my little cottage home,
The revenue men were waitin' there for me.
I was comin' down the hill when they caught me with the
    still
I'll be with you when the roses bloom again.
    When the roses bloom again beside the river,
    And the robin redbreast sings his melody.
    I was feelin' pretty frisky when they caught
        me with the whiskey;
    I'll be with you when the roses bloom again.

They took me to the courthouse, the old judge he was there,
He didn't show me any sympathy —
"They have caught you with the wine, so I'll send you
    down the line —
You'll be with them when the roses bloom again."
    When the roses bloom again beside the river,
    And the robin redbreast sings his melody.
    I was feelin' mighty fine when they caught me with
        the wine —
    I'll be with you when the roses bloom again.

They took me to the jailhouse to serve my ninety days,
Now I'm out on the county road to pay.
But my heart will fill with cheer, for I know we'll drink
    the beer —
I'll be with you when the roses bloom again.
    When the roses bloom again beside the river,
    And the robin redbreast sings his melody —
    But my heart will fill with cheer, for I know we'll
        drink the beer —
    I'll be with you when the roses bloom again.

After a length of time the creative work of a poet is allowed to fall into a collective stew pot called Public Domain, where another poet may find it and reshape it to his convenience. A prime example of this treatment is *The Cowboy's Lament*. There are probably people who haven't seen this ancient lyric, so from a fourteen-verse text claiming to be the original, I quote a few of the more popular verses:

As I walked out in the streets of Laredo,
As I walked out in Laredo one day,
I spied a poor cowboy wrapped up in white linen,
Wrapped up in white linen as cold as the clay.

"I see by your outfit that you are a cowboy,"
These words he did say as I boldly stepped by,

"Come, sit beside me and hear my sad story;
I was shot in the breast and I know I must die.

"Let sixteen gamblers come handle my coffin,
Let sixteen cowboys come sing me a song,
Take me to the graveyard and lay the sod over me,
For I'm a poor cowboy, and I know I've done wrong.

"It was once in the saddle I used to go dashing,
It was once in the saddle I used to be gay;
First to the dram-house, then to the card-house;
Got shot in the breast, I am dying today."

We beat the drum slowly and played the fife lowly,
And bitterly wept as we bore him along;
For we all loved our comrade, so brave, young, and
    handsome;
We all loved our comrade, although he'd done wrong.[109]

Within the last half century *The Cowboy's Lament* has picked up a few hundred variants on as many subjects as there are people to walk out in the street lamenting about: a lineman, a skier, a brick layer, ad infinitum. The last parody I heard worth mentioning is based on the haberdashery of the drugstore cowboy:

THE DYING OUTFIT*

As I walked out in the streets of Laredo,
As I walked out in Laredo one day,
I spied a poor cowboy wrapped up in white linen,
Wrapped up in white linen as cold as the clay.

I see by your outfit that you are a cowboy
You see by my outfit that I am one too,
We see by our outfits that we are both cowboys
Now you get an outfit an' you can be a cowboy too.

Now you got no outfit, so you're not a cowboy
I got two outfits, you take one of mine.
Now you got an outfit, and I got an outfit
And in our outfits now don't we look fine?

You fit in my outfit, I fit in your outfit,
We fit in our outfits, we're outfitted fine.
They're fine-fitted outfits, they're out-fitted fine-fits,
They're fit-outed b-b-l-l-r-r-b-b, I'm fit to be tied.

As I walked out in the streets of Laredo
As I walked out in Laredo one day,
I spied a young outfit wrapped up in his cowboy,
Wrapped up in his outfit, so I let him lay!

Vaudeville songs of the twenties were preoccupied, it seems, with boozing; since there was so much of it when there was supposed to be none. Another favorite of Speed's, Irish in melody and deed is:

The Night I Stole Old Sammy Morgan's Gin *

Listen folks I'll tell a funny story;
You may think it's sad, but I was in my glory.
'Twas a cellar I crept in,
Cobwebs brushin' by my chin,
On the night I stole old Sammy Morgan's gin.

As my hand fell on the jug I had to snicker,
But when I started for the door I went much quicker,
For up above my head
Someone jumped right out of bed.
On the night I stole old Sammy Morgan's gin.

As I left the cellar b'lieve me I was listing,
And I hops from one arm to the other shifting,
Then I stopped and hauled the plug,
Set there till I drained the jug,
And I'm tellin' you no spare drops was I missing.

Then on my feet I thought I was, but wasn't,
And for roads I must have seen about a dozen.
When I reached my old porch door,
I went smacko on the floor;
On the night I stole old Sammy Morgan's gin.

I just made one step and landed in the coal box,
Then from off the mantle came the Big Ben 'larm clock,
But I finally got upstairs,
After passin' seven bears,
'Twas the night I stole old Sammy Morgan's gin.

I saw mice as big as horses washin' dishes,
As an ape came in the door dressed up in britches,
Then the floor fell on my head
As I tried to get in bed,
On the night I stole old Sammy Morgan's gin.

When I woke next morning, guess 'twas closer evening
And the room was still a rockin' and a weavin',
Someone else had took my head,
Left an elephant's there instead,
The morning after drinking Sammy Morgan's gin.

Because Speed is so obviously a Westerner, I'm puzzled by the eastern kidney plasters hanging in his tackroom. The mere sight of that kidney plaster, postage stamp, pancake, punkin' seed, in effect, Eastern saddle, can turn a cowboy's stomach. They've been cause for open warfare since the first one made its appearance in cattle country. Some of Buck's saltiest lingo has been vented on these things — I can hear him now:

"Ain't that a clever way to air your rear end at a trot! . . . Lookit how she spills out that saddle, like bakin' powder biscuits over the pan! . . . A wonderous secure spot fer settin', just like a goddam pea on a breadboard! . . . There goes one of them pore embarrassed horses with a little belly-band around his middle . . . Hey, lookit, Mac — somebody stole the seat off your rockin' horse! . . . *That's* a funny way to ride, with your knees up in your ears!"

Anyone who's ever worked at wrangling dudes has a few stories tucked away about his experiences. Reams of poetry and song have been written on the subject — almost enough to put it all in a single category, except that they weren't all written in a single period. Dude songs are being written still, if not by cowboys, by river guides, jeep drivers, anyone who takes the greenhorn to obscure trails and introduces him to the secrets of the land.

Speed recalls a time when the boss's son took the beat-up Ford wagon into town to pick up a guest at the railroad station.

"Peck was about ten years old I guess, but he could drive the *Ford*, and then some — kids *worked* on that ranch when they was old enough to shed the safety pins outta their *diapers*. This lady come every year and all the hands knew her, so he locates her and helps with her bags when she gits off the train.

" 'My lands, Peck,' she says, 'how you've grown since last year! Did you come alone to meet me?'

'Yes 'um,' he says.

'Look, I want to do a little *shopping*,' she says, 'before we start for the *ranch* — do you have anything to get for your father, groceries or anything?'

He says, 'Yes'um, I got to stop at the *feed* store fer some grain and seed.'

'That's just fine. You meet me here in half an hour,' an' she turns to go, but she remembers somethin' *else* she needs t'know. 'By the way, Peck, what size conveyance do you have?'

"Well, the pore kid turns all red, wiggles his toe in the dirt and hangs his head, not able to look at her — then he says, 'Un — I — I dunno ma'am, I guess it's about the same size as any *other* little boy's my age.' "

Castle Hot Springs, some thirty-five miles from Wickenburg, Arizona, was famed near and far as one of the finest dude ranches in the West. In those years when the eastern market was flooded with yearlings and beef took a dive, the cowboy had to learn to sing and play the guitar, tell jokes and woolly stories, and more often than not, stay up half the night spooning some young lady — that is, if he wanted to keep himself in steak and eggs.

Billy Simon said that he got through that period of his life without too many scars, and no new earmarks. He told me of a doctor and his wife who wanted to go to Crater Canyon one day — the bottom of said canyon, like many in Arizona, was about wide enough at the bottom to sit a wagon, and sides reaching up some five or six hundred feet to the top.

"This doctor's wife was a real nice woman, and she's one of those heavy thinkers. Anyway, we come to the head of the canyon and she looks up and wants to know if there's a way up there so we can go and look back down. I tell her, yes, but it's gonna take us a while to get there. Sometime in the afternoon

151

we hit the rim of Crater and she's looking down in, fairly fascinated! We git off our horses and she asks me to roll a boulder down to see how long it takes to drop. We wait quite a spell b'fore it hits — then all of a quick she says to me, 'Bill, do you know what made this canyon?' 'No,' I says, never havin' thought about it much, an' not really carin' if I think about it then. 'Why, a glacier made this canyon,' an' she goes on t'explain t'me how this big sheet of ice come through here grindin' out rocks an' stuff. Well, I figured she was a smart lady, so I says, 'Well, that sounds good to me,' an' we git back on our mounts and start home. Ridin' along, she gets to musin' some more about that damn ice cube and says, 'I wonder what happened to that glacier?' 'I dunno,' I says, 'maybe it went back after another canyon.' "

> We used to run a cow-ranch
>   In all that old term meant,
> But all our ancient glories
>   In recent years have went;
> We're takin' summer boarders,
>   And, puttin' it quite rude,
> It's now the cowboy's province
>   To herd the festive dude.[110]

And Billy said, "One damn cold and frosty mornin' I had to drive the *buckboard* to Castle Hot Springs Junction t' round up a bunch of people comin' out from Chicago who wanted the full treatment! I mean, they wasn't satisfied to come over on the stage, they wanted to rough it like we did b'fore the automobile. I get there early and I'm stompin' my feet and bangin' my hands together to keep warm when the train pulls in. A woman gits off, just frisky as a chiggered goat, her cheeks puffed out red and rosy, and strides up and down the platform. Purty soon she "sets up" in front of me and says, '*Isn't* this *invigorating?*' 'No, ma'am,' I says, 'This is Castle Hot Springs Junction and I'm here to get you folks in the buckboard.' "

> We used to brand our cattle
>   And ship 'em wide and far;
> But now we import humans
>   From off the Pullman car;
> The dudes have got us captured
>   And tied and branded, too,
> And the cowboy's readin' Ibsen
>   When his daily toil is through.[111]

Time's up with Speed and Mary.

I must get ready to go to work, or as we say in my business, ready to go play. Hopefully, there'll be some cowboys as well as dudes stringing into my camp these next few weeks — I'm thinking how fine one or two of Speed's parodies will go.

"Swap you a song I know for *My Blue Heaven*, Speed."

"Hell's fire, Katie, *Old Dolores* is worth ten of them things, and you've already given us that."

152

"I've got another you can sing for your rug rats and your friends. They'll love it. It's made for you."

With a promise to come back a couple more times for good chuck line chili and beer, if they'll be my guests at Portofino's, I depart Richardson's Riding Stables, leaving behind:

A PEON NAMED PANCHO*

A peon named Pancho
Out on a sheep rancho,
  Down old Mexico way,
Was weary and dry
One day in July,
  As under a wagon he lay.

As he watched his sheep
Neath the mountain so steep,
  No water was there to be found;
He concocted a brew,
Called it locoweed Dew;
  His siesta took place on the ground.

He dreamed of Aliente
And far-off Caliente,
  Señoritas abundant with charms
Then, one night in June,
Neath the Mexican moon,
  He held one so tight in his arms.

He held her so tightly
And kissed her so lightly,
  Her lips were as red as the rose.
He awoke from his sleep
To find an old sheep
  A grazin' southeast of his nose!

Chapter 13

Goin' Back to Arizona*

I left old Arizona,
And went back East to stay,
With my stetson hat and cowboy boots,
I looked like a half-picked jay.
But I'd pack'd my duds, my spurs and ropes.
I'd packed my saddle too,
I'm here among the city folks
And gosh I'm feelin' blue.

Chorus:

Goin' back to Arizona
That's where I want to be,
There's a gal in Arizona
That I'd like mighty well to see.
There's a cow in Arizona that's
Got a calf I'd like to brand;
And my hoss in Arizona
Is runnin' with a mustang band.
Goin' back to Arizona
And round 'em up someday.
And I'll whoop and yell
In the big corral
With a ki-yi-yip-pi-ki-yay.

154

I saw the town from end to end
Cabarets and movies too,
A jillion folks, but not a friend
To holler, "how-de-do."
Oh, give me back my pony
And the range that I love best,
I'm homesick and I'm lonely,
So I'm goin' back out West.

Living in Phoenix in August is like building extra fires in hell, but desert rats don't get too upset with that; nearly everyone has a swamp cooler, and in 1960 (before mass conversion to refrigeration) the heat didn't bother too many people.

An ex-dude wrangler and star performer of radio's old and famed WLS Barn Dance now lives here in the center of town. Romaine Lowdermilk — Romy — has written a number of songs and has set melodies to many range poems, then sung them not only to the dudes at his own ranch, the <u>KL</u> (K L Bar) near Wickenburg, but for the whole creation on that famous network program, beginning in the mid-twenties. Romy quite clearly represents a bridge between the authentic cow songs and those that were made and remade for that radio audience.

Long, long, I have heard of Romaine Lowdermilk from the Arizona cowboys who speak affectionately of him, praise his songs and his singing of them. Billy Simon remembers:

"Romy had a dude ranch of his own out Wickenburg way, and he only came over to the Springs on special occasions. He was really a fine singer, and writer of songs, and he sure did have a sense of humor. Had the biggest damn feet I ever saw on a man — looked like two hogs fightin' when he walked. We used t' say it would take two bullhides and a bushel of tacks to make him a pair of boots."

Naturally, the first thing I look at when I'm admitted through his front door are his feet. They are wondrous large! — as is his smile, the heart and humor of this old-timey performer.

The Lowdermilk clan originated in America around Ashboro, North Carolina, from two brothers who had fought through the Revolution against England and were given land grants in 1779. Romy was born in Chetopa, Kansas, on the Oklahoma border in 1890. As a boy he worked on farms and ranches in Oklahoma and New Mexico, and in 1908, at the age of eighteen, he and his folks came to Arizona Territory. About 1911 he established himself on a ranch along the Hassayampa River four miles north of Wickenburg — 1918 he began taking in dudes. By 1922 he was singing on a Phoenix radio as one of the very *first* Western singers. His contemporaries in the professional singing and writing field at that time were Curley Fletcher, Tex Ritter, Gene Autry, "Haywire Mac" McClintock, John I. White, Patsy Montana — the non-professionals from whom he got real cow songs were the Gail Gardner types, men who worked the Arizona ranches.

Like others before him, Romy began singing cowboy songs when he came

155

West — old songs in the Public Domain like *I Ride An Old Paint, The Chisholm Trail, Cowboy's Lament.* Since he was a good singer, he was called on to sing more than others and therefore wanted more songs. The next step is to do like Billy Simon did — take a poem you like and whip up a tune for it, borrowed or new-made, whatever you have the talent for. Romy developed a flair for melodies that were interesting and out of the ordinary for cowboy verse. He also knew where the verse originated and if the song was to be used on radio or put in a songbook, he'd make arrangements with the author to copyright the song in both their names — if that's how the author wanted it. Some of his better known "put-togethers" are a Lowell Otus Reese poem *Great Grandad,*[112] *Punchin' the Dough* by Henry Herbert Knibbs,[113] *Out in the Short Grass Country, His Trademarks* and *A Spoiled Outfit,* poems by E. A. Brininstool.[114] Some that he wrote from the ground up — words and music — are *The Rodeo Parade,*[115] *The Big Corral,*[116] *Goin' Back to Arizona, Cowboy Goes to Town,*[117] and his now very famous *Blood on the Saddle.*

There has been some controversy about who wrote the latter, but in this text it is ascribed to Romy. Shortly before he died, he wrote to me:

> John I. White, who is a sincere and painstaking researcher of old songs, says my song *Blood on the Saddle* has been copied far and wide.[118] I'd never thought much of it and didn't think it'd ever been heard outside Arizona, but it has spread. I sang *Blood on the Saddle* for the first time anywhere at Castle Hot Springs where Everett Cheetham was working and singing. Everett went to Hollywood and asked me to give him the song as he could get a part in some show or other (movie) and I gave it to him and he gave me a good one called *Jose Cuervo's Daughter* in exchange.[119] It's a good one all right. In the picture he worked in they attributed the "Blood" song to Cheetham which was all right with me, but the company copyrighted it, attributed it to Tex Ritter who still sings it after a fashion. Mr. J. R. Williams who was a noted cartoonist of cowboy doings needed something real gory for a "Balloon" in a picture he was drawing when he lived near Prescott, Ariz., and we were talking about it in a restaurant there and between us cobbled up the first verse which he used and later on I added a couple more and made it longer and goryer.[120]

Blood on the Saddle*

There was blood on the saddle
And blood all around,
And a great big puddle
Of blood on the ground.

The cowboy lay in it
All covered with gore,
And he won't go riding
No broncos no more.

Oh, pity the cowboy
All bloody and red,

For his bronco fell on him
And mashed in his head.

There was blood on the saddle
And bloo-o-od all around
And a great big puddle
Of bl-o-o-o-od on the ground.

Now here is a song that would fit exactly Alan Lomax's misplaced description of Gail's *Sierry Petes* — "A ranch poet, desperate to find something to match the tourists' idea of the wild and wooly West . . ." Indeed Romy admits having tried to make it "goryer." I mean, if you don't have in mind the dressing up of a song to go out among strangers you'll dress it like Curley Fletcher for the cowboy who's *getting* thrown, and you'll not be talking about the gore which he knows is all too likely, but which he has put clean out of his mind in order to ride said rodeo broncs.

I thought I was up on the hurricane deck
Of an earthquake and a cyclone a-havin' a wreck.
I was doin' my best and was just gettin' by,
But he's doin' better with blood in his eye.

He was bawlin' and gruntin' a-humpin' the hump;
He turned wrong side out with every new jump.
At ridin' bad horses I'm no crippled squaw,
But he showed me some tricks that I never had saw.

With a giratin' jump he goes over the gate,
And I grabbed for the horn, but I was too late.
He hit with a jar that 'most shed his hair;
It busted me loose and I quit him right there.

Of all the bad horses that I ever rode,
None was like him, for he seemed to explode.
He busted me up and I'm still stiff and lamed —
The Ridge Runnin' Outlaw will never be tamed.[121]

I ask Romy to remember as many boys who sang at Castle Hot Springs as he can. I asked Billy Simon the same and between them they came up with almost a dozen, over half of them gone to the Big Roundup In The Sky.[122]

"There were some mighty good storytellers and singers among those fellows," Romy says.

I said, "Billy Simon tells me there were some fancy goins-on at the Wickenburg dude ranches back then, like not-so-sweet, not-so-young, not-so-innocent things, bored with bathtub gin parties and ready to paw new pastures, coming West to do the 'in' thing — have an affair with some cowboy."

"Oh, sure, that's right," Romy grins. "Castle Hot had its fat share of those."

I've got the feeling Billy should know. He was one very handsome man in those days — still is. He once told me that a person could get sued for highway robbery and attempt to rape if he told what he knew about The Marriage Corral — but said he'd describe an incident not using any names:

157

"So-'n-so had a regular route every night, and 'bout two in the mornin' he silently cracks the door of a little filly's room to let himself out in the hall. Coast is clear so he takes his boots in one hand and quietly steps out. As he's walking down the hallway, one of the other boys comin' from another room passes him. They both put their fingers to their lips and go, 'sh-s-s-sh,' an' tiptoe on. Just ships that pass in the night."

> Old cowboys claim they knew for shore
> If a nester was married or not,
> By the way he hung the cabin door
> On his little ol' homestead plot.

> If the doors swung in, without a doubt,
> He was free from wedded worry.
> But a married man swung his door *out*
> So he always could leave in a hurry! [123]

What the dude business didn't do to change the character of cowboy songs, radio accomplished in nothing flat — radio and the song publishing racket.

In the early twenties, characters like Powder River Jack Lee and certain New York and Chicago song pulps found a most lucrative business in the rustling of cowboy ballads — those being sung nightly around cowboy camp and dude fires. Without stopping to find if they were already famous poems put to music by some poke, or were the compositions, branded or unbranded, of some local cowhand, said rustlers began slapping them at random into songbooks altering tunes beyond recognition and changing words to get by the law, then copyrighting them in the name of their publication and/or the radio singer whose public was demanding more *Western* songs. Once in a while they were sued — but not often enough.

Radio devoured songs in those days like television devours personalities now. Ravenous beasts that must be fed constantly, they soon find that things in the Public Domain won't satisfy their famished appetites. Radio audiences wanted more than the same melody for each four-line verse sung eight to twenty-eight times. That spelled monotony. And so the "bridge" entered the cow song.

Thus began a chain reaction that was to take the cowboy song completely away from the cowboy and from its home range. Before now, people came West and heard these songs, heard them mostly as written. Came radio and the songs were taken to them, altered, changed, padded, spliced, cut — made "goryer."

The WLS Barn Dance was a melting pot for these items, as was Grand Ole Opry for hillbilly or *country songs*. But many WLS performers began appearing on Grand Old Opry in Nashville, and vice-versa. Here's a very conspicuous place where the two became jumbled enough to lose their identity. By the mid-thirties the whole bag had been labeled *country-western* — a misnomer that hasn't been shaken yet, and probably won't be.

No more alike, really, than the Rocky Mountains and the Tennessee Hills, these musical heritage roots have entangled to form a jungle of confusion.

Tennessee Hill kids are born with strings as an extension of the hand. Before they quit lisping the four-letter words they can play the be-Jesus out of any instrument from a whisky jug to a curled leaf. Because of the time they can spend at it, they become true artists on the variation of themes that stem from backwoods play-party songs, Child Ballads, blues (gutbucker to them) and frenzied religious hymns. If it involves a lyric, this is sung high and through the nose in tight harmonies which produce a distinctive thrilling sound, almost primitive. Small tree-covered pocket valleys in the hills produced instrumentalists of high quality, along with singers whose harmonies huddled so tight you couldn't break them open with a wedge. And they didn't move around. They stayed at home.

Isolated folk music.

The range riders, on the other hand, were concerned with words, story and feeling about a *place* that belonged to cows. The music became indigenous to that place, slowed to the pace of said cows, and the horses moving with them. It was music that came from other places, as hill music first did, but which was altered to fit each need. Here on the range the instrument was rarely played well, if at all, and cowboys sang (sing) together almost never. And the cowboy didn't stay at home; he moved on his hundred thousand square miles of open range, singing to himself and other cowboys.

Again, isolated folk music, until . . .

Collectors came to both places, changing the songs in both camps for reasons I have stated — to make somebody (hardly ever the author) some loot, and to make the songs appealing to city folks.

Today's *City Eastern* music (more accurately, Southeastern but still called C & W) is rankly adolescent, didactic music, concerning itself with the recapture of childhood, returning to the womb, escaping from any real problems or responsibilities, adolescent bravado, death (preferably someone else's), getting even with women, and breaking down in tears. "Thought to celebrate the wide-open spaces it is actually fraught with tight, closed-in areas like jail cells, cabs of trucks and locomotives, little honky-tonks, telephone booths, small truck stop cafes, cottages or railroad shacks, and mines and tunnels . . ."[124] The hero is usually bewildered and seems to *enjoy* his bewilderment, is either running away, drinking, going to prison or turning to religion — *escaping*. The old Western hero was proud in his solitude, "which implies a self-sufficiency, an ability to endure loneliness, whereas the C & W hero, like a child, is afraid of being alone."[125] He still seeks solitary, clandestine relationships but if said relationships become complicated he will immediately flee — "entanglements like marriage, children, debt, hard work, hard thinking — for the free comfort of childhood which [he] subconsciously desires."[126]

Are there any truly *Western* songs today? Yes. Are they still open-space conscious? Yes. But the spaces are closing in and the songs reflect this stricture — they deal with the reminiscence and nostalgia about a *place* that used to be. Steve Fromholz tells it in *The Man With the Big Hat*. I would call Steve The Larry McMurtry[127] of Western balladry, he and Travis Edmonson.[128]

The Man With the Big Hat*

In a bar in Arizona on a sultry summer day
A cowboy came in off the road just to pass the time
  away.
He pulled a stool up to the bar, pushed his hat back
  on his head,
I listened to the stories told, to the words the
  cowboy said,
He said . . .
I can tell you stories 'bout the Indians on the plains,
Talk about Wells Fargo and the comin' of the trains,
Talk about the slaughter of the buffalo that roamed,
Tell of all the settlers come out lookin' for a home.

Chorus:
Now the man with the big hat is buyin',
Drink up while the drinkin' is free.
Drink up to the cowboys a-dead or a-dyin'
Drink to my compadres and me
Drink to my compadres and me.

Well, his shirt was brown and faded and his hat was
  wide and black,
And the pants that once were blue were grey and had
  a pocket gone in back,
He had a finger missin' from the hand that rolled a
  smoke
While he smiled and talked of cowboys but you knew
  it weren't no joke.
He said . . .
I've seen a day so hot your pony could not stand
And if your water bag was dry don't count upon
  the land,
And winters, I've seen winters when your boots froze
  in the snow
And your only thought was leavin' but you had no place
  to go.

Chorus:

He rested easy at the bar, his foot upon the rail
And laughed and talked of times he'd had while livin'
  on the trail.
The silence never broken as the words poured from
  his lips.
As quiet as the .45 he carried on his hip.
He said . . .
I rode the cattle drives from here to San Antone,
Ten days in the saddle and weary to the bone.

160

I've rode from here to Wichita without a woman's smile,
And the fire where I cooked my beans was the only
    light for miles.

Chorus:

He rolled another cigarette as he walked toward the
    door.
I heard his spurs a-jinglin' as his bootheels hit the
    floor.
He loosened up his belt a notch, pulled his hat down
    on his head,
Turned to say goodbye to me and this is what he said,
He said . . .

Now the highlines chase the highways and the fences
    close the range.
To see a workin' cowboy is a sight that's mighty
    strange.
A cowboy's life was lonely and his lot was not the
    best,
But if it wasn't for the life he lived there wouldn't
    be no West.

Chorus:
Now the man with the big hat is buyin',
Drink up while the drinkin' is free.
Drink up to the cowboys a-dead or a-dyin'
Drink to my compadres and me . . .
Drink to my compadres and me.

Travis's roots are deep in . . .

OLD ARIZONA*

Rocky old canyons, old dusty roads,
We can remember where the old rivers flowed
We were all young then, now we've gone gray,
Springs of our childhood have all dried away.

Chorus:
Mockin'birds warble, turtledoves call
Up on Red Mountain where the black walnuts fall.
Old Arizona, where did you go?
They've drained your waters for the cities below.

Cellophane wrappers, rusty tin cans,
That's all you get now from the Family of Man,
And the beautiful mountains and clean desert sands
Of Old Arizona are sold just for land.

Chorus:

The snows in December, the rains in July
You can remember and so can I
But all of these waters now drain to the West,
To California, and you know the rest.

Chorus:

Sighs on the night wind heard in the dawn,
Are me and Red Mountain wonderin' where life has
    gone?
It doesn't matter to the cities and mines
That steal our rivers and choke off our vines.

Chorus:

And there was that segment of the American West at the turn of a Victorian century that was rarely spoken about above a whisper, let alone put into song. It remained to be researched and talked of openly at a much later date. Ultimately it was made into poetry, prose, plays, songs and documented as history.

Long have we heard about the men who made the West, but little about the *women* who made the men who made the West. As Billy Simon says: "If a man stays too long in the dog house he'll wind up in the cat house." Many did. Famous "Ladies of the Evening" like Silverheels, Ma Brown, Julia Bulette, Lola Montez and Silver Dollar, have waited long to have their praises sung, as Travis sings of a southern Arizona lady.

LAVINIA'S PARLOUR*

Once when I was six or seven
Granny's thoughts of heaven came to me,
And I could see
Angels with their harps and things
All flyin' 'round on snowy wings of prayer,
And I was there.
Yes, I thought I was in heaven
Sittin' high among the Saints,
Watchin' herds of heavenly horses,
Blacks and bays, and roans, and paints,
As they reared and wheeled and cantered
'Cross the pasture in the sky —
And a daydream when you're seven
Can be real as you and I.

Chorus:

Drinkin' pink lemonade
In the shade of Lavinia's Parlour.
Rockin' the rockin' chair,
Feet almost touchin' the floor.
Drinkin' pink lemonade
In the shade of Lavinia's Parlour,

As the angel Lavinia murmured
Like perfume of more.

Now the ride's a torture,
For the day has been a scorcher, hot and dry,
Clear summer sky.
Saddle leather burns me
And my dizziness returns me through the haze
To better days —
When I thought I was in heaven
Made of crinoline and lace,
And the lady who was kind to me
Who hummed "Amazing Grace."
There were pretty peacock feathers
Stuck 'round pictures on the wall,
And her dress it whispered gently,
But her face I can't recall.

Chorus:

Now the sun is higher
And the desert is on fire as I dream
My boyhood dream.
The reins are burnin' through my hand,
As heat and stillness rule the land I ride . . .
And smile inside;
For I know now someone left me
On that day so long ago
In a painted lady's parlour
'Cause he had someplace to go.
And to him it may have been a joke
Or not, I'll never know,
But I'd give a month of cowboy's pay
Just one more time to go.

Chorus:

My letter to Bell Sweet came back the second week of my Phoenix engagement marked "return to sender — no forwarding address." Unexpectedly, my plans to try and pull *Old Dolores* from oblivion while on the way to Denver fell through because I was held over an extra week. I would have to return to Santa Fe after my Denver gig, end of September, and after I visited Mr. Rogers in nearby Georgetown.

Dolores had waited this long for me, she would wait a bit longer. I did receive a most encouraging note from Rogers while in Phoenix.

> . . . I will try to find out more about the film of Old Dolores which I
> saw in Mexico, but I don't know quite how to go about it. Yes, the song
> was sung in Spanish for the movie. I thought it delightful, but can't recall
> if they stuck to a literal translation or not.

163

It seems to me your theme of a book tracing the evolution of cowboy songs from folk chants to its parlor-typewriter-sophistication stage is a sound literary theme and good history. In fact literature is full of similar literary history. The Idylls of Theocritus and the Bucolics of Vergil were both fashionable and artificial refinements of the supposed delights and songs of shepherds. . . . We're waiting to see you when you come by. J.G.R.[129]

Shorely was some mighty high-blown fancy lingo for a cowboy-song writer to be flangin' around!

Speed, Mary and the Tumbleweeds keep their promise to come as my guests on closing night at Portofino's. The kids watch the show, transfixed — not a peep. When I ask for requests, young Larry says he would like to hear *Old Dolores*. His dad bends down and whispers something in his ear, whereupon the seven-year-old, prompted to courtesy, blurts out . . . *"Please,* goddam it!" . . . to a near standing ovation from an audience that is no longer mine.

Chapter 14

THE WHITE BIRD and I race along the big artery that leads to Denver. Not a leisurely trip now — no time to take lonely back roads that go and flow with the land, no time to note the season's subtle change, or smell it on a clean wind. An occasional cluster of yellow making a ragged patch high on some mountain warns that soon that patch will be white.

I recall how Shorty Mac and his old bones hated winter. No matter how thick the gloves, his bony hands still froze, nor how thick the socks — same for his toes. And just below his neck, between the shoulder blades, he said it always felt like he'd been hit with a giant snowball "that jist kept meltin', and meltin' an' meltin' till it run clean down m' back to m' butt and froze m' balls!" I would pity him something awful when I was twelve years old and he would cry like that, but as I grew and learned that they would most likely warm up again, I didn't feel such pangs.

Still, in all, Shorty Mac was a gent — nearly a S.W. Raleigh around women. Most things I heard him say that weren't meant for my tender ears were said to Buck or some other hand in what he thought was a private conversation. He would try not to express his uncensored male opinion when I was around, but when he'd hear me repeat a couple days later what he'd whispered in confidence, he finally gave up and said, "Well, button, it don't look like them bumps on the front of yer shirt is gonna go away, an' I s'pose you kaint walk through as many corrals as you have without gettin' some of that stuff on yer boots . . . but," he added, "if I'uz you, I wouldn't try to educate your mother and the whole goddam Southwest with what you overhear on this side of the fence, 'er Buck 'n' me'll be ridin' off into the sunset one fine morning."

Along about then — when the bumps wouldn't go away — I heard his finest story:

"Worked up north a couple years fer an outfit near Globe, an' we used t' go t' town every so often to get whiskey'd 'n' dehorned and talk to an ancient Injun who spent most of his time a-settin' on the courthouse steps smokin'. What I mean is, we *tried* t' git him to talk — do somethin' more'n grunt anyhow. It was a kind of gamblin' game among us. We'd make bets to see who could get a few words out of him.

"We come in one day t' find the whole dang town in a big hubbub an' the square so full of people it looks like there's gonna be a hangin'. Seems this skinny little ol' gal who looked like she was jist walkin' round t' save funeral expenses, come a-cryin' t' her folks a few days back so distracted she couldn't speak, make signs or shake a bush. When they finally gits 'er calmed down, they deduce that she's had the feathers of her cuckoo's nest ruffled up by this here young Indian brave — Globe's up t' here with Injuns, ya know; it's jist off the San Carlos Apache Reservation. He probably imbibed in a bit of tonsil varnish b'fore makin' this here alleged stab at her and was a mite swacked — but anyhow, he was smart enough to tail out for the tall timber. Couple days later the sheriff found him, or some Indian who'd do, an' brought 'um back t' town. They made such a big hullabaloo in the local papers that by the time his trial come up, the town is overflowing with reporters from all over hell 'n gone.

"Well," Shorty continued, "Our ol' Injun sets there on the courthouse steps as usual, smokin' his cigarettes and saying nothing. Us cowboys is layin' round in the shade killin' time, punchin' the spots off each other in the local bars, lookin' fer excuses not t' go back t' camp until the trial's over, and speculatin' on how long it'll be before she looks like she'd backed up to a free-air hose.

"Amongst the reporters is some 'she stuff,' a little filly from the Coast and she's stoppin' anybody she can corral askin' what they know about the case. She lassos one of us and we tells her, 'Ma'am, see that Injun over there? He is the *only* fella in town knows *everything* what goes on — you go ask him.' So, she trots over like a billygoat on a string with her little pad and pencil perched, starts talkin' to the Injun. We follers — makin' our usual bets. She tells the ol' boy she wants a real sincere story with a lot of human interest — surely he can be very helpful in giving her some of the true background of this young brave.

"Injun jist sets there plumb dumb, puffin' his cigarette, lookin' straight ahead as if he never heared a word she says. Then, jist as she's about to go through the whole barnyard again, he spits through his teeth, grunts a couple times, an' says:

'Unh! Fifty year. Cowboy chaseum squaw. Catchum. Fuckum. All *right*. Now. *One* brave. Chaseum paleface. Catchum. Fuckum. Whassa matta now? Sheeeee-it!' " [130]

"Ladies and Gentlemen . . . the Exodus proudly presents the return engagement of one of its favorite entertainers . . . direct from the Playboy Club in Chicago . . . Miss Katie Lee . . ." House lights dim, the applause drops as the bass picks up the beat, and I'm back in the saddle again.

My old friend "Durdy" Ed McCurdy is on the bill with me — a folksinger who is deeply sincere about researching material, as both his performance and his recordings bear out. One night during the gig he pulls out a song that has not been heard by anyone before — written by Jack Guinn, a by-liner on the Denver Post. That day Ed had been to see him and came away with the poem. That same night he put it to the basic melody of the shady little ditty, *In The Hills of West Virginny,* and before he'd finished singing, had everyone rolling on the floor. Then and there I picked the song for a winner and went to see Jack about adding some choruses and getting it copyrighted as a song. Jack had given away his punch line in the first verse — that's bad theatre, so I altered that verse and with the help of a friend composed the choruses.[131] Otherwise, I sang it after Ed McCurdy's interpretation. *The Ballad of Alfred Packer** or *Waste Not Want Not* is written about a well-known historical event:

> In the Colorado Rockies
> Where the snow is deep and cold,
> And a man a-foot kin starve to death,
> Unless he's brave and bold,
> They sing of Alfred Packer,
> And some of them still rave
> 'Bout the Hinsdale County Democrats
> Who never saw a grave.
>
> Old Packer set out on a trip
> With five of his old friends,
> In the Colorado Rockies,
> In the snow and howlin' winds.
> But the way was long and weary
> And the food got mighty short,
> But Alfred had his dinner
> On the very last resort.
>
> *Chorus:*
> Oh, Alfred Packer, you'll surely go to hell.
> While all the others starved to death,
> You dined a bit too well.
>
> Old Packer, fat and healthy,
> Came down onto the plains;
> He was lonely, he was horny,
> But he had no stomach pains.
> When he told his story
> It made the strong men pale,
> So they grabbed old Alfred Packer
> And they flang him into jail.
>
> They brought old Packer to the court
> And had a speedy trial.
> A gory tale it was he told
> That went into the file.

167

The testimony shook the judge
Who trembled where he sat.
He was horrified — but then, of course,
He was a Democrat.

Chorus:
Oh, Alfred Packer,
Please tell me for my sake,
Did the Hinsdale County Democrats
Give you a tummy ache?

Old Packer didn't kill 'em,
He just et 'em when they died.
So they couldn't call it murder,
Or even fratricide.
But they sent old Al to prison
To settle up his debt
For all the votin' Democrats
That Alfred Packer et.

When the judge pronounced the sentence
He was in a righteous rage;
And what he said can still be read
Upon the yellowed page;
He wished that he could hang old Al
Until completely dead,
So when he banged the gavel,
It was in anger that he said:

Chorus:
"Oh, Alfred Packer,
You should be skinned alive!
There was only seven Democrats —
And you bastard, you et five!"

Two years later found me still searching out the *real* plot of the famed
Alfred Packer story. The search led in a full circle right back to the *Denver
Post* and another by-liner, Red Fenwick. He was preparing a booklet on the
gastronomic event, but did not know that Jack Guinn had written a poem about
it. Nor did Jack know of Red's book, yet they saw each other every day of the
week. Jack died about 1966, never gleaning a cent from this goldhill of a song-
poem. Red did somewhat, but not much, better.

Briefly, the historical facts are these:

The story begins in Provo, Utah, late fall of 1873 (an election year), when
Packer offered to take a group of men into the Colorado Mountains with him
for a grubstake. The men were all strangers to each other with only one common interest — gold. By the time he reached Colorado Territory, there were
twenty-one men with him, none of them from Hinsdale County, and Packer is
thought to have come from Minnesota some years before.

They were beset by early snows and by a scarcity of food, and were jumped by Ute Indians who took them to Chief Ouray's camp on the Uncompagre River. Ouray invited them to spend the winter, but instead they bitched, argued and mumbled about pushing on towards Breckenridge to stake their claims, snow or no snow. Part of the group left (how many is not known) and barely made it to the Los Pinos Indian Agency. Then, on February 9th, Packer departed Ouray's camp with five men: Bell, Humphrey, Miller, Noon and Swan. That was the last seen of them, except Packer, who staggered gaunt and wild-eyed into the Agency sixty-six days later.

He set up camp in James "Larry" Dolan's saloon in Saguache, began spending money like a gambler, and aroused suspicion among the townfolks. He was arrested on suspicion of homicide, questioned by General Adams of the Los Pinos Agency, and ordered to lead a search party to the scene of the banquet, which for some reason he could not find.

Then began Packer's pack of lies.

The more he "confessed" about who killed whom and who ate what, the more confused he became. The only part of the menu that remained unchanged was the first course — Swan — who, he insisted, had died of starvation and the others "cut up a piece of his body and ate that." All was told in Packer's high-pitched nasal whine, making the story even more unsavory. Finally, after the tangled plot failed to unravel, he was locked in the Saguache jail for the summer of 1884, pending trial. Some time in August the bodies (skeletons) of the providers of the gourmet feast were found. All had hatchet wounds in their skulls except one — Miller. His was completely gone. The bodies had not been hidden, no attempt had been made to cover them, and there was no way, really, to tell if they'd been cannibalized.

At word of this bizarre discovery Packer was placed in irons within his cell. That night he disappeared and was not heard of again for nine years!

On a night in March of 1883 at John Brown's roadhouse on La Prele Creek in Wyoming, Jean (Frenchy) Cabazon, a drummer and one of the original twenty-one who knew about Packer's confessions and escape, and who truly hated his guts, heard through the thin partitions of his room a nerve-grating, whining voice which he had never forgotten. Next morning he met the owner of that voice who called himself John Swartze. Frenchy recognized him immediately as Alfred Packer. Packer did not recognize Cabazon, who went for the sheriff. Alfred was arrested and brought back to Denver, where his "confession" again changed. At his trial, April 6, 1883, he stated:

> When I came back to camp after being gone nearly all day, I found the red-headed man (Bell) who acted crazy in the morning, sitting near the fire roasting a piece of meat which he had cut out of the leg of the German butcher (Frank Miller). The latter's body was lying the furthest off from the fire, down the stream. His skull was crushed in with the hatchet. The other three men were lying near the fire. They were cut in the forehead with the hatchet. Some had two, some three cuts. I came within a rod of the fire. When the man saw me, he got up with his hatchet towards me when I shot him sideways through the belly. He fell

on his face, the hatchet fell forward. I grabbed it and hit him in the top of the head. I camped that night at the fire, sat up all night.

[In the morning] I covered the men up and fetched to the camp the piece of meat that was near the fire. I made a new fire near my camp and cooked the piece of meat and ate it. I tried to get away every day but could not, so I lived off the flesh of these men the biggest part of the sixty days I was out.

He confessed taking $70.00 off the men before he finally made it to the Agency. (He admitted taking $133.00 from Humphrey at an earlier questioning). He told the jury he couldn't face going back to his camp with the search party so he led them around it, and he disclosed that someone had slipped him a key made from a penknife which let him escape that August night nine years before — but he wouldn't reveal his accomplice.

There is one detail which has never been explained. Why was he tried and *convicted* of killing Swan when he never once, in all the confessions said that he had?

But whatever the table setting and arrangement of the guests, I believe the laurels go to the after-dinner speaker — Judge Melville B. Gerry — especially since history has ignored his garden of words and preferred those of the Saguache saloon keeper, Larry Dolan. The judge was a regular hothouse of euphuistic speech. His sentencing of Packer is a literary jewel which should be quoted in its entirety; space not permitting, I quote the juiciest morsels:

> A jury of twelve honest citizens of this county have sat in judgment on your case and upon their oaths they find you guilty of wilful and pre-meditated murder. A murder revolting in all its details.
>
> At that time the hand of man had not marred the beauties of nature. The picture was fresh from the hands of the great Artist who created it. You and your companions camped at the base of a grand old mountain, in sight of the place you now stand, on the banks of a stream as pure and beautiful as ever traced the finger of God upon the bosom of the earth. Your every surrounding was calculated to impress your heart and nature with the omnipotence of Deity and the helplessness of your own feeble life. In this goodly favored spot you conceived your murderous designs.
>
> You and your victims had had a weary march, and when the shadows of the mountain fell upon your little party and night drew her sable curtain around you, your unsuspecting victims lay down on the ground and were soon lost in the sleep of the weary; and when thus sweetly unconscious of danger from any quarter, and particularly from you, their trusted companion, you cruelly and brutally slew them all. . . . Close your ears to the blandishments of hope. Listen not to the flattering promises of life, but prepare for the dread certainty of death. Prepare to meet thy God; prepare to meet the spirits of thy murdered victims; prepare to meet thy aged father and mother, of whom you have spoken and who still love you as their dear boy.
>
> Alfred Packer, the judgment of this court is that you be removed hence to the jail of Hinsdale County and there confined until the 19th

day of May, A.D. 1883, and that on said 19th day of May, A.D. 1883, you be taken from thence to a place of execution prepared for this purpose, at some point within the corporate limits of the town of Lake City, in the said county of Hinsdale, and between the hours of 10 a.m. and 3 p.m. of said day, you then and there, by said sheriff, be hung by the neck until you are dead, dead, dead, and may God have mercy on your soul.[132]

Judge Gerry, fighting for composure, could hardly get out the last words. But Larry Dolan, who'd been a witness at the trial, didn't have any trouble getting out his words, or having them stamped forever into the history of the West. Dolan dashed from the courtroom to the nearest bar shouting the now famous sentence that has completely eclipsed the Judge's declamation.

"They're gonna hang Packer. The Judge, he says, 'Stahnd up, y' man-eatin' son-iv-a-bitch; stahnd up.' Thin, pintin' his finger at him so ragin' mad he was, he says, 'They was sivin Dimmycrats in Hinsdale County, and yez ate foive iv em, Goddam ye. I sintins ye t' be hanged be th' neck until yez are dead, dead, dead, as a warnin' ag'in reducin' th' Dimmycrat population of th' state.'"

But Packer was never hanged at all. His attorney appealed on grounds that Colorado was a Territory when Packer had been first arrested, and was now a State. Three years later, in another trial, this time for manslaughter in each of the five deaths, Packer pleaded not guilty, but was sentenced to forty years in the state penitentiary. This time Packer spoke the eulogy, saying he'd had a fair trial, but could he please be sentenced for the killing of one man — Bell — not for all the others whom he did *not* kill? No, the law didn't permit that, said Judge Harrison.

Old Al served seventeen years in jail before Polly Pry of the *Denver Post* stirred up enough sentiment to get him released. Before stepping down from his seat, the Governor signed the document to parole him on the grounds that he'd remain the rest of his life in the state of Colorado. That was January 8, 1901. He moved from Littleton to Sheridan to Deer Creek Canyon before he died in April of 1907.

Coloradans savor this bit of their history, reminding each other in various ways that their outdoor picnic was not as grizzly as the Donner Party's disaster. Five miles from Lake City on what is now called Cannibal Plateau is a historical marker to Alfred Packer erected by the Republican Women of Hinsdale County — so I'm told. In Boulder on the University of Colorado campus is the Alfred Packer Memorial Cafeteria (now Grill) which serves Democrat steaks as a specialty, and there are Alfred Packer Clubs throughout the state which have such mottoes as "Join the Club and Eat a Democrat" or "Since 1873, Serving Our Fellow Man."

And for dessert this news item appeared in the *Englewood Enterprise*, December 2, 1940.

> Just after the turn of the century, on the sunny banks of the Platte . . . children gathered around a white-bearded story-teller who came in from his lonely cabin 'Deer Creek way' and stocked up with groceries. He was Alfred Packer, 'the man eater,' the most famous of Colorado's

criminals . . . Paroled from the penitentiary by Governor Charles S. Thomas, the gentle old man was the 'Pied Piper' to the youngsters who followed him in droves each Saturday afternoon to thrill to his stories and munch his candy beside the old mill that ground their father's wheat.[133]

On a warm Indian Summer afternoon, as Denver lies squirming in its own bile, I remove Thunder's hard-top and drive to Georgetown for the long awaited meeting with James Grafton Rogers.

I am apprehensive.

After all this build-up, do I really want to know any more about Old Dolores than I do right now? She has been *my* town, in *my* way for seven years. Should I hold her under the microscope, expose her flaws, pick at her secrets, or just love her? It's something to consider. Seeing Mr. Rogers is going to bring the town's past closer to me and perhaps beyond that I shouldn't venture. The last phone conversation with Mekeel sticks in my mind . . . "Don't go any farther."

Georgetown is long and skinny of necessity — laid in a glacial trench between towering rocky mountains. Clear Creek sparkles in the gorge, abandoned mills and mines head and foot the town, colorful wounds dot the steep slopes on either side where little beaver men have dug out the innards in search of the glittering ore. Backed against one of these ridges is a white Victorian house surrounded by a picket fence — a stand of clacking cottonwood trees embracing all.

Not exactly a cowboy's house.

A tall, fair-skinned, freckled man with a quick, warm smile looks down from an opened screen door, saying in a soft voice, "Well, well, Katie Lee, at last!" Taking my hand, he ushers me inside.

Another early Fred Harvey house! I could be back at the Gardners in Prescott. The cowboy image glows a bit brighter.

Mr. Rogers has about him a quiet repose, appears distinguished, and I might say even wise. Though in his seventies, there's no trace of absent-mindedness, no glaze over the eyes, no preoccupation with things past. He seems very active in his retirement, even *hip*, as his eyes flash little pin-points of light with each ready smile. He offers a drink, and while he goes to the kitchen to prepare it, I look around. Framed diplomas and awards hang on the walls, gifts and knick-knacks from around the world, war souvenirs, modern paintings, books, books, books, and magazines — *Scientific American, National Geographic, Harper's,* the *New Yorker, Saturday Review* lie about on tables and chairs. Once again my illusion of the range rider shows a tarnish.

When he returns, handing me a tall, cool rum collins, we clink glasses. "Here's to a long and interesting friendship," he says, sitting in a rocker by the lace-curtained window.

"Mr. Rogers," I ask, a bit woefully, "weren't you *ever* a cowboy?"

"No," he laughs, "I never was. I started out in life as a newspaper reporter for the *New York Sun*. Then I studied law and after that came back to Colorado to go into university work. In the spring of 1912 I was invited down to

Santa Fe, by the railroad of the same name, as part of an advertising campaign for Fred Harvey. My invitation stemmed from the fact that I was a lawyer for an irrigated land project near Las Animas at the time. As a little side trip the railroad officials took us to visit the owner of the Ortiz Mine Grant and the relics of this old town of Dolores. We spent the whole day getting there and back. The next day, on board the Santa Fe train to Denver, I composed the song."

"How did she look then — Old Dolores?"

"Oh, pretty much like the song says, I guess. It was more than half way up the mountain, it seems to me, situated in a beautiful little pocket valley over-looking the Galisteo River below."

"It's south*west* of Santa Fe, you know. You said southeast. My friend Bill Mekeel, who's been looking for it from the air, claims he could see nothing, but he finally drove to it from somewhere near Los Cerrillos, or Madrid. He won't tell me what he saw — says he's going to let me discover it for myself."

"I think you should go and look for yourself. From what I know of your adventuring, you wouldn't be satisfied not to, but I'm afraid I don't hold much hope of your seeing it like I did. Fifty years ago it was a lovely, nostalgic place, but now. . . . I don't know."

> Dream back beyond the cramping lanes
>   To glories that have been —
> The camp smoke on the sunset plains,
>   The riders loping in.
>
> The trail's a lane, the trail's a lane.
>   Dead is the branding fire.
> The prairies wild are tame and mild,
>   All close-corralled with wire.
> The sunburnt demigods who ranged
>   And laughed and lived so free
> Have topped the last divide, or changed
>   To men like you and me.[134]

"Seems to me you're quite a romantic yourself, in spite of your work. Do you ever get the feelings I do when you walk through a ghost town? I have the sensation that people who once lived there are still there and that they're peeking out at me through the old boarded-up windows as my heels click down the boardwalks."

He laughs softly. "True romantics are like that. Yes, I often get those feel-ings — they're essential to writers — certain kinds of writers. My plays, *The Fire of Romance, The Third Day* and *The Goldenrod Lode* contained some verse on Western themes, and were what you'd call 'romantic pieces.' It's the sort of writing that comes and goes with the times and there are many books on these literary fads. Milton's *Lycidas* and Shelley's *Adonais* come to mind; they were pastorals, that is, cloistered fakes."

"But don't you think that romanticising an event often turns it from a dull affair into a legend, and in a way, though probably not a truthful way, preserves it; whereas otherwise it would have slipped off into oblivion? You've done that for *Old Dolores* it seems to me, since I'm sure she was a grubby little mining town full of mud and murder, greed and stench, racial hatred and brawling, before she was gutted and left for the cowboys as an idyllic watering hole."

"Yes, I'm sure that's so. That kind of writing, whether verse or prose, is fun. My earnings in life have all been as an executive, but I've truly enjoyed writing the romantic plays, jingles and verse."

I tell him about Gail Gardner, of his very definite opinions about the altered lingo in his songs — of how they've been stolen and branded over — and remind him that the same has happened to his own creations. I wonder how he feels about it.

"It is my experience that anyone who writes something to be performed ought not to try to direct its performance, because a skillful artist will often completely depart from the author's conception and improve on it. I've never been interested in directing, or even following the direction, of plays or songs that I wrote — someone else can do it better."

"All right, it's nice you feel that way; it gives the artist a chance to be creative in his own right, but it's quite another matter to have someone walk away with your creations. *The Santa Fe Trail* was stolen early on, and *The Town of Old Dolores* acquires a new author almost every year. Doesn't that upset you?"

His smile broadens at my concern. "Oh, I think anyone can find out that I wrote them, and many people *know* that I did, especially here in Colorado. I've written over a dozen books, several plays, written scores of articles and verse — most of the verse under the name of Roger West — and many hymns, and I don't think there's any question of proving authorship. I doubt that these people make any money off my little songs, and when I get requests to use them for something they don't appear to be suited for, I simply say no."

"Will you sing *The Santa Fe Trail* for me? Perhaps I can follow on the guitar."

"I'm a very poor singer, Katie, but I can possibly hum the air for you — or better yet, if you've heard it already somewhere else, I'd like to listen to the version you sing. I put it to an adaptation of an old British song called *The Witch* which I never hear any more. The melody that's usually sung to it was written by Dr. J. H. Gower of Denver and appears in Lomax's *Cowboy Songs*, 1948 edition. I much prefer his melody to the one I concocted."

THE SANTA FE TRAIL*

Say, pard have ye sighted a schooner
A-hittin' the Santa Fe Trail?
They made it here Monday or sooner
With a water keg roped on the rail,
With daddy and ma on the mule-seat
And somewhere around on the way
A tow-headed gal on a pony
A-janglin' for old Santa Fe
    Oh — Ah — Oh
A-janglin' for old Santa Fe.

I seen her ride down the arroyos
Way back in the Arkansas sand,
With a smile like an acre of sunflowers,
An' her little brown quirt in her hand
She straddled the pinto so airy
And rode like she carried the mail,
And her eyes near set fire to the prairie
'Long side of the Santa Fe Trail
    Oh — Ah — Oh —
Alongside of the Santa Fe Trail.

Oh, I know a gal down on the border
That I'd ride to El Paso to sight;
I'm acquaint with the high-steppin' order,
And I've sometimes kissed some gals goodnight;
But Lord, they're all ruffles and beadin'
Or afternoon tea by the pail
Compared to the kind of stampedin'
That I get on the Santa Fe Trail
    Oh — Ah — Oh —
That I get on the Santa Fe Trail.

I don't know her name, and the prairie
When it comes to a gal's pretty wide,
Or shorter from hell to hilary
Than it is on this Santa Fe ride,
But I guess I'll make Cedars by sundown
And campin' may be in a swale,
I'll come on a gal and a pinto
Alongside of the Santa Fe Trail
    Oh — Ah — Oh —
Alongside of the Santa Fe Trail.

During this mellow afternoon we walk outside in the garden where a little stream trickles peaceful accompaniment to the cottonwood's chatter. I meet Cora Rogers, quiet pixie of a lady, gentle and quick and witty, a perfect match for Jim Rogers. I try to sing *Old Dolores* for them and become so overwhelmed with the proximity of both the town and its author that I puddle up and am unable to finish. He is touched by this and says that I have gone far beyond the point most singers go to learn about a song they sing.

I begin to take notice, reluctantly perhaps, that throughout the afternoon's conversation he has referred many times to various government projects in which he's been involved, and has added to his sentences an off-hand "as you know." Well, I *don't* know, and I have not wanted to appear stupid. I suppose I haven't tried to discover the things about James Grafton Rogers that I usually try to discover about the subjects of my research, but when he tells me that his first job in politics was Assistant Attorney General of Colorado, I stare at him with a kind of disbelief and shake my head.

"I can see how an educated, literary man can write a nostalgic little song like *Old Dolores* or *The Santa Fe Trail*, but how does a man like that ever fall into politics?"

"Well, a lawyer's life is so tied up with politics that the division is slight, and my government post. . . ."

"That's right, you're a lawyer. I keep wanting to forget that somehow in view of my not-quite-shattered image. . . ."

The little pin-points of light dance in his eyes. "Not shattered, even yet, Miss Katie?"

"No," I insist. "You're not bowlegged like Gail Gardner, but there are other things about you, and this house, that transplant warm reminders of the early West."

Again he smiles in that luminous way I've come to know so well. Then, almost as an apology he says, to the tinkle and crash of my last cowboy illusion falling,

"I was Assistant Secretary of State under Hoover's Administration."

In 1961 I left the Eastern USA forever.

I moved to Aspen, Colorado, and made many trips to and from Denver during the eight years I lived there. Each time I came over the pass, I stopped to see Jim and Cora. If it was winter, a hot rum toddy was brewed in the grand old kitchen; if summer, a collins or iced tea. We would have dinner there or go to town and eat at the Black Cat. Once or twice I was able to coax him into singing *Old Dolores* with me, and often we would talk of literature and my most unfavorite subject, politics. I have never known a wiser man, or one who could explain more clearly the inner workings of government. My favorite subject was to talk of *Old Dolores*, or his most recent project, which was writing a book on Colorado Mountain Natural History.

To my utter horror one day, over Aspen Radio, I heard a male voice singing the unmistakeable strains of *my* song!

I dashed down to the station and demanded the record they had played. It was Randy Boone. Who the hell is Randy Boone? I didn't know or care, but for once, I was able to stir Jim Rogers into some action. He had Ranger write to the record company informing them that Mr. Boone was certainly not the author of the song *Old Dolores*, and waving the threatening "sue" flag of the law — for whatever good that might have done.

One winter night as we sat by the old wood stove in his kitchen drinking our rums, Jim said in his always gentle unruffled voice, "We won't be here this time next winter."

I nearly dropped my cup! Why wouldn't they be here next winter?

"The new Interstate highway is coming through the middle of the house and Cora and I will be moving to Denver in the spring."

The statement fell like a dead rat in my drink. Nothing but *nothing* stays the same. I should be old enough to accept this sort of thing by now, the way Jim does. "Cora's health is not too good," he added. "I believe it will be better for us in the city."

By 1968 I realized that Aspen was hell-bent — a jangly-spirited, juiced-up, joy-junketed resort. Tall buildings rose to cut off my view of Ajax and the Highlands; the view is why I came — that and the camaraderie of skiing. But it was no longer "our mountain" in any season. Suddenly skiing was *the* thing to do and Aspen was *the* place for the world to do it.

Bye.

And Jim Rogers's letters followed me south to Arizona, keeping me abreast of his doings in Denver.

Lovely Cora died.

Jim moved into the University Club of Denver.

His handwriting became more shaky with each communication, and after I'd finished the pilot for *The Last Wagon* series, I drove from Arizona to Denver with the Bolex and tape recorder to get Jim telling of *Old Dolores* on film before it was too late.

He looked a bit tired, but otherwise was the chipper, soft-smiling Jim. The conversation and communication were there, the rum was there, the astute intellect; he spent the whole day with me, even sang *Old Dolores* again, and dining in the big plush dining room that evening, told me exactly what would happen in the high seats of government and to the attitudes of the American people for the next fifteen years. To the letter he has been correct. I showed him *The Last Wagon* pilot and he glowed with pleasure for it, and for me, telling me he was pleased that I should want to do an entire half-hour film on his little insignificant song!

Two weeks later, on April 23, 1971, Jim Rogers signed in on the "no breakfast forever" list.

> Men in the rough — on the trails all new-broken —
>   Those are the friends we remember with tears;
> Few are the words that such comrades have spoken —
>   Deeds are their tributes that last through the
>   years.[135]

Chapter 15

HE FIRST WEEK in October closed my engagement at the Exodus in Denver.

With snow showing on the highest ranges of the Rockies, the white Thunderbird raced for the lowest passes, heading west by south. Before I could turn my undivided attention to the finding of Old Dolores and the putting to rest of a seven-year curiosity itch, I had to pick up a quick concert in Albuquerque. From the stage that night I experienced some rather odd sensations. Would it be the last time I saw the piñon smoke rising from the village and heard the clinking chips, the greaser girls laughing, saw the streets bright with candlelight and the crick tumbling down? And if tomorrow changed it all, how then would I sing of Old Dolores?

October is new and on this morning smells and looks new. I leave Albuquerque for the southern end of the Ortiz mountains and State Route 14, which cuts between the Ortiz and Sandia range over broad mesas peppered with piñon that twist sensuously and press low to the warm earth. It passes around and between hills and rock buttresses, following little streams where the sweet smell of autumn lies like perfume in the sheltered creases. White plumes crest the Sandias and above them streaks of soft opaque blue are layered between more trailing plumes. It looks fake, this sky, hanging so innocently over man's folly. A new road flattens firmly down over the snake wiggle of an old one that went around each foothill and followed the contours of the earth — the new one gives off a gassy smell of asphalt. Names on the land clearly indicate who was here before: Zambora, Tijeras, La Madera, Sedillo, Cedro. Nice Cortezy sounds. I pass Golden, all the while staring intently at each trail breaking through the cedars on my right.

A windmill back from the road, standing very still.

Soft warm wind sweeps up from the valley, alternating with the brittle cool resistance of fall winds off the peaks nearby. Is Dolores up there, overtaken by the brush? Reclaimed?

I swing Thunder off the road, dismantle the art form which holds the gate closed and walk up foothills strewn with boulders. Hard summer rains have creased the soil like the face of a weathered old hag. I pick some piñon gum from a tree and crunch it, letting the undammed juices run over my chin, as slowly the sawdust forms into a soft pungent ball that tastes like the whole wild, fresh outdoors. Keeping my eyes to the ground, I look for — who knows? — something from time past — a cart wheel, a burro shoe, a gold pan — some symbol of what must have been there.

Before I'd left Denver, of course I saw Jim and Cora Rogers again and he had given me a book — *The Wind Leaves No Shadow* — which vividly tells of Dolores's early mining days. Vividly and perhaps a bit romantically. A tale of Doña Tules Bárcelo, a mistress of the notorious Manuel Armijo, last Mexican governor of New Spain's northern territory, in Santa Fe. What the author said about the finding of gold, the strike, the upper mine, rang true to the research I had done — at least she knew as much about its history as I — and she painted a picture typical of such a town, deep in mud and liquor and fighting people, gambling, Mexican intrigue and manipulation of the written laws, which surprised no one, since Mexico City was almost two thousand miles south and could care less. Dolores's posture grew . . .

> Last year Dolores Springs had been a quiet water hole in the remote Ortiz mountains. This year the discovery of gold brought swarms of people to the springs to live in warrens on the side of the red gulch. A road twisted through the bottom and crossed level ground where oxcarts unloaded before the long adobe store, dance hall, and cantina. [Okay, Willie, so it *wasn't* called Ramon's!] Above the springs Tules could see the flat roofs of the Ortiz hacienda and the chapel of Nuestra Senora de Dolores. [Humf! even a church, Mr. Mekeel — those things were pretty solid built. I suppose there's nothing left of it either!] . . . Ten leagues south of Santa Fe a Spanish King had given the Ortiz family land that included mountains, valleys, and an ever-flowing spring. At that time a mountain range, more or less, was not important in the wilderness of New Mexico, but a dependable source of water was of the utmost importance for grazing cattle.[136]

And again my belief was fortified that Mekeel hadn't seen Old Dolores. Not all of Dolores, anyway, probably only the part that had fallen down.

As I walk the crusty hillside, there is a sudden scuttle in the brush and I jump back. I've spooked some cattle who stand pawing and bellowing. They stare at me like the Indians must have stared at Cortez when he came apart from his horse. "Woof!" I stomp, and they rattle their hocks through the juniper, leaving the dusty air full of their acrid smell. Stepping over a bunch of ripe road-apples, I make a few more turns before the thicket coughs up the windmill. It looks very formal on its stiff legs braced high above the curvey trees. Beside it sits a water tank where two steers drink, slobbering green from their cuds.

Maybe this is the little well in Hell.

No, that was a pond, not a windmill-type thing. I climb the ladder to have a look at *the country down below* through the stopped-down blades, blades that whine and bicker with a wind they have to sift, instead of rolling and romping with. Off to the northeast, perhaps fifty miles, lies the haze of Santa Fe, and to the left, the Sandia mountains. Winding down the valley comes the Rio Grande, gathering in the Galisteo. No red earth to make those *red mud walls,* no water for the *water falls,* not even a clearing where a town might have been, no mine tailings, only dry arroyos and stream beds wandering and re-tracking, searching for the water they've dropped somewhere along the way.

No Dolores.

I climb down, moo at the steers who follow me back to the fence, jackknife into Thunder and drive away, leaving the old crabs to themselves.

Four or five miles down the road I slow up to inspect a wagon wheel rut clawing into an arroyo's side, but it's too close to the mountain to go anywhere, so I pass on to some old and sad-looking relics of an abandoned mine. Narrow-gauge tracks tilt and buckle where their roadbed has slithered away and dropped the rusty ore buckets into a tangle of bobwire over the side. A decrepit building of purple and red rusted tin lurches from its moorings, leans against a sagging cable tower, the ground about a tangle of pipes, cables, fly-wheels, sprockets and gears. Was this the mine? The twenty-stamp mill built by Edison? No. The earth is black and it was coal they mined here.

What in hell have they done with my town?

Sunlight leaves the arroyo as clouds play roundup over the Ortiz peaks. From the coal mine the road plunges between foothills to where Madrid squeezes out like a stepped-on banana. Through an avenue of ill-kept cotton-woods which roof a housing project for ghosts — shag-eared little cracker-boxes with front and back doors agape, each staring hollow-eyed into a deserted yard collared by rickety pickets — I go swirling yellow leaves in my wake.

> The echoes roused by hoof-strokes of my steed
> > Strike on the heart;
> How many tragedies the eye may read
> > In this dead mart;
> From cabins, windowless, faint voices plead
> > And specters start.[137]

At the banana's fat end I come upon boarded windows and a rusty hand-pump gasoline tank. One weary windowpane spells GROCERY STORE in an arch of peeling gold letters. The door is open. I walk the long, worn oiled floor past foggy showcases filled with all sorts of dusty, once essential things. The ancient owner I find in the dim bowels of the store reading a newspaper. I ask if he's ever heard of Old Dolores.

"Yeah, it's around here somewhere."

"Where, please, which direction?"

He thumbs through the mountain behind him. "Over thattaway, back of *Mad*rid."

"Where's *Mad*rid?" I ask, not even recognizing the real word.

"This *here's Mad*rid," he scowls.

"Oh, yes, sure. Mad*rid*. Do you know how to get to Old Dolores?"

"Not zackly, but t'ain't far. I heared they was mebe gonna open the mines agin."

"Is it just a mining town, or *was* it?"

"Yup."

"Not a watering stop for cattle drovers back in the seventies?"

"Hell, lady, I dunno, I ain't been here *that* long. [Christ, I could be in Vermont!] Why'nt ya go down to Cerrillos n' ask them people; they been here since the ground was first put in."

Three more miles and I see the adobe houses of Cerrillos glowing pink in the afternoon light. There are splashes of red earth along the river bank, some mesas, and yellowing tamarisk swishing in the breeze, making a bold foreground for the sleepy village. The new road has passed it by, letting it suckle by the creek of Galisteo, growing a little corn, squash, beans and a few peppers. The old bridge, washed out now, lies crumpled against the bank, its abutments standing starkly mid-stream supporting the blue cloud-spattered sky. Here time passes gently, the Mexican way. An old gravel road into the village is lined with giant cottonwoods; their trunks creak and their leaves make a soft snare-drum sound. I stop in front of the store where dogs lie in a patch of damp earth beneath a dripping faucet. Three old men hold up the front of an ancient wooden building as they draw in the dirt talking. An old Señor looks up.

"*¿Hóla, mi amigo, vivio aqui mucho tiempo?*" I ask.

"*Si, mucho tiempo, y mi familia tambien.*"

"Do you know where is the — *¿Donde está el pueblo, muy viejo, de Dolores?*"

"*Ah, Dolores. Si conosco* — *pues, mira usted alla, otro lado del rio, y de la carretera. . . .*"

"*Habla me en Ingles, por favor, Señor,* or I won't understand all you say — my Spanish is not that good."

"*Ah, no, es muy bien, Señorita, muy bien. Pues* — see back across thee reeber? — is a leetle dirt road beside thee peenk house. Joo follow dees road for seven kilometros. . . ."

"Kilometros or miles, Señor?"

"Seven mile, *mas ó menos.* Dolores Ranch now own by a new Meester, I theenk. He only joos buy."

Then the town *was* where the topo map now indicates Dolores Spring Ranch, I conclude, but to make sure I ask, "Are you certain this is where the town was, Señor?"

"*Si, seguro* — *wass* there, but all fall down now."

"Is anyone living there? Any houses left?"

"*Creo que si; El Rancho* . . . an' thee mine steel there . . . mebe one, mebe two house more."

"Any ghosts?" I smile.

"Gho — ah! *Alma* . . . *espiritu? No se, Señorita,* I don't know. You like ghosts?"

"I want them there."

We shake hands, say *gracias, de nada* and *que vaya al bien.* Back across the river and turn up the dirt road. Thunder dips down, up and out of several high-banked arroyos, crossing quickly even though they're bone dry. There are dark clouds now over the Ortiz peaks and I don't care to get trapped in a flash flood. On high ground I flank more foothills, creep up the skirt of one of those

alluvial fans beside a fence and before long rattle over a couple cattle guards.
"Whoa, hoss. A sign."

DOLORES SPRING RANCH
Private Property
POSITIVELY NO TRESPASSING

In we go.

Climbing now between and around hills, I look back to see how the view matches the song. It's there — *the country down below where the little piñons grow, the whole wide world before us,* the Galisteo twisting below, *half a day to water.* Only the crick is missing. Ahead is a cuddled spot between two high ridges where Dolores must be nestled in her mountain throne — the back of soft, light green willow and cottonwood, the ridges of dark piñon, juniper and scrub oak. Maybe her ghosts will greet me when I cut through the crick.

It is dry.

Slowly, out of the rocky arroyo around the base of the mountain, I turn. And there in a small pocket valley on near level ground, is *The Town of Old Dolores.*

Crumbling walls of an old village? Tattered graveyard with wobbly crosses? An old wagonbed lying overgrown with weeds? A gentle waterfall?

No. None of these things. What I see hurts the heart and hurts the mind and touches a vein of angry blood that gushes hotly to the surface. This spot of earth, bought and paid for by someone else, doesn't belong to me. Maybe that someone didn't know about it, what it was long ago. Maybe he came too late to do anything about it, or he may even know and not care. But *I* care. I'm shocked and feel betrayed that the ghosts of Old Dolores don't ramble here any more — they've long since moved away, their homes leveled, crumbled back to dirt and clay by the squirming, blunt-nosed rutter, the bulldozer. Now, only the mountain that cradled Old Dolores stands. A dusty breeze irritably wheezes and nothing is left of the *streets bright with candlelight, the red mud walls, the crick tumbling down.*

What is she now?

A large new corral, sleek horses inside, an adobe ranch house stuccoed and painted white, a *Cadillac* standing by, a bone-yard of old car and truck carcasses strewn over an acre of ground. I go to the fly-laden screen door and knock. A young girl with a child slung from her hip comes to the door and gives me a questioning stare.

"I came to find an old ghost town, a mining town, a cattle stop, Old Dolores," I explain. "Is . . . is this where it . . . was?"

"I believe so, but it's all gone except this building — once the assay office for the mine, they tell me. One of the former owners had all the other buildings . . ."

"Bulldozed to the ground — yes, I see. What about the town square, the spring, the creek? Could you point out where they were?"

"I don't know, that was a long time ago and we're relatively new here. There's *no* creek, and the spring's not very lively — we only use it to water the horses."

182

I ask her if I may look around, to which she assents, and I leave her, picking my way around the devastation, over bobwire fences . . .

> And every man in sight
> Let his cattle drift at night
> Just to mosey to the town of Old Dolores.

. . . threading a path through the jungle of rusting-away fenders, springs, axles, bell-housings, looking for a remnant of her past — a grave? . . . maybe Ramon's. ("You know goddam well there couldn't be any cantina named Ramon's — he *invented* Ramon!")

What's this? An old sawmill, huddling close by the south arm of the mountain; around it, deep, soft piles of piñon chips that give off a sharp, live smell . . .

> And the scented smoke that came
> From the piñon wood aflame
> Smelt like incense to Our Lady of Mañana.

. . . making me think this ghost is lingering. The *smell* of Old Dolores has not entirely vanished. Head down, I look for memorabilia — an old bit from a Spanish bridle, a Mexican rowel. ("Now, listen, Tinkerbell, you've got to quit playing games with yourself.") There's been a whole other civilization on top of this spot since then. I kick up a long hand-forged nail with a T-shaped head — from the mining days when Dolores first felt the strike?

> But the 'dobe walls are gone
> And the goat bells in the dawn
> Ain't a-jingling in the streets of Old Dolores.

Feeling like a hillbilly version of Camille, I wander sadly through the junk to come suddenly upon an old well with side and hoist-braces and a weather-beaten frame. The bucket is long gone, but looking down I can see the bottom, black and still. Did it once stand in the Plaza? A dry wash erodes past it now.

Dark clouds stride for the valley below letting the sun cast its last reddish rays on Dolores. Touched by this wand, a tiny adobe leaps from the shadowy, dejected heap of litter and etches itself against the flame. Surely *this* is from her torn, ravaged scrapbook. The roof has caved in, the lintels have collapsed, vigas poke in every direction, cactus grows rakishly out the top and a fallen match-stick rail fence half encloses it. I stare in wonder. Just as suddenly the sun is covered again and the adobe fades back into nowhere.

A puff of cold air makes my skin tingle. One of Dolores's ghosts still here perhaps . . .

> And the strings of peppers hung
> On the house-fronts in the sun,
> Blazin' red as some young puncher's new bandana.

Following the old creek bed down the mountain a way, I come upon many diggings and several foundations of well-laid rock cemented together by hard clay and pieces of straw. One or two of these rough structures stand with a yet unbuckled lintel. I failed to see them on the way in because they line the creek bed and are below the level of the road. Slowly the town begins to take shape in my head. Whatever there had been of the plaza, the square, the assay office, the mine, the town was obviously concentrated on the flat ground where the ranch house now stands, but the other houses, those of the gold seekers and mine workers, had been strung out along the creek where they gave easy access to placering and panning gold. This is what Hamilton Rogers meant when he mentioned that above the townsite is a steep canyon, which I could see from the corral, with remnants of several stone structures, probably like these here below. The town took on much larger proportions and I wondered why I was beginning to feel this *gold town* estranged and removed from the sleepy little Mexican *watering hole* known to the cowboys of the seventies.

Because the two eras were separated by some forty years!

When the cowboys came all this hubbub had died down and left the Ortiz grant much like it had been before the nuggets and the large vein were discovered, 1828–1833. But now the main component that linked Dolores's *old* past with her *late* past, and was responsible for her attracting my attention in the present, seemed to be missing.

> . . . a view over this country where anybody can own a whole mountain but nobody can afford a water supply. J. G. Rogers

> . . . but a dependable source of water was of the utmost importance for raising cattle. Ruth Laughlin

> *There us't to stand a town,*
> *Where a crick come tumbling down,*
> *From a mesa where she surely hadn't ought'a.*
>
> *And if there's any little well*
> *Down inside the Gates of Hell*
> *Why I know the boys have named it, Old Dolores.*

Beside a scummy little pond beneath yellowing willows I stand crying.

> *The greaser girls that fool*
> *On the Plaza — in the cool*
> *There was one, I us't to meet her by a willer,*

How could this *ever* have been the Plaza, or the place where the crick come tumbling down? There's not even a whisper of water, just a few frog bubbles bulging on the surface. Springs dry up, retreat back into the womb, are covered over, diverted, blasted, tapped, and sometimes, sometimes, with care, come to life again.

But not this one.

Old Dolores, for all the song has to say for her, is dead. Gone and crumbled under. Forgotten by all save a few romantic fools like me who sing a memory to her glorious past. She has hustled off her ghosts to some other camp before the last calamity, before the living finally desert her and before the weary, torpid beating of her pulse finally stops.

Old Dolores's springs are drying up.

I stumble, misty-eyed, back to the car and drive on to Santa Fe.

> *But the friendly lights are dark,*
> *And the coyote's lonesome bark*
> *Is the only music now in Old Dolores.*

I have just seated myself in a big easy chair by the fire in the Indian house of my friends Dr. Stanley Leland and his wife Isobella. It is later that same night and Mekeel is there.

"Give her a drink, Stanley," says Bill watching me closely. "She's just come from Old Dolores."

"Oh, you found it, did you?" Isobella stands in the kitchen doorway drying glasses. "How was it — like you thought it would be?"

"Uh-huh, just like I thought." I hear Stanley dropping ice into glasses. Bill comes over by the fire and gives me a fishy look. "The red mud walls are there, kinda broken and crumbled, but you can see where the square was, and the willows by the stream, some graves, and the crick comes tumblin' down. I could almost hear the goat bells and see the cowboys' horses standing with their reins a-draggin'." Mekeel looks at me like I'd just wet the floor and drops an aside from the corner of his mouth.

"Are you out of your middle-class mind? I was there at the same place exactly; there's only one way in, and not a damn thing is left but the ranch house!"

Stanley hands me a tall rum and smiling, says, "So it really looks like that. Wonderful, Katie. I'm glad for you, and for me, glad it didn't spoil our illusions."

Mekeel looks hard at me, raises his eyebrows, glances at Isobella and Stanley, then back at me. "Uh . . . ah . . . where *is* it, exactly?"

I stare into my frosty drink and beyond into the fire, smile and flip my hand nonchalantly over toward the mountains. "Oh, over there in the Ortiz range like Jim Rogers said. Pretty much overgrown with cedars now, and very hard to find. I very nearly got lost."

> Gone are the silent riders,
> And only the sun beats down
> On the trampled, bare arena
> And the chute gates weathered brown:
> They've ridden back to the Days That Were;
> But before a play is made —
> Three cheers for the unseen men who passed
> In the old cow men's parade.[138]

185

Epilogue

I HAVE JUST SEATED MYSELF in a big easy chair by the fire in the Indian house of my friends Dr. Stanley Leland and his wife Isobella. It is later that same night and Mekeel is here.

"Give her a drink, Stanley," says Bill watching me closely. "She's just come from Old Dolores."

"Oh, you found it, did you?" Isobella stands in the kitchen doorway drying glasses. "How was it — like you thought it would be?"

"Uh-huh, just like I thought." I hear Stanley dropping ice into glasses. Bill comes over by the fire and gives me a fishy look. "The red mud walls are there, kinda broken and crumbled, but you can see where the square was, and the willows by the stream, some graves, and the crick comes tumblin' down. I could almost hear the goat bells and see the cowboys' horses standing with their reins a-draggin'." Mekeel looks at me like I'd just wet the floor and drops an aside from the corner of his mouth.

"Are you out of your middle-class mind? I was there at the same place exactly; there's only one way in, and not a damn thing is left but the ranch house!"

Stanley hands me a tall rum and smiling, says, "So it really looks like that. Wonderful, Katie. I'm glad for you, and for me, glad it didn't spoil our illusions."

Mekeel looks hard at me, raises his eyebrows, glances at Isobella and Stanley, then back at me. "Uh . . . ah . . . where *is* it, exactly?"

I stare into my frosty drink and beyond into the fire, smile and flip my hand nonchalantly over toward the mountains. "Oh, over there in the Ortiz range like Jim Rogers said. Pretty much overgrown with cedars now, and very hard to find. I very nearly got lost."

> Gone are the silent riders,
>   And only the sun beats down
> On the trampled, bare arena
>   And the chute gates weathered brown:
> They've ridden back to the Days That Were;
>   But before a play is made —
> Three cheers for the unseen men who passed
>   In the old cow men's parade.[138]

186

A Compendium of Songs

(Arranged Alphabetically)

Note: There is no way a collector can include (or even find) all publications, song folios and recordings that contain a particular song, nor is it necessary. The listings here are partial — in some cases more complete than others. I believe there is enough information for student and layman alike. I have tried to cover enough ground so that whatever digging is left will be fairly easy. In order to keep each song score intact on one page, they sometimes precede or fall in the middle of an entry. When I know there is music with the lyric, none, or some, I have made the following notation. . . . If I don't know, it has been omitted.

w/m: With Music   n/m: No Music   s/m: Some Music

About period classification: A date at times being impossible to determine, I have arranged the songs according to the four phases of cowboy history mentioned on pages 8–12, 158–162. There will be some bleed-over from period two which ran through to number five.

(1) First Period: Songs from other cultures, popular melodies of the day, minstrel tunes, the beginnings of his own inventions.

(2) Second Period: Those that other people wrote about him; his own derring-do creations that lived up to that image.

(3) Third Period: The real cowboys and the real cowboy writers, writing with know-how about themselves.

(4) Fourth Period: Commercializing the cowboy for radio audiences. Tinpan Alley at work on his songs.

(5) Fifth Period: Newer songs written in the idiom of events past and present.

ADIOS* (3)
pp. 29–30

S. Omar Barker. First heard sung in Taos, N.M., 1959, by Jenny Wells Vincent, who wrote the melody. At the time she owned the Music Center Record

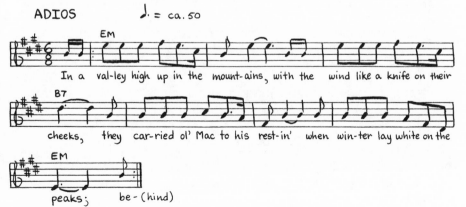

ADIOS   ♩. = ca. 50

EM
In a val-ley high up in the mount-ains, with the wind like a knife on their

B7
cheeks, they car-ried ol' Mac to his rest-in' when win-ter lay white on the

EM
peaks; be-(hind)

---

*These songs included in a two-volume album, *Ten Thousand Goddam Cattle*, Katydid Records, KD-10076

Store and was collecting and singing southwestern songs. Barker wrote the poem after an actual happening — the funeral of McMullen. It was copyrighted as a song by agreement between them (Class E:Eu 920597) in 1966.

Publications:
Barker. *Songs of the Saddlemen.* n/m

Recordings:
Katie Lee. *Ten Thousand Goddam Cattle.* KD-10076

ARIZONA KILLER, THE (4) pp. 100–101

Katie Lee. A gen-u-wine rewrite, with very little of the original showing, save structure of the ballad and gist of the story. Place names all changed from the South to the West. Randolph collected it as *The Tennessee Killer* in MS. from Dr. George E. Hastings, Fayetteville, Ark., Jan. 6, 1942, "who had it from a man named Steel, who credits it to a Negro beggar in Conway, Ark." In 1955 I taped my version for Harry Belafonte. To my knowledge he never used it. No music accompanied the original lyric.

Publications:
Randolph, Vance. *Ozark Folk Songs* Vol. 2. n/m

THE ARIZONA KILLER

BAD BRAHMA BULL
See *Flyin' U Twister*.

BALLAD OF ALFRED PACKER, THE* (5)   pp. 167–68

Jack Guinn. Additions and alterations: Katie Lee, Natalie Gignoux, Ed McCurdy. Letter from Jack to me says a piano playing friend of his, Max Morath supplied music once for the Ballad, but he's never heard it. My version was copyrighted in 1964 in both our names. Alterations were really miniscule. Jack's first verse read:

> They sing of Alfred Packer,
> And they never will forget
> The Hinsdale County Democrats —
> The fellows that he et.

His one and only chorus was the last one printed in the text and used only at the end of the song. October, 1974 (preceeding record release below) I taped it for Studs Terkel's WFMT show in Chicago.

Recordings:
Katie Lee. *Ten Thousand Goddam Cattle*. KD-10076

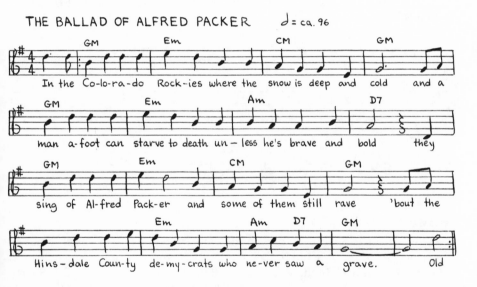

THE BALLAD OF ALFRED PACKER   ♩ = ca. 96

In the Co-lo-ra-do Rock-ies where the snow is deep and cold and a man a-foot can starve to death un-less he's brave and bold they sing of Al-fred Pack-er and some of them still rave 'bout the Hins-dale Coun-ty de-my-crats who ne-ver saw a grave. Old

BALLAD OF BLACK BART, THE Po8
See *Corrido de Bartolo Negro, El*.

BLOOD ON THE SADDLE (4)   pp. 156–57

Romaine Lowdermilk. A letter from John I. White to KL: "In *Folk Songs of Canada* there is a note with 'Blood' to confuse everybody: 'Seldom have so few words painted such a gory picture with so much relish.' Just when or where this bloody ballad originated has never been definitely settled. Tex Ritter said it was written by two Arizona cowboys to describe a rodeo accident, and it was popularized by him and Tony Kraber in recent years. However, it is not a modern song, for Dr. E. A. Corbett remembers a cowboy called Oklahoma Pete singing it on the Cochrane Ranch west of Calgary back in 1905." Well, at least there seems no question that it came from Arizona, and I'll lay my cash that Romy was its composer.

Publications:
Fowke & Johnson. *Folk Songs of Canada*. w/m
Lynn, Frank. *Songs for Singin'*. w/m
Cazden, Norman. *A Book of Nonsense Songs*. w/m
Coleman & Bregman. *Songs of American Folks*. Note: "As told us by Tex Ritter, the tune originated among the cowboys at Wickenburg, Arizona, and the words of the song were written at Florence, Arizona by Everett Cheetham and another cowboy named 'Slim.'" w/m
Gardner & Chickering. *Ballads and Songs of Southern Michigan*. w/m
Lomax, John A. *Cowboy Songs* (1948 ed.). Finds it under the title "Trail End" and credits it to Cheetham on the authority of Ritter. n/m
Ritter, Tex. *Cowboy Songs*. Credits Cheetham. w/m
Fife. *Cowboy and Western Songs*. They mention a Kathy Dagel who sang it in a pensive, tragic mood, and say: "the melody and basic imagery are traceable to 'Halbert the Grim,' a romantic ballad of the early 1800s." They do not mention Romy's name. w/m

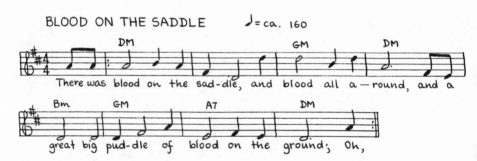

BLOOD ON THE SADDLE ♩= ca. 160

There was blood on the sad-dle, and blood all a-round, and a great big pud-dle of blood on the ground; Oh,

BOOMER JOHNSON * (3)   pp. 93–95

Henry Herbert Knibbs. Range cooks were famous for their rotten tempers mostly because they were old broken-up and broken-down cowboys who would rather have been back in the saddle than on the business end of a skillet. Shorty Mac swore he *knew* Boomer Johnson, but I doubt that. He would say this poem with gestures, and once while demonstrating the doughnut shooting scene with cowpies, blew open a ripe one and fell backward into the fire trying to dodge flack. The melody is mine; written sometime in the early fifties. I've never seen it anywhere else as a song, nor heard any recordings of it.

Publications:
Knibbs. *Songs of the Lost Frontier*. n/m

Recordings:
Katie Lee. *Ten Thousand Goddam Cattle*. KD-10076

BOOMER JOHNSON ♩=ca.96

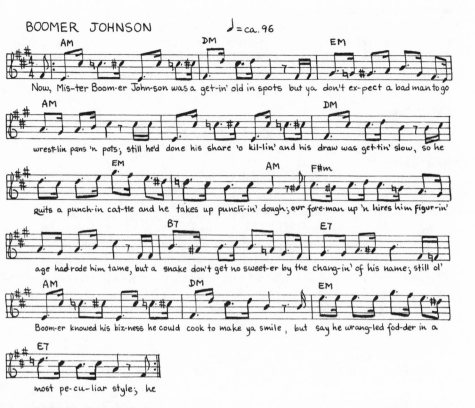

Now, Mis-ter Boom-er John-son was a get-in' old in spots but ya don't ex-pect a bad man to go wrest-lin pans 'n pots; still he'd done his share 'o kil-lin' and his draw was get-tin' slow, so he quits a punch-in' cat-tle and he takes up punch-in' dough; our fore-man up 'n hires him figur-in' age had rode him tame, but a snake don't get no sweet-er by the chang-in' of his name; still ol' Boom-er knowed his biz-ness he could cook to make ya smile, but say he wrang-led fod-der in a most pe-cu-liar style; he

A BORDER AFFAIR

See *Spanish Is the Lovin' Tongue*.

BOSKY STEER, THE (3)   pp. 92–93

Henry Herbert Knibbs. For all its singing years among the cowboys, this song has traveled as "Jake and Roany" and whenever written out in musical form, spelled Roney. The tune is unique; not a variant of any well-known melody. It probably wasn't put to music until after the mid-thirties, but I have

THE BOSKY STEER   ♩=ca. 144

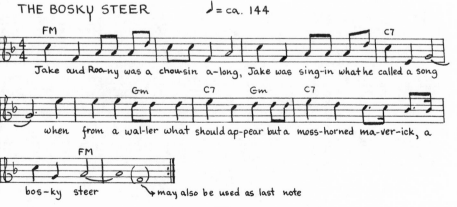

Jake and Roa-ny was a chou-sin a-long, Jake was sing-in what he called a song when from a wal-ler what should ap-pear but a moss-horned ma-ver-ick, a bos-ky steer   ↳may also be used as last note

191

never found anyone who could tell me where the tune came from. *Bosque,* which Knibbs probably spelled wrong on purpose, means woodsy, timbered, brushy — the Arizona cowboys say "bald-faced steer." A story by Russell in his *Trails Plowed Under,* "Safety First — But Where Is it" tells this exact tale; an elk replacing the steer. We have only the publication dates to help us guess whether chicken or egg came first — Russell, 1927; Knibbs, 1930.

Publications:
Knibbs. *Songs of the Lost Frontier.* Used by permission. n/m
Ohrlin. *The Hell Bound Train.* No credit. Listed, *Jake and Roney.* w/m

Recordings:
Sam Agins. *Singin' Sam's Saddlebag of Songs.* Haywire ARA 6419.

CORRIDO DE BARTOLO NEGRO, EL* (5)   p. 39

Barbara James, David Zeitlin, Katie Lee. A note from David: "Barbara wrote the thing, I'd guess 1952 . . . she was about fifteen at the time. The words will take a lot of fixing, Katie, but you must keep in mind they were written by a teenage girl who was brought up on a diet of Corridos, Rancheros *and* too much Edward Lear. Fix 'em up and have fun with 'em — they are copyright in my name though, so let me know what the changes are." The first verse is as she wrote it. Her other originals were:

He took the box in the woods
And left it where he could throw it,
He left the note, not the goods
And signed it Black Bart the Po8.
He robbed more than 80 stages
Until a boy, passing by,
Brought to his sin its wages,
And shot Bart in the thigh.
He then was caught, jailed beside,
But came out soon, and Wells Fargo
Paid him pension till he died,
So he would not rob their cargo.

Another version, entirely different, came out with the early thirties song folio rash. The words to this version are claimed by Milton Bethwyn, the music by our ubiquitous friend Sterling Sherwin, in the Sam Fox publication of *Bad Man Songs of the Wild and Woolly West*. I know of one recording other than mine, which may be the above version — I've not heard it — titled simply *Black Bart*.

Recordings:
Dickson Hall. *Outlaws of the Old West*. MGM 3263.
Katie Lee. *Ten Thousand Goddam Cattle*. KD-10076.

COWBOY'S PRAYER, A* (3)   pp. 75–76
Charles Badger Clark. Of the hundreds of poems written about cowboys praying to the stars, this is probably the best. I've heard any number of cowboys recite it, but have never heard one sing it. The language is true to his free-roving spirit and gives insight to the code he lived by — the things he expected of himself. According to Austin and Alta Fife, Clark wrote it while living on a ranch near Tombstone, Arizona, and it was first published in *The Pacific Monthly*, Dec. 1906. John I. White, in *Git Along, Little Dogies*, notes that Tex Ritter used to recite the poem against the music of *The Cowboy's Dream*, and that Clark had it stolen from him and put on postcards as "Anonymous" so many times that he made a collection of more than sixty thievings from his original.

Publications:
Clark. *Sun and Saddle Leather*. n/m
Fife. *Heaven on Horseback*. w/m
———. *Cowboy and Western Songs*. n/m
Thorp. *Songs of the Cowboys*. 1921 ed. n/m
White. *Git Along Little Dogies*. n/m
Williams. *Collection of Favorite Songs*. (This melody written in 1937 sounds very un-cowboy and severely churchy.) w/m

Recordings:
Katie Lee. *Ten Thousand Goddam Cattle*. KD-10076

A COWBOY'S PRAYER ♩= ca.112

FM .... B♭M FM

Oh Lord, I've nev-er lived where church-es grow I

C7

loved cre-a-tion bet-ter as it stood .... that day you fin-ished

B♭M .... CM C7

it so long a—go .... and looked u-pon your work and called it

FM .... B♭M FM

good .... I know that oth-ers find you in the light .... that's

B♭M

sift-ed down thru tint-ed win-dow panes .... and yet I seem to

FM .... CM C7

feel you near to night .... in this dim qui-et star-light on the

FM

plains I

COWMAN'S TROUBLES, THE (3)

pp. 135–37

Gail I. Gardner. Roughly the melody is *Whoopie Tie-yie-yo, Get Along Little Dogies,* which he lassoed for it some time in the late twenties. The song stems from the actual experiences of the author when he had a little "greasy sack" outfit south of Prescott, Arizona, during his cowboying days.

THE COWMAN'S TROUBLES ♩. = ca 72

AM

I used to make mon-ey a run-nin' wild cat-tle in them good ol'

EM .... AM

days 'fore the bus'-ness went wrong, when a hot run-nin' iron and a

F#m DM E7 AM

good long ri-a-ta was all that was need-ed to start you a-long; I

194

Publications:
Gardner. *Orejana Bull.* n/m

DEEP WATER, ICE AND SNOW* (5)   pp. 134-35

Ben Perkins. Benny was kind of a talking singer with a wide range of inflection. So the tune, which didn't matter much anyway when he sang it, often got lost or pushed around by his interpretation. *Deep Water* has a lilt that makes you feel you're swinging up into the saddle and taking off. The night that Ben told me about writing this song, he sat shivering out the memory of the ice cakes floating in the river and the slick freezing mud that made the horses stumble and fall. The "vain man" was Old Nick and there was some bitterness in the way he said it. There's been no other publication of the song, and only one taped version exists with Benny singing.

Recordings:
Katie Lee. *Ten Thousand Goddam Cattle.* KD-10076.

DEEP WATER, ICE AND SNOW ♩ = ca. 160

We had deep wa-ter, ice and snow, with a thou-sand cat-tle we had to go to get those cat-tle to the oth-er side, you can bet your life we had to ride thru deep wa-ter, ice and snow, with a thou-sand cat-tle we had to go; the

'DOBE BILL* (2)   pp. 10-11

Sometimes called *The Killer,* at least in one place I know it appears in print. The Arizona cowboys always called it "Dobe Bill." I composed this music about

'DOBE BILL ♩ = ca. 112

'Do-be Bill he came a ri-din' from the can-yon in the glow of a qui-et Sum-mer eve-nin' from the town of An-ge-lo ri-din' ea-sy on the pin-to that he dear-ly loved to strad-dle with a six-gun and som-bre-ro that was wi-der than his sad-dle and he's

NOTE: last half verse repeats from *

195

1950. Cisco Houston heard me sing it and wanted to record it, but I told him only the words were PD (Public Domain) so he made another tune. I heard yet another record of it done "Hollywood Style" in the mid-fifties. The words had been hacked all to pieces and it was an *awful* piece of crap — like it had been written by some dude who operated the rolly-coaster at Santa Monica — and was not Cisco's version.

Publications:
Lomax, John A. *American Ballads and Folk Songs.* n/m
Lomax, John and Alan. *Cowboy Songs.* n/m

Recordings:
Cisco Houston. *Folk Songs.* Folkways. FH2346.
Katie Lee. *Ten Thousand Goddam Cattle.* KD-10076.

THE DUDE WRANGLER (3)   pp. 56–57

Gail I. Gardner. Written, he says, for his cowboy friends who turned to dude wrangling around Castle Hot Springs in the twenties. For the melody Gail used an old turn-of-the-century popular song in the floral, sentimental genre, *The Convict and the Rose* — truly a tear-jerker.

Publications:
Gardner. *Orejana Bull.* n/m
White. *Git Along Little Dogies.* Uses excerpts. n/m

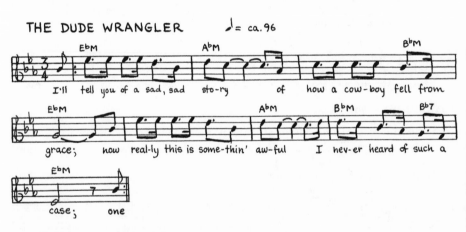

THE DUDE WRANGLER   ♩ = ca. 96

I'll tell you of a sad, sad sto-ry of how a cow-boy fell from grace; now real-ly this is some-thin' aw-ful I nev-er heard of such a case; one

THE DYING OUTFIT (5)   p. 149

I believe Jack Thorp is the only person who gave credit to someone for writing the original *Cowboy's Lament.* In his *Songs of the Cowboys* he credits Troy Hale, Battle Creek, Nebraska, and says, "I first heard it sung in a bar-room at Wisner, Nebraska, about 1886." It appears in one form or another in almost every known book of cowboy songs. The music sticks to two basic themes, one very Irish in character, the other close to blues which beds it with St. James Infirmary. The music here is the Irish version. I learned these words from Paul Hansen, of the first batch of The New Christy Minstrels. Later heard Tom and

Dicky Smothers using them and suspect most were composed by an itinerant, Gene Farmer.

THE DYING OUTFIT ♩. = ca. 42

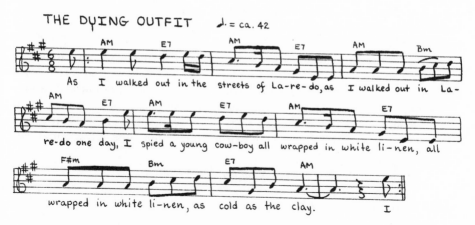

As I walked out in the streets of La-re-do, as I walked out in La-re-do one day, I spied a young cow-boy all wrapped in white li-nen, all wrapped in white li-nen, as cold as the clay.

EMPTY COT IN THE BUNKHOUSE TONIGHT*(4)   pp. 137-38

Arizona cowboys have always thought this to be a Curley Fletcher song, and if I told them I'd found it published in a Gene Autry song folio with the famous "words and music by" line, they'd say "then howcum I heard it in 1928 or 9?" Nevertheless, I'm happy to have permission from Jay Morgenstern of ABC Music to reprint that version here.

Publications:

Autry. *Cowboy Songs and Mountain Ballads.* "There's an Empty Cot in the Bunkhouse Tonight," © 1934, renewed © 1961 (Gene Autry) by ABC/Dunhill Music, Inc. Used by permission only. All rights reserved. w/m

EMPTY COT IN THE BUNKHOUSE TONIGHT ♩ = ca. 104

There's an emp-ty cot in the bunk-house to-night, there's a pin-to's head hang-in' low; his spurs and chaps hang on the wall, he's gone where the good cow-boys go; there's a range for ev'ry cow-boy, where the fore-man takes care of his own; there'll be an emp-ty sad-dle to-night, he's hap-py up there I know; he was

197

Recordings:
Rex Allen. *Rex Allen Sings Western Ballads*. Hilltop JM6009. No credit.
Katie Lee. *Ten Thousand Goddam Cattle*. KD-10076.

FIROLERA, LA* (2)   pp. 26–27

Heard first in the late forties, sung in Spanish. It seems to have found its way into New Mexico by some route other than the cowboys who rarely bothered to translate a Mexican song. Operetta, being a late form of musical expression, would take the song out of antiquity, but I suspect it has folk roots, that it came from Europe to Mexico City first. Jenny Wells Vincent has turned up a Venezuelan version, La Pirolera (the twirling one) same tune, a few variations.

Publications:
Van Stone. *Spanish Folk Songs of New Mexico*. w/m
Silber. *Reprints from Sing Out Magazine*. w/m
Luboff & Stracke. *Songs of Man*. w/m

Recordings:
Jenny Wells Vincent. *American Records*. Children's Music Center, Los Angeles, Calif. 78 rpm
Katie Lee. *Ten Thousand Goddam Cattle*. KD-10076.

FIRST YOU RING THE BELL (4)   p. 63

I have no clues to the authorship of this song, but I later met the woman who taught it to Gail at a bankers' convention in Phoenix in the late thirties. She is Gertrude White of Prescott, and she said it (the first verse only) was sung by the girls in her dormitory when she was away at college in the east.

The second verse was written by Romy Lowdermilk, but when I don't know. He'd heard Gail sing number one, and for a lark made the addition "for the boys."

FIRST YOU RING THE BELL ♩ = ca. 88

First you ring the bell and then you ask for An-na; then you put a nick-el in the 'Bell' pi-a-na,* down comes An-na in a silk ki-mo-na, all dressed up in pa-her-fume and co-lo-na; then you pay two dol-lars for the mus-ic that you hear, then you pay two dol-lars for a lou-sy bot-tle o' beer then you pay two dol-lars for a couple o' weeks o' fear down the line well, ya down the line and the dream that was walk-in' and the dream that was talk-in' and the hea-ven in my arms was you; good eve-nin' friends

(* say " pie-anna.")

FLYIN' U TWISTER (Bad Brahma Bull) (4)   pp. 129–31

Curley Fletcher. Though many Arizona cowboys sang, and still sing, this song, none I know call it anything but *Bad Brahma Bull*. Finding success with *Strawberry* and *The Ridge-Running Roan* no doubt made him add a third. *Flyin' U* has more rodeo than home corral setting and has not been widely recorded. Austin and Alta Fife (*Cowboy and Western Songs*) call RRR and FUT "parodies", which they are not. The Twister was published in 1934 by Kellaway-Ide-Jones, Los Angeles.

Publications:
Fife. *Cowboy and Western Songs.* n/m

Recordings:

Peso Dollar. *Peso Dollar Sings Trail Rider Songs.* Ranch Records, 1410 Birch St., Globe, Ariz.

FLYIN' 'U' TWISTER ♩. = ca. 80

I was snapp-in' out broncs for the old fly-in' U, at for-ty a month a plumb good buck-er-oo; when the boss comes a-round and he sez say my lad, you look pret-ty good rid-in' hor-ses that's bad, now you see I ain't got no more out-laws to break, but I'll buy you a tic-ket and give you a stake, at rid-in' them bad ones well you ain't so slow, and you might do some good at the big Ro-de-o, lay (Chorus) off of hard liq-uor and don't you get full, and think you kin tame that there bad brah-ma bull, Go right down and choose him and when you get through, just tell them you learned on the Old Fly-in' U

GLORY TRAIL, THE (3) pp. 58–60

Charles Badger Clark. Most places where it appears in print after Clark's original it is labeled *High Chin Bob.* N. Howard Thorp in his 1921 edition of *Songs of the Cowboys* says, "This song was brought to Santa Fe by Henry Herbert Knibbs, who got it from southern Arizona where it was sung by the cowboys." It's even possible that Knibbs could have heard the melody that Billy Simon put to it sometime between 1915 and 1920.

Publications:

Clark. *Sun and Saddle Leather.* n/m

Lomax, John A. *Songs of the Cattle Trail and Cow Camp.* No credit to the author in the 1919 ed. It was reprinted in his 1947 edition with Clark's permission along with the *High Chin Bob* version. All n/m.

Botkin. *Treasury of American Folklore.*

Coleman & Bregman. *Songs of American Folks.*

Fife. *Cowboy and Western Songs.* w/m

Ohrlin. *Hell Bound Train.* w/m

White. "Poet of Yesterday's West — Badger Clark," Article. *Arizona Highways.* Feb., 1969. *Git Along Little Dogies.* n/m

Recordings:

George Gillespie. *Cowcamp Songs of the Old West.* Thorne TR200. Scottsdale, Ariz.

Merrick Jarrett. *The Old Chisholm Trail.* Riverside RLP 12-631.

Glenn Ohrlin. *Glen Ohrlin.* Philo 1017. Philo Records, The Barn, North Ferrisburg, Vt.

THE GLORY TRAIL

Way up high in the Mo-go-llons a-mong the moun-tain tops a li-on cleaned a year-lin's bones and licked his thank-ful chops when on the pic-ture who should ride, a trip-pin' down the slope but high-chin'd Bob with sin-ful pride and a ma-ve-rick hung-ry rope "oh glo-ry be to me says he and fame's un-fad-in' flowers all medd-lin' hands are far a-way; I ride my good top horse to-day and I'm top rope o' the La-zy 'J' hi kit-ty cat you're ours; that

GOIN' BACK TO ARIZONA (4)

pp. 154–55

Romaine Lowdermilk. In a letter Romy wrote to John I. White, he says, "Patsy Montana liked it and wanted to sing it on her road appearances, so I just called it *Goin' Back to Old Montana* and she recorded it for Victor and it was on the juke boxes for quite a spell. You can sing it Back to California or Oklahoma or Wyoming — or any damn place you want to go back to. So I figured it was an all-around western. I got paid for it by WLS, so I didn't really care where the singer went back to." His original version was "Back to Arizona" which is the way I have always heard it. Patsy Prescott sang it often over station KOA in Phoenix in the thirties.

Publications:

Lair, John. *100 WLS Barn Dance Favorites.* (Goin' Back to Old Montana) w/m

Recordings:

Patsy Montana. *Goin' Back to Old Montana.* RCA Victor, 78 rpm.

George Gillespie. *George Gillespie Sings Cow Camp Songs of the Old West.* TR200. Scottsdale, Arizona. (Goin' Back to Arizona)

GOIN' BACK TO ARIZONA ♩ = ca. 176

I left old Ar-i—zo-na, and went back East to stay, with a stet-son hat and cow-boy boots I looked like a half-picked jay I packed my duds and spurs and ropes, I packed my sad-dle too, I'm here a-mong the ci-ty folks gosh I'm fee-lin' blue go-in runn-in' with a mus-tang band go-in' back to Ar-i—zo-na, and round 'em up some day, I'll whoop 'n yell in the big cor-ral with a ki-yi-yip-pee-yi-yay yee hah ki yi yip-pee yi yay

HAIR TRIGGER NEWT (4)

Lifted from Singin' Sam Agins who isn't what you'd call a painstaking researcher, and can't now recall where *he* lifted it, or when. Discussing its bloodlines, one day, we decided it had come from the dudin' period — a guess reinforced by Billy Simon who dimly recalled it from way back then.

Recordings:

Singin' Sam Agins. *Saddlebag of Songs.* Haywire ARA 6419.

203

I'LL BE WITH YOU WHEN THE ROSES BLOOM AGAIN (4)   p. 148

A parody from the vaudeville circuit that Speed Richardson played; born no doubt, in the backstage trunk of some comic singer. The original was a mushy popular song of the twenties.

I'M A RAMBLER, I'M A GAMBLER (1)   pp. 8-9

Sprouting many titles, this basic set of lyrics has grapevined all over the world. *The Wagoner's Lad, The Rose of Saline* (Madine in Ireland), *I'm a Poor Boy, My Horses Ain't Hungry, The Rabble Soldier, The Texas Cowboy,* whatever, it took its place early in the cowboy's repertoire, and along with *Green Grow the Lilacs, The Cowboy's Lament, Little Old Sod Shanty,* it night-herded cattle. The Gaelic melody stayed with this title, whereas other versions leaned toward an *On Top of Old Smokey* pattern. There's no doubt about who wrote the song. Everybody. And everybody from Joan Baez to Ken Maynard has recorded it. Look for it under *The Wagoner's Lad* in just about any book of folksongs.

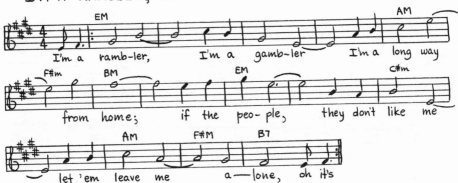

I'M A RAMBLER, I'M A GAMBLER   ♩ = ca. 106

I'm a ramb-ler, I'm a gamb-ler I'm a long way from home; if the peo-ple, they don't like me let 'em leave me a—lone, oh it's

NOTE: piece ends on dominant 7

JOHNNY RINGO (1)   p. 109

Katie Lee. This version anyway © Greenwitch Music, is explained in Fife's *Songs of the Cowboys,* pp. 122, 123, 134. Generally titled *My Love Is A Rider, Buckin' Bronco, The Cowboy's Hat,* it was the cowboy's free-for-all "blue" song but whenever it was printed those verses were left out. They passed from mouth to mouth, you can be sure and weren't all lost. I was able to drag one out of Shorty Mac that's heading from blue into purple!

> My Love is a rider, he rides me at will
> And each time he does it, he gives me a thrill
> The first time I saw it was early one Spring,
> Like a hair-over brand, a big red and blue thing.

Vance Randolph says, "It was first printed in a story by Stewart Edward White, *McClure's Magazine,* 'The Rawhide,' 24, Dec. 1904." Thorp in his *Songs of the Cowboys,* 1921, said the song had been expurgated by him. (I'll bet it had!). Dobie mentions a James Hatch of San Antonio as claiming authorship. But it's doubtful the authors of the random blue verse will ever come to light.

Publications:

Thorp. *Songs of the Cowboys.* Credits Belle Starr. n/m

Fife. *Cowboy and Western Songs.* (Buckin' Broncho) w/m

Fife & Thorp. *Songs of the Cowboys.* w/m

Randolph. *Ozark Folk Songs.* Vol. 2. w/m

Larkin. *The Singing Cowboy.* Credits Belle Starr. w/m

Lomax, John A. *Cowboy Songs.* 1916. Calls it *The Cowgirl.* In his 1948 printing with Alan Lomax he credits Belle Starr and calls it *Buckin' Bronco.* Both are w/m

Lomax, Alan. *Folk Songs of North America.* Suggests Starr. Calls it *My Love is a Rider.* w/m

Allen, Jules Verne. *Cowboy Lore.* Under title *Bucking Bronco.* w/m

Clark, Kenneth S. *The Cowboy Sings.* Listed under *Bucking Broncho* and *My Love is a Rider* (folio). w/m

———. *Buckaroo Ballads.* Same notations (folio). w/m

White, Stewart Edward. *Arizona Nights.* n/m

Ohrlin. *Hell Bound Train.* Under *My Love is a Rider.*" w/m

Recordings:

Katie Lee. *Spicy Songs for Cool Knights.* (Title: *Johnny Ringo*). Specialty, SP-5000.

Carolyn Hester. *The Badmen.* Columbia Records Legacy Collection. L2L-1011 (My *Johnny Ringo* version).

Dickson Hall. *Outlaws of the Old West.* MGM-3263. (This *Johnny Ringo* song

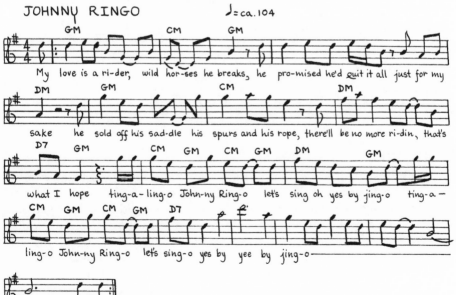

may be an entirely different song from mine and about the outlaw himself, or it may be my version of *Buckin' Bronco* — I've not heard the record).

Hermes Nye. *Texas Folk Songs*. Folkways FA-2128.
Jeane Richie & Oscar Brand. *Courting Songs*. Elektra EKL-22.
Dick Deval. *Girls of the Golden West*. Bluebird 5752; Montgomery Ward 7204.
Powder River Jack Lee. Singles — 78 rpm. Bluebird 5298-A; Sunrise 3379.
Glenn Ohrlin. *Hell Bound Train*. Puritan Records — 500. P.O. Box 946, Evanston, Ill. 60204.

JOSE CUERVO* (3)   pp. 74–75

Romaine Lowdermilk says that Everett Cheetham gave him this song in the mid-twenties. Billy Simon probably got it from the same source, but never have I discovered who might have composed it. Billy gave me a typed copy titled *"Tales Uv Ole Mekiko* and signed Mescal Ike (pout lariut uv h. & m.)" The manner of spelling seems to be done more for a lark than for lack of literacy, but it points up the sentiments of the time — the cowboy put-down of his Mexican counterpart. Shorty didn't sing it often — possibly it offended him. At one time he had been much in love with a Mexican girl whose father would have killed her rather than let her marry a *gringo*.

Recordings:
Katie Lee. *Ten Thousand Goddam Cattle*. KD-10076.

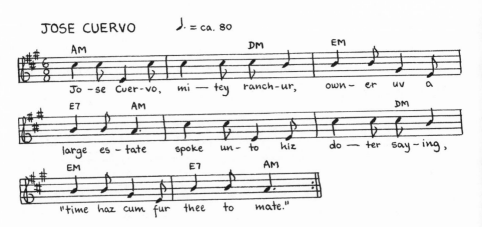

LASCA* (1)   pp. 107–8

Frank Desprez is the author of the poem; Katie Lee the composer of the music and cut version of the poem. A search through the Library of Congress showed no *song* remotely resembling the poem, but did turn up something written in 1921 which suggested the authors had at least *heard* it. They called it *Laska* — words by Laverne Taylor Zundel, music by A. Leopold Richard. Copyright 1921, Published by *Legters Music Co.*, 189 N. Clark St., Chicago.

    Chorus:
    When the ev'ning breeze steals softly all around,
    And the birds their goodnight sing,

There's a missing one that will never be found,
Fading days sad memories bring.
There's a heart buried deep in the gleaming sand,
Oh, a heart that's pure and true,
Buried deep, or so deep in the Rio Grande;
'Tis my heart buried, Laska, with you.
Innocence was her name, and God was love
Naught on earth did she blame, nor in heaven above
As the morning sun rose, it stole 'way all my mirth
For the fairest that grows, had now fled from this earth.

Now, that's bad, folks, *Really bad.*

Zundel and Richard have produced pure bullshit from no farther west than the Chicago Stockyards. Shows what can be done with a two-page rhyming dictionary and a very blunt instrument on the shoulders.

In the Gordon Collection at the Library of Congress written by hand after part of the poem is the signature Vern Stall. He probably sent it to the poet's corner of a western pulp as something he'd heard or learned. The Fifes tell me of a first printing in the U.S., 1888, *The Montana Livestock Journal,* June 16th.

Publications:

George, David L. *Family Book of Best Loved Poems.* n/m
Mackenzie, Richard. *New Home Book of Best Loved Poems.* n/m
Stevenson, Burton. *New Home Book of Verse.* n/m
Thing, Walter. *Best Loved Story Poems.* n/m
Lomax, John. *Songs of the Cattle Trail and Cow Camp.* n/m
Shay, Frank. *My Pious Friends and Drunken Companions.* n/m
Kennedy, Charles. *American Ballads.* n/m

LASCA   ♩= ca. 98

I long for the can-ter af-ter cat-tle for the crack o' the whips like shots in bat-tle for the me-lee of the hooves the horns and heads for the free life, the fresh air and star-lit beds for the green be-neath, and the blue up a-bove and dash and dan-ger and life and love and Las-ca; all

Lee, Katie. "Songs the Cowboys Taught Me." *Arizona Highways*, Feb. 1960.

Recordings:
Edgar Davenport. *Lasca* — with incidental music by orchestra. Victor Talking
   Machine Company, September 22, 1903, 78 rpm. #31529, May, 1912.
———. *Lasca*, Edison Amberol Record 296, November, 1909. 78 rpm.
William S. Hart. *Lasca* — I've been unable to find this disk, also an old 78 rpm.
Katie Lee. *Ten Thousand Goddam Cattle*. KD-10076.

THE LAST WAGON* (3)   pp. 98–99
    Words by Bennett Foster, music by Slim Critchlow. Slim has to say about
the song, "To the old time cowboy the coming of the wire fences was the signal
that the old days and the old ways had gone for good. To add a word of explanation about 'circles,' in the old days of free range a cowboy used to occa-
sionally be detailed to ride 'circle,' just like it sounds, to keep cattle from drift-
ing too far from their home range, pushing back any he found during the course
of his circle. During the spring and fall roundups, on the larger outfits, several
riders would fan out at considerable distance from the gathering ground and
start pushing the cattle into the gather. Where their circles crossed a puncher
going left would pick up the cows started by the rider heading right, and eventually as the circles narrowed the cows would wind up with the rest of the
gather — except for the one missed, of course. A too-simple explanation of geo-
metrical cow-gathering which worked well except in rough country." From the
jacket notes of Slim's record.
    A letter from Doubleday, publishers of Foster's books, I learned that Bennett
Foster wrote also under the pseudonym John Trace. He died September 29,
1969. His wife Arleen Foster lives in Albuquerque. Slim Critchlow died October
31, 1969.

Publications:
Padell Books Company. *Cowboy and Mountain Ballads.* n/m

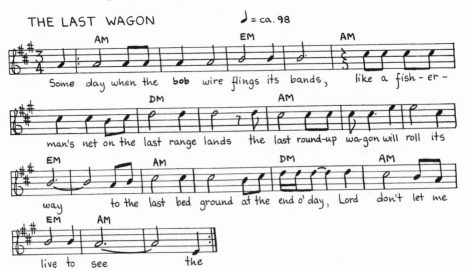

208

Recordings:

Slim Critchlow. *The Crooked Trail to Holbrook.* Arhoolie 5007, Berkeley, California.

Katie Lee. *Ten Thousand Goddam Cattle.* KD-10076.

THE LAVENDER COWBOY (4)

p. 120

A poem by Harold Hersey in *Singing Rawhide.* Published and recorded many times without a mention as to where the tunes originated — they vary widely. Mine from the singing of Burl Ives, is what Harrydick Ross remembers as sheet music during the twenties. Billy Simon and the Castle Hot Springs gang sang it then, but to this melody or not, I haven't a clue.

Publications:

Hersey. *Singing Rawhide.* n/m

Lomax, John. *Cowboy Songs.* 1938 gives no credit to Hersey. w/m

Lomax, John and Alan. *Cowboy Songs.* Rev. ed. 1948 credits Hersey. w/m

Fife, Austin and Alta. *Cowboy and Western Songs.* No credit. w/m

Recordings:

Burl Ives. *Wayfaring Stranger.* Columbia CL-628.

Ed McCurdy. *The Folk Singer.* Dawn DLP-1127.

Peter LaFarge. *Peter LaFarge Sings of the Cowboys.* Folkways FA-2533. (He claims words *and* music).

George Gillespie. *Cow Camp Songs of the Old West.* Thorne TH-200.

Alan Arkin. *Once Over Lightly.* Elektra EKL-21.

Katie Lee. *Spicy Songs for Cool Knights.* Specialty SP-5000.

Ewan Hall. Single 78 rpm. Brunswick 141-8.

Vernon Dalhart. *Vernon Dalhart and His Big Cypress Boys.* Single, Bluebird B-8229-A.

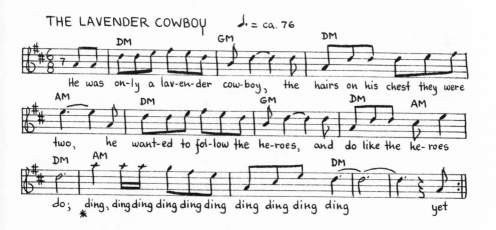

THE LAVENDER COWBOY ♩. = ca. 76

He was on-ly a lav-en-der cow-boy, the hairs on his chest they were two, he want-ed to fol-low the he-roes, and do like the he-roes do; ding, ding ding ding ding ding ding ding ding ding ding yet

✳ NOTE: these syllables are sung nasally to produce a sound similar to that of stopped strings.

209

LAVINIA'S PARLOUR (5)

Travis Edmonson. Based on an actual happening, as are most of his songs of the West, Travis lets us in on how cowboys felt about the bad women who were so good to them. When Travis was a kid his parents farmed him out in the summertime to uncles who owned a ranch in Safford, Arizona. On Saturday's the relations would go to town for weekly supplies, leaving Travis with the cowboys who had another kind of "baby sitting" in mind. He recalls being taken to a fancy house, sitting downstairs with a pretty lady who fed him pink lemonade, while the boys went up and down, stopping now and then to pat him on the head and say, "Howz everything, Trav? Lavinia, give the kid another pink lemonade, we'll be down in a while." I suppose it was years before he knew where he'd been, and years more before he went back on his own. This is the song's first printing. Travis gave it to me for a special show that I do about Ladies of the Evening, now a record album.

Recordings:

Katie Lee. *Loves Little Sisters.* Katydid Records KD-1006. Box 395, Jerome, Arizona 86331.

(continued →)

LAVINIA'S PARLOR (continued)

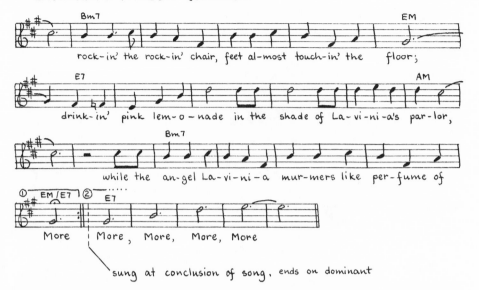

rock-in' the rock-in' chair, feet al-most touch-in' the floor;

drink-in' pink lem-o-nade in the shade of La-vi-ni-a's par-lor,

while the an-gel La-vi-ni-a mur-mers like per-fume of

More ¦ More, More, More, More

sung at conclusion of song, ends on dominant

LITTLE JOE THE WRANGLER'S SISTER NELL* (1) pp. 122–23

Said to have been written by N. Howard "Jack" Thorp as a sequel to his *Little Joe the Wrangler*. Not one of the collectors has proven that Thorp did indeed write it, and nowhere has it been found that he claimed it. My personal conviction is that he did not. His Little Joe, written in 1898 after what he claims was a true incident, doesn't teeter on the edge of bathos as does the Sister song. I think it was written some time later, after the writer had heard Texasized versions where all place names are changed. To be four hundred miles north of Llano you still have to be in Texas. Even for the trail herding days, Little Joe was on a long drive if he was headed for Cinnabar (Basin) which is north of Gardiner, Montana on the northern boundary of Yellowstone National Park. Several things don't fit the characters. In the original, Little Joe joins the outfit in brogan shoes and overalls, a Southern kack, an O.K. spur on one boot, and a "hot roll" in a cotton sack. His daddy's married twice and his new ma beat him, but he never mentioned a sister. He did say, he didn't know "straight up" about a cow, and maybe that's why he was killed one night, down by the Pecos, when the cattle stampeded. But Nell was wearing raw-hide chaps well greased and worn, her rig all scarred from working in the brush. For a farm kid, or a nester, she sure knew a bunch more about working cattle than her twin brother. He'd been gone "a year from last April" before she set out to look for him. My guess, the two writers were miles, and years, apart.

Publications:

Randolph, Vance. *Ozark Folk Songs*. Vol. 2. n/m

Fife, Austin and Alta. *Songs of the Cowboys* with Thorp. w/m (music in all
   cases is the same as *Little Joe*).

Clark, Kenneth. *The Happy Cowboy*. Thorp is given authorship. w/m

Ohrlin. *The Hell Bound Train*. Learned from Dick Smith of Buffalo, S.D. w/m

Recordings:

Harry Jackson. *The Cowboy*. FH-5723.

George Gillespie. *Cowcamp Songs of the Old West*. Thorne TH-200.

Katie Lee. *Ten Thousand Goddam Cattle*. KD-10076.

LITTLE JOE THE WRANGLER'S SISTER NELL ♩ = ca.144

She rode up to the wa-gon as the sun was go-in' down,
Slen-der lit-tle fig-ure dressed in grey; He asked her to get
down a while and pull up to the fire, red hot chuck 'd
soon be on the way; an

LOLITA (2)   p. 28

Poem by Captain Roger Pocock. Music and added verses 3 and 4 by Katie Lee after the faded memory of some Arizona cowboy's singing at Ruby, Arizona, 1938 or thereabouts. Years after I'd been singing this version, I ran across another in an old song folio. Apparently this fellow Sterling Sherwin, who got around to a lot of other people's material in the twenties and thirties, either by writing music or "assisting in the publishing" to the extent that he added his name to the copyright, did so with the Captain's poem. His melody in no way resembles the one here.

Publications:

Pocock, Capt. Roger. *Curley*. n/m

Lomax, John A. *Songs of the Cattle Trail and Cow Camp*. n/m

Sherwin, Sterling. *Singing in the Saddle*. w/m

Lee, Katie. "Songs the Cowboys Taught Me." *Arizona Highways*, Feb., 1960.

LOLITA   ♩ = ca. 96

The ca-ba-lle-ros throng to see thy laugh-ing face, Se-ñor-i-ta, but
well I know thy heart's for me, thy charm and grace, my Lo-li-ta

212

THE MAN WITH THE BIG HAT (5)

Steve Fromholz, words and music. © 1968 by American Broadcasting Music, Inc. Used by permission only, all rights reserved. For the frustrations of Fromholz one may read a chapter of *The Improbable Rise of Redneck Rock*, by Jan Reid, Heidelberg Publishers, Inc., Austin, Tex. Steve wants very much to make it big in the gigantic world of chrom-music. Given his sensitive, intuitive songs, that's like saying he wants to steel-plate a hummingbird. There is *no way* the market of muckrakers and tin-eared teenieboppers will buy his intelligence, so I hope he can settle for that smaller, beautiful, oh-so-hip and joyful audience that digs him . . . before he goes bananas. They are the ones who deserve songs like his *Texas Trilogy*.

MY BLUE HEAVEN* (4)

p. 147

A parody — not the same hue of blue as the one we all remember from the

213

late twenties or early thirties, but *blue* nonetheless. Many a cowboy's creation was tagged to a tune of the times such as this; his talents, such as they were, gravitating to the "put-togethers" of words more than music. If this parody has ever reached the printed page, I have never heard it.

Recordings:
Katie Lee. *Ten Thousand Goddam Cattle.* KD-10076.

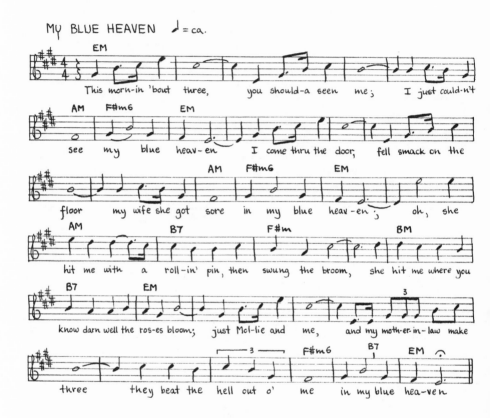

MY BLUE HEAVEN ♩ = ca.

This morn-in 'bout three, you should-a seen me; I just could-n't see my blue heav-en I come thru the door, fell smack on the floor my wife she got sore in my blue heav-en, oh, she hit me with a roll-in' pin, then swung the broom, she hit me where you know darn well the ros-es bloom; just Mol-lie and me, and my moth-er-in-law make three they beat the hell out o' me in my blue hea-ven

MY HOMESTEAD* (5)   p. 85

Stephen Gay (George) Pendleton. In 1949 I acted on the first state-wide television program to come out of Hollywood with Steve — *Armchair Detective.* In the early fifties he composed a woman's version of *Homestead* that I used in my nightclub act for years. Stephen is an actor, born in a stage trunk, played banjo in vaudeville (and whorehouses) in the twenties when but a pup. His resonant voice makes him money in the audio-viz ad-biz, talking. He does not write songs for a living. The original poem was longer and has some beautiful lines I'd like to share:

> And I felt the great rush of her love as she left me
> To seek out her children and comfort their cry . . .
> With mothering tresses all gold in the moon-rise
> She nestled each critter from earth to the sky . . .

With the blush of the sunrise the rustle an' creakin'
The wailin' and squeakin' has quietly died . . .
An' I stare at my desert an' know why I'm livin'
To take of her givin', an' swellin' with pride . . .

Recordings:

Katie Lee. *Ten Thousand Goddam Cattle.* KD-10076. (Woman's version).

MY HOMESTEAD   ♩ = ca. 120

Em   GM   Em

I dreamed of a home-stead way out on the de-sert, on the

Am   Em   B7   Em

great san-dy de-sert, but I did-n't know why; a fe-vered with

GM   Em   Am   Em

yearn-in' I wan-dered a burn-in' 'til I found my old home-stead just a

B7   Em   B7   Em

patch on the sky; there I watched and I wait-ed to find what I'd

B7   Em   B7   Am   B7

come for to end all my seek-in', to love or to die then I

THE NIGHT I STOLE OL' SAMMY MORGAN'S GIN * (4)   p. 150

I don't even know if this song's mother came from Ireland, since it has left no

THE NIGHT I STOLE OL' SAMMY MORGAN'S GIN   ♩ = ca. 120

BbM

List-en folks and I will tell a fun-ny stor-y you may

FM

think it's sad but I was in my glo—ry 'twas a

BbM   EbM

cel-lar I crept in, cob-webs brush-in' by my chin, on the

BbM   FM   BbM

night I stole ol' Sam-my Mor-gan's gin as my

215

tracks to follow. Speed is the only person I've heard sing it, and he learned it where he learned others of its ilk, on the vaudeville circuit. If it ever spread among the Arizona cowboys, it did so, as Speed says, "like a dose of crabs — on the sly."

Recordings:
Katie Lee. *Ten Thousand Goddam Cattle.* KD-10076.

ODE TO BENNY PERKINS (5) pp. 142–43

. . . words by Al Schauffler, sung to the music of *Mustang Gray.* This is probably a one-time-sung composition, since it is hardly likely to fit another personality. It is too personalized to stand with Omar Barker's *Adios*, and isn't likely to inspire anyone to write a new melody for it, which might extend its journey into the future beyond the day of Benny's funeral. A good melody will invite new words, as did *Mustang Gray.* It is documented here simply to show that a tradition is still being carried out; one that is carried out all over the world, not just here in the West.

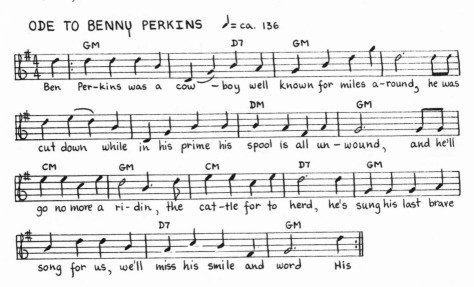

OLD ARIZONA *(5) pp. 161–62

Travis Edmonson, who hates to be called Trav, is the composer of several classics, *Scotch and Soda* for one, as Dave Guard of the old Kingston Trio has admitted in front of witnesses. (Travis was one of the original members). He is one of the best song writers and performers that I know. *Old Arizona* was scribbled off one day inside half an hour when Travis had been out on horseback, riding territory he'd known intimately as a younger man. It was gone. Desert growth was stripped and ticky-tacky houses stood all in a row, selling for fifty thousand clams. Considering that, the song shows great restraint.

Recordings:
Katie Lee. *Ten Thousand Goddam Cattle.* KD-10076.

OLD ARIZONA

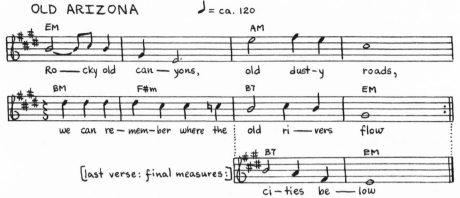

♩ = ca. 120

Ro——cky old can—yons, old dust-y roads,
we can re—mem—ber where the old ri——vers flow
[last verse: final measures:] ci—ties be——low

OLD BACH (3)

pp. 46–47

Gail I. Gardner, who spelled it Batch — meaning a whole bunch. He told me he'd never put a tune to it, but Billy Simon says they used the same one as *Sierry Petes* when singing it at Castle Hot Springs. Most any tune will do, it's the *words* that say it. Incidentally, it's spelled both ways.

Publications:

Gardner. *Orejana Bull.* n/m

OLD BACH

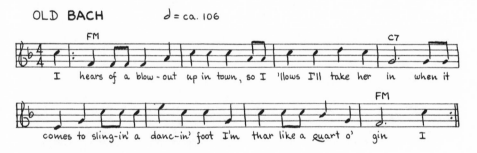

♩ = ca. 106

I hears of a blow-out up in town, so I 'llows I'll take her in when it
comes to sling-in' a danc-in' foot I'm thar like a quart o' gin I

OLD DOLORES

See *The Town of Old Dolores.*

A PEON NAMED PONCHO

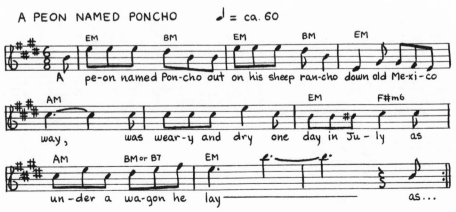

♩ = ca. 60

A pe-on named Pon-cho out on his sheep ran-cho down old Me-xi-co
way, was wear-y and dry one day in Ju-ly as
un-der a wa-gon he lay as...

217

A PEON NAMED PANCHO (4)

p. 153

A song on loan to me by Singin' Sam Agins, who borrowed it from a dude wrangler named Red Lawson, who lifted it from a bartender in Los Alamos. I've never seen it in print or heard anyone sing it but Sam. I doubt that it is an old song — probably "thunk up" some time in the thirties.

Recordings:

Singin' Sam Agins. *Singin' Sam and Friends.* Haywire Record Co., Box 3057, West Sedona, Ariz.

REAL COWBOY LIFE (3)

pp. 48–49

Gail Gardner's verse, which he made into song for himself and other cowboys around Prescott. Says he lifted the melody from an old song of the twenties, *My Canoe Is Under Water,* words of which have fled from his head. But Dr. Leland Sonnichsen (see acknowledgements) came up with a couple of verses from minstrel days, the tune, roughly, *Little Old Sod Shanty On My Claim:*

> I am gettin' old and feeble now,
> I cannot work no more,
> I have laid my rusty-bladed hoe to rest.
> Ol' Massa and Ol' Missy now are sleepin' side by side.
> Their spirits now are roamin' with the blessed.

Publications:

Gardner, Gail I. *Orejana Bull.* n/m

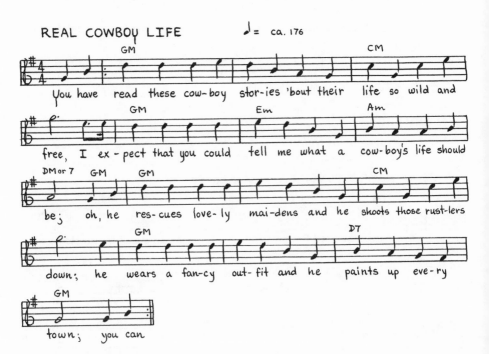

REAL COWBOY LIFE ♩ = ca. 176

You have read these cow-boy stor-ies 'bout their life so wild and free, I ex-pect that you could tell me what a cow-boy's life should be; oh, he res-cues love-ly mai-dens and he shoots those rust-lers down; he wears a fan-cy out-fit and he paints up eve-ry town; you can

ROUNDUP LULLABY* (3)   pp. 79–80

Charles Badger Clark poem. As a song it was used in a Bing Crosby movie in the thirties. Also recorded by him on an old Decca 78. The melody used here might be the work of a professional songwriter like Bob Nolan of the Sons of the Pioneers. Whoever "re-tuned" it from the earlier, simpler, one made it stick, because it's not heard to the old melody any more.

Publications:
Clark. *Sun and Saddle Leather.* n/m

Recordings:
Bing Crosby. Decca 78 rpm. Number lost.
Katie Lee. *Ten Thousand Goddam Cattle.* KD-10076.

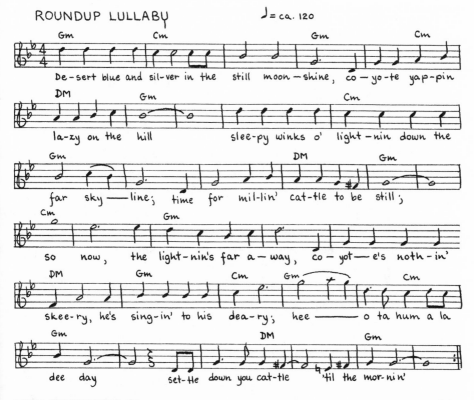

THE RUSTLER* (3)   pp. 16–17

Henry Herbert Knibbs poem. Music and revision by Katie Lee. I did not "jingle into to town" to copyright my version until long after it was composed, but Larry Shane Publishers, Hollywood and New York, holds the copyright now. His Knibbs original before my tinkering:

> From the fading smoke of a branding-fire in a
>   mesquite hollow close and dim,
> We followed a phantom pony-track, over the range
>   and down

Into the cool, deep canyon gloom, then up to the
    mesa's ragged rim;
And the foam-clots flew from our swinging reins as
    we loped to the desert town.

Gray in the dusk at the hitching-rail there loomed
    the shape of a lean cayuse,
His gaunt flanks streaked with dust-dried sweat in
    the doorway's golden glow;
A rider stood at the lamplit bar tugging the knot
    of his neck-scarf loose,
And some one sang to the silver strings in the
    moonlit patio.

He flung a coin as we crowded in. He knew us all,
    but with no surprise:
We had run him down and he faced us square, a
    fighter from hat to heel:
The music stopped and a Spanish girl came from the
    dusk, her wondering eyes
Filled with a strange and fearsome light; but his
    were cold as steel.

Tense as a lion crouched to spring he poised on
    the midnight brink of fate;
But she, with a smile, drew near the lamp, playing
    the woman's game:
A crash — and the room was black and still: a
    whispered word and we knew, too late,
As hell surged up in our hearts, we drew and the
    dark was streaked with flame.

We heard the thud of a pony's stride and shuffled
    back to the open door,
Ringed by a sudden crowd that came, questioning,
    shuffling, till
A light was made in the 'dobe bar, and a shadow
    lay on the beaten floor —
We saw an arm and an upturned face, girlish and
    white and still.

Gray in the dusk at the hitching-rail there loomed
    the shape of a lean cayuse,
His gaunt flanks streaked with sun-dried sweat in
    the lamplight's golden glow:
But no rider stood at the lamplit bar tugging the
    knot of his neck-scarf loose,
And no one sang to the silver string in the moonlit
    patio.

Publications:
Knibbs. *Songs of the Trail.* n/m

Recordings:
Katie Lee. *Ten Thousand Goddam Cattle.* KD-10076.

THE RUSTLER ♩ = ca. 144

We found his smok-in' brand-in' fire in a hol-ler dark and dim; we
fol-lered his faint and lone-some track all the way to the me-sa's rim;
we rode thru the cool of a cañ-on's gloom and o—ver the range then
down and the foam flew hot from our swing-in' reins as we
loped thru the bor-der town (not sung.............................) All

THE SANTA FE TRAIL* (3)   pp. 174–75

Song by James Grafton Rogers. It was written in 1911 when Jim Rogers was working on an irrigation project near Las Animas, New Mexico — not digging it, but in the capacity of lawyer. The song was copyrighted by Rogers and Comet Publishing Co., Denver, long before the thieving began. It was copyrighted illegally after that a dozen times by: Jules Verne Allen; in the agile name of that fellow Sterling Sherwin (with Henri Klickman, 1934) and again in 1948 after he'd been notified, he credited *John* Grafton Rogers; the old Rustler Powder River Jack Lee slipped away with it in 1934, got lassoed and used the name Rogers in his 1937 printing, *arranged* by PRJL; Lomax in his 1948 edition credited Sherwin. One place, at least, it has been printed with permission of the author; the song book of the University Club of Denver. George Gillespie says he got his version from Romy Lowdermilk. Both the Fifes and John I. White gave me a reference which I question being the same song, a Dick Jurgens dance band record done in the late thirties. It was called *Along the Santa Fe Trail* and had quite a different melody and lyric.

Publications:
Allen, Jules Verne. *Cowboy Lore.* w/m
Sherwin and Klickman. *Songs of the Roundup.* w/m

Sherwin. *Saddle Songs.* w/m

Lomax, John A. and Alan. *Cowboy Songs.* w/m

Lee, Powder River Jack. *Cowboy Wails and Cattle Trails of the Wild West.* w/m

University Club of Denver. *A Golden Treasury.* n/m

Ohrlin, Glenn. *Hell Bound Train.* w/m

Recordings:

Jules Verne Allen. Montgomery Ward -4344. Victor V40118. (both 78 rpm.)

George Gillespie. *Cow Camp Songs of the Old West.* Thorne TH-200.

Glenn Ohrlin. *Glenn Ohrlin.* Philo 1017. The Barn, North Ferrisburg, Vermont 05473. No credit to Rogers, gotten from Jules Verne Allen.

Katie Lee. *Ten Thousand Goddam Cattle.* KD-10076.

THE SANTA FE TRAIL ♩. = ca. 63

Say, Pard, have ye sight-ed a schoo-ner a hit-tin' the San-ta Fe Trail? They made it here Mon-day or soo-ner with a wa-ter keg roped on the rail; there was Dad-dy and Ma on the mule seat, and some-where a—long on the way was a tow-head-ed gal on a pint-o just a jang-lin' for old San-ta Fe, yee hah! just a jang-lin' for old San-ta Fe

THE SIERRY PETES* (3)   pp. 43–44

. . . is by Gail I. Gardner, the music by Billy Simon. It was written in April of 1917 with no assistance whatever, from anybody but the Muse.

Publications (and comment thereon):

German, George. *Cowboy Campfire Ballads.* March 5, 1929. This was a paper-back pamphlet, privately printed, with credit to the author and is used with his permission. Verses appeared with alterations and deletions from Gail's original, but here is where it was first copyrighted in his name. n/m

German, George. *Cowboy Song Book No. 5.* (1939). *Cowboy and Hillbilly Ballads. Tyin' Knots in the Devil's Tail.* Words by Gail I. Gardner, Music by George B. German. (And lucky Billy Simon didn't care). w/m

Lee, Powder River Jack. *The Stampede*. (No date of publication). Printed without music, without permission, and with the following quote: "I wrote this as a poem but later made a song of the story and it describes two typical cowboys . . . etc." Jack Lee is deceased, or Gail would be tempted to "dress him out" on the spot.

———. *Powder River Jack and Kitty Lee's Song Book*. (1931). *Tyin' A Knot In the Devil's Tail*, Words and music by Jack and Kitty Lee.

———. *Cowboy Song Book*. Words and music by PRJ Lee. (1936)

Larkin, Margaret. *The Singing Cowboy*. (1931) A corrupt version titled *Rusty Jiggs and Sandy Sam*. Author states she learned it from Everett Cheetham. Gail mentioned that Cheetham heard him sing the song in its original version using the phrase that is so often commented on — "I'm tired of cowpyrography" — but Larkin uses "cowpography." No credit to Gail. w/m

Ivins, Joseph William. *Library of Congress Copyright Notice*. Hollywood, Calif., Feb. 5, 1932. *Tyin' Knots in the Devil's Tail*. Words and Music by J. W. Ivins. (A little late, Joe).

Street & Smith. *Wild West Weekly*. Under "Fiddlin' Joe's Song Corral" with comment: "Robert Rankin of Mass, who's sure been sendin' us some right interestin' material, gives us the following song which he says is pretty old. Nobody seems to know who wrote it." A letter from Gail straightened this out right away and it was printed again in its original form and with explanation of terms from the author — appearing in Joe's Corral, Nov. 5, 1932. n/m

Lomax, John A. *American Ballads and Folk Songs*, (1934) "Author unknown. Contributed to the collection of Dr. Hazard by Helen Becker of Mills College." Note to Lomax from Gail: "Several girls from Prescott, Arizona attended Mills College during the years 1924–34, any one of whom may have heard the song sung by the author." w/m

Gardner, Gail T. "Orejana Bull," *Collected Poems for Cowboys Only*. Library of Congress Certificate of Registration; Class AA, No. 192120, Dec. 14, 1935. Printings, 1935, 1950, 1960, 1965.

Ford, Ira W. *Traditional Music in America* (1940). "Sandy Sam and Rusty Jiggs." No credit to author. w/m

Loesser, Arthur L. *Humor in American Song* (1942). "Rusty Jiggs and Sandy Sam." No credit. w/m

Carlson, Raymond, ed. *Arizona Highways*. Vol. 2 (1944). With credit to the author using his own version. Illustrations by Ross Santee. n/m

Lomax, Alan. *Folk Songs of North America* (1960). Alan to Gail, Feb. 22, 1961: "The song was sent to my father, by the way, as a dude ranch song sometime in the twenties or earlier and this is the source of my misunderstanding." Delia Gardner states: "Gail sang this song in public in the early twenties at Prescott Community sings, broadcast at the Old Ball Park and frequently at the winter resort area, Castle Hot Springs, Arizona, and other dude ranches, where many cowboys were employed as wranglers. It is interesting to note that almost all the early published versions where source is mentioned at all, trace directly back to the self-styled singing cowboys who were employed at the dude ranches of that area; many of whom later exploited it in their own versions, some of them wildly different from the original." w/m

Western Horseman. Pub. Colorado Springs, 1961. With permission from the author using his second version which replaced "cow-pyrography" with the smell of burnin' hair." Illustrated by George Phippen who was commissioned to do the painting for him. n/m

Gail I. Gardner. *Certificate of Claim to renewal of Copyright,* No. 313825, April 15, 1963.

Houston, Cisco. *900 Miles.* 1965. "Tying A Knot in the Devil's Tail." No credit. w/m

Silber, Irwin. *Songs of the Great American West.* (1967). In 1959 I wrote Moe Asch and Irwin Silber of Folkways records telling them the song was Gail's. They said I'd have to prove it, which I did, with a letter from Gail, saying they were about to be sued, and sending copyright numbers. Moe sent him a "token check" of $25.00 saying they would send him more when they counted up the royalties from all the records on which they'd recorded his song without credit. That was the last heard from them. He gave *me* the twenty-five dollars for making them budge that far. Irwin's book is the first publication by anyone connected with that outfit to acknowledge Gail as author, even though Oak Publications, their subsidiary, published Cisco's book (above), they knew the song was Gail's. w/m

Sackett, William R. *Cowboys and the Songs They Sang.* (1967) "*Tying Knots in the Devil's Tail.*" No credit.

Fife. *Cowboy and Western Songs.* (1969) With full credit and accurate text, and music credited to Billy Simon. w/m

Ohrlin. *The Hell-Bound Train.* (1973) Printed as Gail wrote it and with credit to him. But the many references in the book about Powder River Jack Lee's fine contributions to cowboy songs, set the old one-eyed cowboy off on another tear, since he knows that a great number of the songs Lee claimed were *not* written by him. w/m

White. *Git Along Little Dogies.* w/m

Recordings:

Rosalie Sorrels. *Songs of Utah and Idaho.* Folkways FH-5343.

Harry Jackson. *The Cowboy.* Folkways FH-5723.

Cisco Houston. *Cowboy Ballads.* Folkways FA-2022.

———. *Traditional Songs of the Old West* (with Bill Bender). Stinson SLP-37.

———. (Title missing). Disc Album 608.

Peter LaFarge. *Peter LaFarge Sings of the Cowboys.* Folkways FN-2533.

Frank Hamilton. *The Folksinger's Folksinger.* Concert-Disk M-1054.

Sam Hinton. *Singing Across the Land.* Decca DL — 8108.

Jack Eliot. *Ramblin' Cowboy.* Monitor MF-397.

George Gillespie. *Cowcamp Songs of the Old West.* Thorne TH-200.

Rex Allen. *Mr. Cowboy.* Elanco Cattle Products Record, Privately pressed. Phoenix, Arizona.

Singin' Sam Agins. *Saddlebag of Songs.* Haywire ARA6419.

Powder River Jack Lee. Singles, Victor 23527.

———— with Kitty — Montgomery Ward -4462.

Gail Gardner. *Cowboy Songs*. The Arizona Friends of Folklore at Northern Arizona University. AFF 33-1. Released 1971.

Katie Lee. *Ten Thousand Goddam Cattle*. KD-10076.

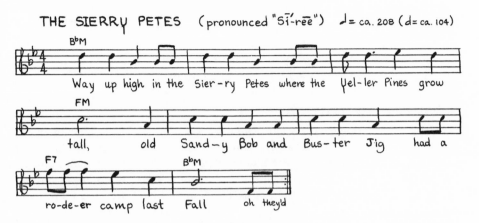

THE SIERRY PETES (pronounced "Sī-rēē") ♩= ca. 208 (♩= ca. 104)

Way up high in the Sier-ry Petes where the Yel-ler Pines grow tall, old Sand-y Bob and Bus-ter Jig had a ro-de-er camp last Fall oh they'd

THE SOUTH COAST* (5)   pp. 111–14

Lillian (Shanagolden) Bos-Ross. A poem originally titled *The Coast Ballad* and copyrighted as a song by Lillian and Sam Eskin in 1941. She was the author of several novels about Big Sur. One, *The Stranger*, is now the movie *Zandy's Wife*, starring Liv Uhlman and Gene Hackman. The song has been recorded, but never in its entirety, or with the reverence due it's classic style. In the fifties the Kingston Trio butchered it, The Easy Riders, who knew better, and sang it beautifully on stage, hacked it to pieces on record. Record companies then liked things to stay in rhythm and be done in two and a half minutes. Well now, you do not sing *The South Coast* like the hounds was snappin' at yer ass — not if you want to tell the story. I've Rich Dehr to thank for bringing it down to all of us in Hollywood in the late forties, because it fired my curiosity to know more, sending me on the ultimate search that turned up much more than the song itself. The Easy Riders and Kingston Trio versions were published by Montclair Music Co., Hollywood, Calif.

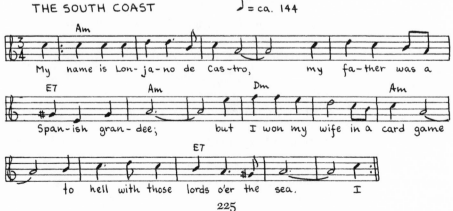

THE SOUTH COAST   ♩= ca. 144

My name is Lon-ja-no de Cas-tro, my fa-ther was a Span-ish gran-dee; but I won my wife in a card game to hell with those lords o'er the sea. I

225

Recordings:

The Kingston Trio. *The Kingston Trio.* Capitol T-996.

Terry Gilkyson and The Easy Riders. *Marianne and Other Songs.* Columbia Records. Number missing.

Herta Marshall. *American Folk Songs for Women.* Folkways FA-2333.

Singin' Sam Agins. *Singin' Sam and Friends.* Haywire Record Co., Box 3057, West Sedona, Ariz. 86340. (Given to him by me about fifteen years ago. He neither credits the author or says where he got it.)

Katie Lee. *Ten Thousand Goddam Cattle.* KD-10076.

SPANISH IS THE LOVIN' TONGUE * (3)   pp. 69–70

Written as a poem *A Border Affair* by Charles Badger Clark in about 1914–15. But in nearly all cases the song took the name of the first line as it passed among the cowboys. Billy always called it *A Border Affair* because he first saw it in print and knew where it came from. There is no credit on any recording to Billy Simon for the music, but I should have listened more carefully to the first primitive recording I heard by "Texas" Jim Robertson — he sang it as Billy sings it. That recording placed back to back with one of Richard Dyer-Bennett's esthetic renditions shows quite a range of possibilities. Billy told me he once had a lady staying at the dude ranch take the melody down for him and play it on the piano, "but," he says, "I dunno what she did with it." The lady was Dorothy Youmans, sister of Vincent Youmans. A letter from John I. White sheds light on some rustlers: "I have two copies of *Bob Miller's Famous Folio Full of Original Cowboy Songs,* both carrying 1934 copyrights. One has words and music of *The Border Affair* about as Clark wrote them, but credited to Bob Miller. The other book is exactly the same in appearance but has the words in a bastardized form credited to Bob Miller and Vasca Suede. In both instances there is a line reading: 'From a theme suggested by Margaret West, the Texas Cowgirl.' My deduction is that Miller got the song from a ballad singer, possibly the mysterious Margaret, and took a chance on its being traditional. When someone told him he was guilty of literary piracy, he quick did a rewrite for the other book." One day over at the Horse Camp, Billy gave me a yellow typed sheet of the following:

SEQUEL TO THE BORDER AFFAIR

Many moons have come and gone
Never more to pass our way.
Each dim sunset, each gray dawn
Means another lonely day.

Still there is no other lover
Takes the place of one I've known.
Oft in dreams I'm saying over.
Mi Amor! Mi Corazon!

Dawn awakens in the patio.
Sunbeams kiss the fountain spray.

Cast reflections in my window
Drive those torturing dreams away.

Then I hear a welcome noise
'Tis Juanita, niña mine.
Up so early with her toys.
Laughing gayly — so Divine.

Silent foot steps drawing near,
Niña's madre bending o'er
Whispers words to me so dear
"Buenos Dias, Mi Amor!"

Eyes that speak and lips that linger
Two small arms that hold me tight.
Matters not if she is Mex.
There's no other soul so white.

And God knows how much I love her,
Juana Mia — Mine alone
Sworn by all the Stars above her
Mi Amor — Mi Corazon!

> Poem by Frank Wilburn
> March 13, 1933

Publications:

Clark. *Sun and Saddle Leather*. Original and first printing in 1915. n/m

Thorp. *Songs of the Cowboys*. 1921 ed. Credits Clark. n/m

Lomax, John A. *Songs of the Cattle Trail and Cow Camp*. Credits Clark. n/m

Kolb. *A Treasury of Folk Songs*. No credit to Clark, taken from a singing arrangement of Richard Dyer-Bennett. w/m

Best. *Song Fest*. No credit to Clark, and with Mi Corazon printed as *micoroso!* w/m

Glazer. *New Treasure of Folk Songs*. No credit. w/m

Lynn. *Songs for Swingin' Housemothers*. No credit and with a verse left out. w/m

Fife. *Cowboy and Western Songs*. Credit to Clark and first known credit to Billy Simon for music. w/m

———. "Collector's Choice — Border Affair," in *The American West Magazine*. Vol. VI, March, 1969. w/m

White. "Poet of Yesterday's West — Badger Clark," Article. *Arizona Highways*. Feb. 1969. (He changed line "She was Mex and I was white" to please Ray Carlson, publisher). w/m

———. *Git Along Little Dogies*. w/m

Recordings:

Richard Dyer-Bennett. (Album name missing) Stinson SLP-35 His own label DYB-5000.

George Gillespie. *Cow Camp Songs of the Old West*. Thorne TH-200. (Learned it from Ev Cheetham at Castle Hot Springs.)

Todd Dylan. *Love Songs Old and New*. Judson J-3010.

Milt Okum. *Traditional American Love Songs*. Riverside RLP-12-634.

Dorothy Olsen. *I Know Where I'm Going*. Victor LPM-1606.

Bob Ross. *American Folk Songs for Men*. Folkways FA-2334.

Glen Yarborough. *Here We Go, Baby*. Elektra EKL-135.

Herb Strauss. *Folk Music for People Who Hate Folk Music*. Judson J-3003.

Ian and Sylvia. *Four Strong Winds*. Vanguard VRS-9133.

"Texas" Jim Robertson. 78 rpm single. Victor P-84. Words and music credited to Miller & Suede.

Billy Simon. *Cowboy Songs*. The Arizona Friends of Folklore at Northern Arizona University. AFF 33-2. Released 1971.

Katie Lee. *Ten Thousand Goddam Cattle*. KD-10076.

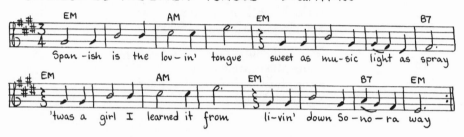

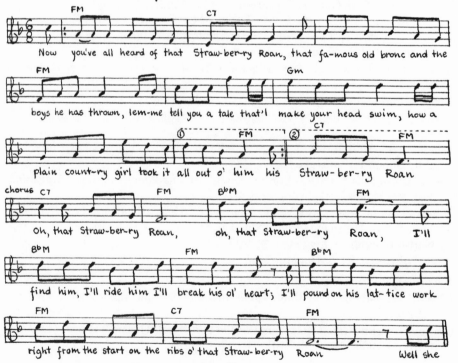

228

THE STRAWBERRY ROAN (New Version of the Old) (4) pp. 72–73

The author has either "deep six'd" or "gone fishin"; — or ten authors will turn up at once and all swear that they wrote it. A letter from Romy Lowdermilk, 3/23/69 states: "By the way, Katie, don't forget that the parody on Strawberry Roan was written (at least I got it from) a man named J. Western Warner, who lives at Goleta, California. So here is another parody on a cowboy song which I am sure had no collusion between the writers as Warner didn't know who wrote the "Roan," although Curley Fletcher was well known around Hollywood. I'm sure Warner wrote 'The Girl on the Strawberry Roan.' I'd give him credit, anyhow." Billy Simon, who got his version from Tex France — "a radio and Western band sort of singer, not a cowboy" — didn't know whether he wrote it or not, and didn't know any more about Tex France. I have asked around Arizona without success, and discovered nothing more about him. I am unaware of either printed or recorded versions.

THE SUBDIVIDED COWBOY (5) pp. 132–33

By James E. Cook, Assistant Editor of *Arizona Magazine*, Sunday supplement of the *Arizona Republic and Gazette*. Jim has been with the paper for thirteen years, was born in Phoenix, but has lived all over the state. His father was with the forest service for a good many years and the family lived in such places as Camp Verde, Happy Jack, yes, even Tucson. In a phone conversation he told me he had never written anything like the Subdivided Blues before, that it "just sort of came to me."

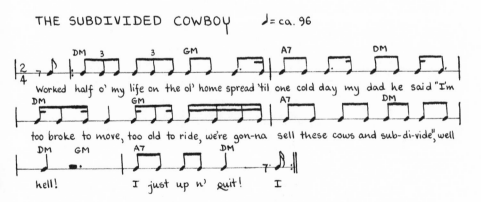

THE SUBDIVIDED COWBOY   ♩ = ca. 96

Worked half o' my life on the ol' home spread 'til one cold day my dad he said "I'm too broke to move, too old to ride, we're gon-na sell these cows and sub-di-vide", well hell! I just up n' quit! I

NOTE: text is rhythmically spoken over chordal accompaniment.

TEN THOUSAND GODDAM CATTLE* (2-5) pp. 123–24

Owen Wister wrote the words to *Ten Thousand Cattle Straying* in 1888 in Wyoming (See Ch. 2. Git Along Little Dogies, J. I. White). He put it to an air from an old French opera, which probably didn't make it sound very cattle-like. Later, in 1904 he composed another melody for it which was published by Witmark and used in the stage version of his famous novel *The Virginian*. That melody is also quite complicated for cowboy-style consumption, and bears no resemblance to the melody or words printed here, nor to what I've heard cow folks sing. This author wonders if Wister might not have heard some Wyoming cowboy make reference to, or sing, the Goddam version, which he could not use? Just as probable is the reverse; some cowboy falling upon Wister's sheet music, decides to tell it after his experience, and with a much less complicated melody. My melody was learned from the singing of Sam Hinton, La Jolla, Calif., 1948, though I had heard Shorty Mac and Buck sing and play different ones. Harland Thompson, a producer at Paramount studios wrote a verse in 1948, and one I have not included anywhere was sung with relish by Shorty Mac ten years before that. While in Hollywood a record company wanted me to do a sanitized version of this great song. I told them to go fry eggs on a spit, and for spite I now include ol' Shorts verse:

> I wisht I had a nickle
> Fer every single mile
> I've chased them fuckers outta the brush
> By Christ I'd have a pile, a pile.
> You bet I'd have a pile.

Publications:

Lomax, John & Alan, *Cowboy Songs*. With two verses only, and music worlds away from that used here.

Recordings:

Katie Lee. *Ten Thousand Goddam Cattle*. KD-10076.

TEN THOUSAND GODDAM CATTLE

James Grafton Rogers. Written in 1912. It has been printed in newspapers, Western pulps, had a movie made of the story, been sung on radio and recorded mostly without permission — when with permission, rarely credited to Jim. The one place where it was used with his consent (and with added verse by George A. H. Fraser) bears no music. Only three recordings have been made with his consent. Mine, Utah Phillips and Oscar Brand. It was used on an LP of many singers, produced by the Exodus Espresso House, Denver, in the late fifties. Someone else in Denver made a 45 single of it, and it was ripped off by Randy Boone of TV's defunct "Cimmaron Strip," who claims he wrote the words and music. Sure, he did! I suspect Randy ain't never been *near* the Town of Old Dolores. Upon request Jim received a record from the company after Ranger, his lawyer son wrote and cited their plagiarism. He wrote to me: "I will follow up this piracy as it is obviously a tune and words heard over the radio and a copy of my work. It is going to be hard to fix responsibility as the whole list of outfits (publishers and recording companies) has a bad reputation for irresponsibility." And later: "I have heard nothing from the stolen Old Dolores. They are, I suppose, relying on time and no copyright but that is not a defense against a misrepresentation and author's common law rights."

Publications:

University Club of Denver. *A Golden Treasury.* n/m

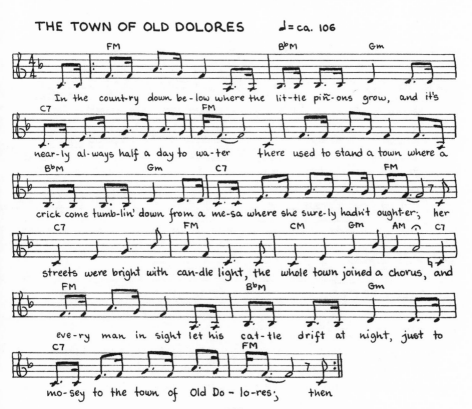

THE TOWN OF OLD DOLORES ♩ = ca. 106

In the coun-try down be-low where the lit-tle piñ-ons grow, and it's near-ly al-ways half a day to wa-ter there used to stand a town where a crick come tumb-lin' down from a me-sa where she sure-ly hadn't ought-er; her streets were bright with can-dle light, the whole town joined a chorus, and eve-ry man in sight let his cat-tle drift at night, just to mo-sey to the town of Old Do - lo-res; then

Utah Phillips Song Book. *Starlight On the Rails,* Wooden Shoe, 1036 Solano
Ave., Sonoma, Calif. 95476.

Recordings:

Oscar Brand. *Oscar Brand Sings for Adults.* ABC Paramount. ABC-388.

Randy Boone. *Randy Boone.* Gre-Gar 22-17-0005.

Utah Phillips. *Utah Phillips.* Philo Records 1016. The Barn, North Ferrisburg,
Vt. 05473.

Katie Lee. *Ten Thousand Goddam Cattle.* KD-10076.

TRAIL HERDING SONG (1) pp. 87–88

. . . has turned up no author among the collectors. In fact it hasn't turned up
many collectors. Vance Randolph has a version, the only one I know of, called
Cowboy Song, and says: "From Mr. Whittier Burnette, 1939. 'Russel Hester,
then a student at Smith A & M College, at Stillwater, Oklahoma, gave it to me
some twelve years ago. His people were large landholders around Vinita, Oklahoma and he got the song from the cowboys there." Bits and pieces were sung
among the Arizona cowboys with nondescript tunes, or tunes as well known
as *Strawberry Roan,* but the one used here is my own, as is the last verse which
I added in the late forties. All I got from the cowboys when I asked about it
was, "it's old — older'n you."

Publications:

Lee, Katie. "Songs the Cowboys Taught Me." *Arizona Highways,* Feb. 1960
(music only).

THE TRUSTY LARIAT* (4) pp. 117–18

By Harry (Haywire Mac) McClintock. Alan Lomax in *Folk Songs of North
America* has a very good piece on Mac's background and how he came to write
these songs, though this particular song is not printed there. It is a product of

the cowboy-on-radio days and has seldom appeared in collected works of Western folk songs.

Publications:

Harry McClintock and Sterling Sherwin. *Mac's Songs of the Road and Range.* (folio) Copyright 1932, Southern Music Pub. Co. w/m

Recordings:

Harry (Haywire Mac) McClintock. *The Trusty Lariat.* Victor 78 rpm. V-40234.
Katie Lee. *Ten Thousand Goddam Cattle.* KD-10076.

THE TRUSTY LARIAT

Thru the high Si-er-ra moun-tains came an Es——pee pass-en-ger train; the ho-boes tried to ride her but found it all in vain; the con-duc-tor took the tick-ets and count-ed ev-e-ry soul, the en-gin—eer looked straight a-head and the fire-man shov-elled coal; the fire-man was a cow-boy, but do not think it strange he could make more mo-ney shov'ling coal than rid-in' on the range but tho he was a fire-man and tho he had to sweat he still re-mained a west-ern guy, and kept his lar-i-at. The

233

WALKIN' JOHN (3) pp. 90–92

Poem by Henry Herbert Knibbs, put to music in the early thirties by Who Knows. The melody that appears here is my own. The traditional tune is simpler than mine and does not vary after the first two lines, which makes monotonous singing and listening unless you're hunkered down by a campfire with a bunch of cowboys. Margaret Larkin in *Singing Cowboy* traced the melody to Arizona and Everett Cheetham at Castle Hot Springs — perhaps he wrote the tune. Billy Simon did not. Nor did Peter LaFarge who claims words and music. Knibbs claimed it was the biography of a real horse, which is not hard to believe. I got pitched off of Billy Simon's mare right smart a while back, it having been some years since I was on a cutting horse, and she knew it.

Publications:

Larkin. *Singing Cowboy.* w/m

Knibbs. *Songs of the Lost Frontier.* Used by permission Houghton Mifflin Co. n/m

Lee. *Cowboy Song Book.* 1938. Actually credits Knibbs!! w/m

Ohrlin. *Hell Bound Train.* No credit. w/m

Recordings:

Peter LaFarge. *Peter LaFarge Sings of the Cowboys.* Folkways FN-2533. (Words and music by Peter — Unicorn Music Pub., New York).

George Gillespie. *Cow Camp Songs of the Old West.* Thorne TH-200. George traded some of his songs for it to a fellow who came down from Montana, but he had no idea of its origin.

Glenn Ohrlin. *Hell Bound Train.* Puritan Records. 5009. P.O. Box 946, Evanston, Ill. 60204.

WARING OF SONORA TOWN* (3)

pp. 89–90

Poem by Henry Herbert Knibbs. Music by Katie Lee. I suppose this poem took my fancy because I lived close to the state of Sonora, Mexico for many years and have seen much of the country. I'm not familiar with a Sonora-*town,* however, nor was Shorty Mac. (Dr. Leland Sonnichsen says there's a Sonora, Texas — maybe that's it). I've not seen it in print other than in the author's book, and I doubt if it ever got sung outside our circle of friends. I still use it in concert now and then.

Publications:
Knibbs. *Songs of the Trail.* n/m

Recordings:
Katie Lee. *Ten Thousand Goddam Cattle.* KD-10076.

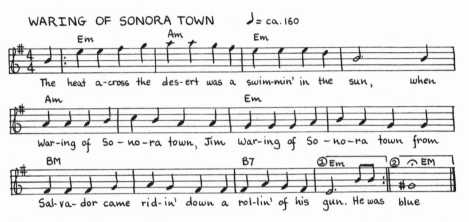

THE WESTERN PLAINS* (4)

pp. 6–7

Called *The Texas Plains* if you're from Texas. In one place that I know about, Stuart Hamblen is credited with authorship, but knowing how these "radio-cowboys" willy-nilly slapped their brand on things, I can't vouch for the authenticity of what I read. I used to hear Patsy Prescott twanging it out of a Phoenix radio station in the thirties — some say *she* wrote it. In Ray M. Lawless's *Folk Singers and Folk Songs in America,* there's a notation of Leadbelly singing "Out On the Western Plains" which is very likely the same song, though I have not heard the album. It is the sort of song that would be appealing to a man who'd spent time behind bars — the steel kind. It boasts the "radio yodel" and reeks of what listening audiences wanted to hear about cowboys in the thirties. The song is used here by special permission of ABC Music. "The Western Plains," a/k/a, "The Texas Plains" by Stuart Hamblen, © 1933, renewed © 1961 by ABC/Dunhill Music, Inc. Used by permission only. All rights reserved.

Publications:
Hamblen. *Stuart Hamblen and His Lucky Stars.* Folio. w/m

Recordings:
Leadbelly. *Memorial Album Vol. 2.* Stinson. SLP 19.
Katie Lee. *Ten Thousand Goddam Cattle.* KD-10076.

THE WESTERN PLAINS ♩=ca.144

Each night in my dreams, some-how it seems that I'm back where I was born, I'm just a count-ry hick from the count-ry sticks, and that's where I be-long; now all your ci-ty life and all your ci-ty ways are dri-vin' me in-sane, I wan-na be a-lone where I feel at home, back on the west-ern plains o-lee-o lay-dee-o-dle lee-o lay-dee-o-dle lee-dle lay-dee-o-dl-lee-odle lay dee dee dee dee

Chapter Notes

Reference   CHAPTER 1

1. *Old Dolores* — Most of the history of this song is revealed throughout the text, so keep reading. What is not revealed in the text can be found in the song compendium.

2. Charles Badger Clark, "On the Oregon Trail," *Sun and Saddle Leather,* p. 156. My quotations from Badger Clark are keyed to the 1962 edition.

3. *Ibid.,* "The Buffalo Trail," p. 176.

4. S. Omar Barker, "Old West Welcome," *Rawhide Rhymes,* p. 60.

5. Henry Herbert Knibbs, "Hash," *Songs of the Outlands,* p. 36.

6. Arthur Chapman, "Ridin' the Chuck-Line," *Out Where the West Begins,* p. 54.

7. E. A. Brininstool, "Rainy Day In A Cow Camp," *Trail Dust Of A Maverick,* p. 66.

8. Elliot C. Lincoln, "Little Roads," *The Ranch,* p. 75.

9. Larry Chittenden, "The Old Texan In New York," *Ranch Verses,* p. 56.

10. John A. Lomax, "Young Champions," in *Cowboy Songs,* p. 81.

11. Larry Chittenden, "A Barefoot Boy," *Ranch Verses,* p. 80.

12. *Ibid.,* "A King's Daughter," p. 50.

13. *A Cowboy's Prayer* — See song compendium.

14. William Doerflinger, "The Ocean Burial," in *Shantymen & Shantyboys,* p. 162.

15. Frank V. Dearing, Editor, "The Hired Man On Horseback," in *Best Novels and Stories of Eugene Manlove Rhodes,* p. 549.

CHAPTER 2

16. Charles Badger Clark, "Plains Born," *Sun and Saddle Leather,* p. 183.

17. Eugene Manlove Rhodes's "Bradford of Rainbow Range," in *Best Novels and Stories of Eugene Manlove Rhodes,* p. 127, says "A certain soulless corporation placed in each package of tobacco a coupon, each coupon redeemable by one paper-bound book . . ."

18. Henry Herbert Knibbs, "The Grand Old Privilege," *Songs of the Outlands,* p. 49.

19. Charles Badger Clark, "From Town," *Sun and Saddle Leather,* p. 47.

20. Charles Badger Clark, "Latigo Town," *Sun and Saddle Leather,* p. 174.

21. Charles Badger Clark, "The Old Cowman," *Sun and Saddle Leather,* p. 92.

22. *Ibid.,* "From Town," p. 47.

23. *Ibid.,* "The Plainsmen," p. 95.

24. S. Omar Barker, "Pinto," *Buckaroo Ballads,* p. 14.

25. Charles Badger Clark, "God's Reserves," *Sun and Saddle Leather,* p. 86.

CHAPTER 3

26. James Grafton Rogers, letter to KL, May 31, 1956.

27. S. Omar Barker, "Thirsty Cowboys," *Rawhide Rhymes,* p. 8.

28. *Ibid.,* "A Cowboy's Christmas Prayer," *Songs of the Saddlemen,* p. 32.

29. Henry Herbert Knibbs, "Mesa Magic," *Riders of the Stars,* p. 16.

CHAPTER 4

30. Charles Badger Clark, "The Border," *Sun and Saddle Leather,* p. 148.

31. Paul I. Wellman, *The Trampling Herd,* pp. 14–17.

32. *Ibid.*

33. Charles Badger Clark, "The Border," *Sun and Saddle Leather,* p. 148.

34. *Ibid.,* p. 148.

35. *Ibid.,* p. 148.

36. Information on rawhide instruments, Mrs. E. Boyd, Folk Art Museum, Santa Fe, N.M.

37. Américo Paredes, "The Corrido on the Border," in *With His Pistol In His Hand.*

38. Charles Badger Clark, "The Border," *Sun and Saddle Leather,* p. 148.

39. Elliott Arnold, From the author's Foreword Note in *The Time of the Gringo:* "Gringo (green-go): (coll) Unintelligible, gibberish: applied to a language. (vulg.) A nickname given to one who speaks a foreign language.

VELAZQUEZ: A New Pronouncing Dictionary of the Spanish and English Languages. . . . A naive but persistent legend has the word 'gringo' originating from the popularity of the song, based on Burns's poem "Green Grow the Rushes, Oh!" which American cowboys in Texas and American soldiers of that time are supposed never to have stopped singing as they went about their business. . . . Dr. Frank H. Vizetelly, however, has traced 'gringo' as far back at least as 1787, to P. Esteban de Terreros y Pando's *Diccionario Castellano,* published in Madrid, where 'gringo' is defined as 'The name given in Malaga to those foreigners who have a certain accent which prevents them from speaking Spanish fluently and naturally; and in Madrid the same term is used for the same reason, especially with reference to the Irish.' . . ."

40. Américo Paredes, *With His Pistol in His Hand,* p. 244.

41. Charles Badger Clark, "The Border," *Sun and Saddle Leather,* p. 148.

42. Oscar Osborn Winther, *Via Western Express & Stagecoach,* pp. 86–91.

43. *Ibid.*

44. Charles Badger Clark, "The Border," *Sun and Saddle Leather,* p. 148.

45. *The Last Wagon* — first of a series of half-hour television documentaries for educational TV — was filmed in Prescott, Arizona, March, 1970 and won the 1972 Council on International Nontheatrical Events (CINE) Golden Eagle Award "for excellence to represent the United States of America in international motion picture events abroad." Harry Atwood of the University of Arizona Film Department was editor and cinematographer. It was written, directed, and narrated by Katie Lee. More are in the making.

46. Arthur Chapman, "In A Deserted Mining Camp," *Out Where The West Begins,* p. 53.

CHAPTER 5

47. Gail Gardner, letter to KL, May 10, 1960.

48. Gail I. Gardner, *The Magic Jug.* Poem. Gail Gardner, letter to Billy Simon, October 7, 1942. ". . . Sometime ago Jerome Eddy sent me a *Gallon Jug* of Scotch, I appreciated this unusual gift so much that I wrote him a poem about it — it isn't intended for a song, but I thought you might find it amusing so am enclosing a copy."

49. S. Omar Barker, "Buckaroo's Brew," *Rawhide Rhymes,* p. 19.

50. See song compendium under *Sierry Petes* for discography.

51. Gail I. Gardner, "For Cowboy's Only," *Orejana Bull.*

52. See song compendium under *Sierry Petes.*

53. George Phippen, well known painter and sculptor of Western scenes, made his home in Prescott, Arizona. Gail's birthday is Christmas Day, and for that event in 1959, his daughter Cynthia commissioned George to paint this scene of "Papa's" famous song. It appeared on the cover of *Western Horseman Magazine,* January, 1961. The poem appeared on page 36 of that issue with more illustrations and a picture of Phippen with Gardner on the Desert Caballero ride. On the mantle in the Gardner's living room is a bronze of the Devil, also by George Phippen — "an even trade to save bookkeepin'," says Gail, "so George and Louise [Mrs. Phippen] could reprint the poem with illustrations on placemats — that ol' devil is my royalty payment." George Phippen died April 13, 1966. Louise Phippen still lives in Prescott.

54. See song compendium under *Sierry Petes.*

55. *Powder River Jack Lee Song Book,* Southern Music Co., 1931, prints Gail's song with words and music by Powder River Jack and Kitty, true enough, but not Curley's "Roan." In a 1938 songbook he credits Frank Chamberlin with "Strawberry Roan," so Gail was mistaken here, about his claiming it then and there.

56. Carmen W. Fletcher, *Songs of the Sage.* Twenty-two of Curley's songs and poems. No music. There is an excellent article by John I. White regarding Curley's trials and tribulation over *The Strawberry Roan,* appearing in *Arizona and the West,* vol. 11, no. 4, Winter, 1969. University of Arizona Press, Tucson.

57. Alan Lomax, *The Folk Songs of North America,* pp. 365, 388.

58. Alan Lomax, letter to K.L., January 25, 1961.

59. *The Writings of Ralph Waldo Emerson,* Essay on "History," The Modern Library, p. 123.

60. Gail Gardner, letter to Alan Lomax, February 6, 1961.

61. Alan Lomax, letter to Gail Gardner, Feb. 22, 1961. The new paperback edition of *Folk Songs of North America* came out in 1975. Alan did *not* change the notes or credit Gail, as promised.

62. Henry Herbert Knibbs, "The Edge of Town," *Songs of the Trail,* p. 71.

CHAPTER 6

63. *Museum of New Mexico Library,* Santa Fe, supplied me with a folder of the Governor's Letters, written in Spanish longhand, June 28, 1827, noting a claim by Santiago Narbrase, Juan José Ruis, José Nicamor Ydalgo. Dr. Jenkins of the Records Center supplied further information on these claims.

64. S. Omar Barker, "Cuttin' Horse," *Songs of the Saddlemen,* p. 111.

65. *Ibid.*, "Big Windies," *Songs of the Saddlemen*, p. 90.

66. Castle Hot Springs was a big dude ranch in the mid-twenties. It was, and still is located out of Wickenburg to the east, some 30 miles by road. Many of the Arizona cowboys spent several seasons there "herdin' dudes," "playing mockingbird to the dudes," and more than one happy puncher walked away with a rich wife from the east — often one that had' belonged to someone else. After the first few successful seasons it became known as the "Marriage Corral." It also housed an occasional fast buck artist, but mostly it was a high class place for the EV's (eastern visitors) to live out their fantasy of the Wild and Woolly West. Today it is called a resort.

67. John A. Lomax, "High Chin Bob," *Songs of the Cattle Trail and Cow Camp*, p. 33. Printed from the cowboy's oral rendition, crediting Charles Badger Clark with the original.

CHAPTER 7

68. Henry Herbert Knibbs, "The Hills," *Songs of the Outlands*, p. 25.

69. James G. Rogers to KL, June 2, 1960.

70. KL, letter to Bill Mekeel, June 6, 1960.

71. Emma Medearis, letter to KL, June 26, 1960.

72. Bill Mekeel, letter to KL, June 13, 1960.

73. Emma Medearis, letter to KL, June 26, 1960.

74. Henry Herbert Knibbs, "The Outland Trails," *Songs of the Outlands*, p. 9.

75. The name used here is fictitious, though the person is very real; also his 'place' is very real, but not at the location described. The events and conversations are true — in other words, Buck exists, but he does not want people to know where.

76. Charles Badger Clark, "Bachin'," *Sun and Saddle Leather*, p. 75.

77. *Ibid.*

78. Lester Parks, letter to KL, July 12, 1960.

79. Charles Badger Clark, "Bachin'," *Sun and Saddle Leather*, p. 75.

CHAPTER 9

80. Henry Herbert Knibbs, "Braves of the Hunt," *Riders of the Stars*, p. 71.

81. The Blue Angel and Julius Monk's Downstairs At The Upstairs, as well as Upstairs at the Downstairs, were very popular supper clubs in New York during the '50's. Julius later moved to Plaza 9 — The Blue Angel closed some time during the mid-sixties, I believe.

82. Jerome Lawrence and Robert Lee — Writers of the musical *Mame*, *Look Ma, I'm Dancing, Shangri-La, Dear World*. Winners of Peabody Award for best radio program, U.N. Series; Outer Circle Award, and British Drama Critics Award. Writers of the plays: *Inherit the Wind, Auntie Mame, The Gang's All Here, Only In America*.

83. Woody Guthrie, letter to KL.

84. *Trailing the Cowboy*, Clifford P. Westermeier, The Caxton Printers, Ltd., Caldwell, Idaho, 1955. Many of the large western ranches were then controlled by English Lords who sent their relations across the sea to work these holdings. These chaps kept to their odd English speech and manners, and were resented by the cowboys. There are numerous snide remarks about them in the poetry and prose of the west — especially the monocle.

85. More Texas tampering which reads:

> Was that thunder? I grasped the cord
> Of my swift mustang without a word.
> I sprang to the saddle, and she clung behind —

86. Walter E. Thing, *Best Loved Story Poems*. London.

87. *Arizona Highways*, "Gunslingers of the Old West," Lea Franklin McCarty, vol. 34, no. 11, Nov., 1958, pp. 6–11.

88. *The Columbia Records Legacy Collection*, Produced by Goddard Lieberson, Notes on the songs by B. A. Botkin.

89. *Arizona Highways*, "Gunslingers of the Old West," Lea Franklin McCarty, vol. 6, no. 11, Nov., 1958, pp. 6–11.

90. The *Johnny Ringo* version (mine) turned up in the *Columbia Records Legacy Collection* album *The Badmen* sung by Carolyn Hester. They were notified of their error, and apologized. But did they pay royalties? No.

91. Henry Herbert Knibbs, "The Hills," *Song of the Outlands*, p. 25.

92. Henry Herbert Knibbs, "I Have Builded Me A Home," *Songs of the Trail*, p. 4.

CHAPTER 10

93. Lillian Bos-Ross was the author of two novels that use Big Sur as their background. *The Stranger* and its sequel, *Blaze Allen*, published by William Morrow, New York, in

1942 and 1944, respectively. Recently the *Stranger* was made into the movie, *Zandy's Wife*.

94. Sam Eskin — An itinerant folksinger born in Washington, D.C. in 1898. Though he didn't set out to be a collector, songs seemed to stick to him; he roamed the whole world singing. He was not one to publish his work except by his singing and records, but he was a scholar about giving credit where it was due. He made an album of sea songs for Folkways Records. Harrydick Ross told me that Sam died sometime in 1974.

95. Slim Critchlow, letter to KL, January, 1965.

96. *Ibid.*, February, 1965.

97. Barry Olivier, of Berkeley, books singers for festivals, universities, etc. He and Slim have been friends for a number of years. He *is* "Arhoolie Records," I believe.

98. Critchlow, letter to KL, July, 1969.

99. Arthur Chapman, "Men in the Rough," *Out Where The West Begins*, p. 92.

100. *Little Joe, The Wrangler* appeared in *one* of the first, if not *the* first collection of cowboy songs to ever see print, *Songs of the Cowboys*, by N. Howard ("Jack") Thorp, 1908. Of Little Joe, he says: "Written by me on trail of herd of O Cattle from Chimney Lake, New Mexico, to Higgins, Texas, 1898. On trail were the following men, all from Sacramento Mountains, or Crow Flat: Pap Logan, Bill Blevens, Will Brownfield, Will Fenton, Lijo Colfelt, Tom News, Frank Jones, and myself."

101. Charles Badger Clark, "The Old Cowman," *Sun and Saddle Leather*, p. 94.

CHAPTER 11

102. Curley W. Fletcher, "Meditation," *Songs of the Sage*, p. 72.

103. Al Schauffler, from Portland, Oregon, his wife, Flea, born in Cleveland, raised in Boston, came from a three year stint at ranching in Oregon, to settle in Cottonwood and hang his Veterinarian shingle some time in the late 50's. Almost immediately they became friends of the Perkins family. Al was already a folk singer of no mean accomplishment, but he was mainly schooled in the Child Ballads tradition by his mother who was a student of Cecil Sharp. Ben taught him western songs, he taught Ben Appalachian songs, and between them they wrote a raunchy ditty or two. Al sings German Lieder and has a high, clear voice something like John Jacob Niles.

104. Charles Badger Clark, "Plains Born," *Sun and Saddle Leather*, p. 183.

105. *Western Words*, Ramon Adams, p. 15.

106. S. Omar Barker, "Boot Galoot," *Rawhide Rhymes*, p. 31.

107. There are people (damn few) who are going to recognize the teller of this story. Being a "city father" type he didn't want his image altered, so I placed it in the untaintable mouth of Shorty Mac . . . who probably knew it anyway.

108. Charles Badger Clark, "The Old Cow Man," *Sun and Saddle Leather*, p. 92.

CHAPTER 12

109. N. Howard Thorp, "The Cowboy's Lament," *Songs of the Cowboys*, p. 41.

110. Arthur Chapman, "The Dude Ranch," *Out Where the West Begins*, p. 24.

111. *Ibid.*

CHAPTER 13

112. *Great Grandad*, Music by Romaine Lowdermilk. In a song folio, "The Lonesome Cowboy Songs of the Plains and Hills," compiled by John White and George Shackley, and copyrighted by Al Piantadosi Music Pub., 1929, with no credit to either poet or musician. The compilers say in a foreword that the authors of these selections are unknown. It appears again, with exactly the same notes, in Jules Verne Allen's *Cowboy Lore*, a book first copyrighted in 1933 by The Naylor Company, San Antonio, Texas. Allen says the authors are unknown to him also. (Piantadosi's address is given by Romy Lowdermilk as 1650 Broadway, New York.)

113. Henry Herbert Knibbs, "Punchin' the Dough," *Saddle Songs*. The melody Romy used was *Sweet Betsey From Pike*. The poem, sans music, appears in N. Howard Thorp's *Songs of the Cowboys*, p. 131, wherein he gives Knibbs credit. Jules Verne Allen in *Cowboy Lore* 1943 edition, states that he has gotten permission from the author to write music to same and that "all rights are reserved." Austin and Alta Fife in *Cowboy and Western Songs* only mention Knibbs.

114. Brininstool, *Trail Dust of a Maverick*. I do not know where these appeared as songs or who published them, with the exception of *His Trademarks*, which appears in John I. White's *Lonesome Cowboy Songs* folio.

115. *The Rodeo Parade*, w & m by Romy Lowdermilk in *Stuart Hamblen and his Lucky Stars* folio, p. 90.

116. *The Big Corral,* w & m by Romy Lowdermilk, was first published in *Lonesome Cowboy Songs,* sung and arranged by John I. White, Al Piantadosi Publishing Co., New York, 1929.

117. "Cowboy Goes To Town," w & m by Lowdermilk, appears in the *Patsy Montana Deluxe Edition of Famous Original Cowboy Songs and Mountain Ballads.* (See why we're getting the hills and the mountains confused already?) It's on page 84 and Patsy has put *her* name along with Romey's as co-author, and called it "Mr. Cowboy Goes to Town."

118. For many years John I. White and I have been in close correspondence, exchanging and hunting down information for each other. I say here and now, he's done more for me than I for him. He has also completed work on a book published by the University of Illinois Press in 1975, *Git Along Little Dogies.* His own song book is mentioned in footnotes 112 and 116, and though he did not confess it there, he is the author of a sequel to the "Great Grandad" song which he called "Great Grandma" — one that got loose from him and fell into oral tradition before he claimed it. "I probably thought it wasn't very good," he said, "but several unwary collectors have labeled it a song of the California goldrush." John was born and raised in Washington, D.C. His brother Lewis had a ranch near Wickenburg and in 1924 John went out there to spend the summer and was bitten by the cowboy song. He sang in New York on radio as The Lonesome Cowboy, and on the early Death Valley Days program, mid-20's. He has written articles for many publications about Western songs, trying to restore authors to their works, hunting down the obscurities he encountered during his days as a professional radio singer.

119. *José Cuervo's Daughter* is the same song Billy Simon and Shorty Mac sang as *José Cuervo,* p. 74.

120. Romy Lowdermilk letter to KL, March, 1969. Anyone familiar with J. R. Williams's wonderful cartoons, syndicated all over the country, can easily see how he and Romy would get their heads together over this "balloon" (the words hanging over the heads of the speakers). He drew the famous *Out Our Way* — *Heroes are made, Not born, Why Mothers Get Gray,* and especially for Gail Gardner, the cover of his little song book, *Orejana Bull.*

121. Excerpt from Curley Fletcher's "The Ridge-Running Roan," *Songs of the Sage,* p. 47.

122. George Champie and his sister Gertrude Champie Walker were guides at Castle before they started a dude ranch of their own nearby. Many people went over to see them from the Springs because they were such a colorful family. The others on that list were Homer Ward, Johnny Green, Omer Maxwell, Jimmie Norman, Yellowstone Chip, George Gillespie, George German, Bill Wheeldon, Jimmie Cameron, Everett Cheetham.

123. S. Omar Barker, "Cow Country Clue," *Songs of the Saddlemen,* p. 16.

124. Peter Thorpe, "I'm Movin' On: The Escape Theme in Country and Western Music," *The Western Humanities Review* of Utah, Autumn, 1970, p. 312. Thorpe is associate professor of English at the University of Colorado, Denver Center.

125. *Ibid.,* p. 313.

126. *Ibid.,* p. 316.

127. Larry McMurtry is the author of *Hud, The Last Picture Show, Moving On,* and *In a Narrow Grave — Essays of Texas.*

128. Travis Edmonson, an old friend and fellow singer, was born in Nogales, Arizona, in 1932. I consider him the best story-telling folk singer on the scene or off it; his talent borders on genius so of course he is crazy, in the kind of way I would like to be crazy, able to write the kind of songs he writes. On stage, the only man who has catalytic powers equal to his is Pete Seeger, and Pete ain't as purty. Travis comes from an old Arizona family whose roots are deep in the state. His "bigtime" years and mine correspond somewhat, but he was much better known in the folk field having sung as a member of The Gateway Singers, Limelighters, Kingston Trio and finally as the heavy side of Bud and Travis. He writes musicals, pageants, symphonies, and when he has a mind to, he tells lies, drinks, and cusses his audiences when they don't listen to him. He has worked for five digits a week, and two, but he ain't for sale if he don't like the job.

129. James G. Rogers, letter to KL, August, 1960.

CHAPTER 14

130. Honesty compels me to point out that the same "city father" of note 107 told me this classic story also. Obviously he's bi-lingual because many folks swear (to play on a word) that he'd never use such down to earth lingo. Let me say that he won't tell the story if he *can't* use the lingo — it would ruin it.

131. Natalie Gignoux, then owner of the Little Percent Taxi and Jeep Tours of Aspen,

Colorado. We have now forgotten who contributed what, but I credit most of the tasty lines to her.

132. The Alfred Packer material was taken and condensed from *Alfred Packer — The True Story of the Man Eater,* by Robert W. Fenwick. After the infamous Nixon pardon, I sent Red a bumper sticker I made — "Pardon Alfred Packer." Someone else who had gotten one wrote to Red questioning him about the spelling of "Alfred," to which he replied: "About poor Alfred or Alferd — take your pick — I stick with Alfred as proper although Packer very likely called himself Alferd. So far as I ever learned, the name used by the army and elsewhere in his prison record, was Alfred Packer. Packer talked in a high nasal voice. I have that on the authority of the old Wyoming sheriff who arrested him at Fort Fetterman."

133. *Ibid.,* p. 40.

134. Charles Badger Clark, "The Passing of the Trail," *Sun and Saddle Leather,* p. 171.

135. Arthur Chapman, "Man in the Rough," *Out Where the West Begins,* p. 92.

CHAPTER 15

136. Ruth Laughlin, *The Wind Leaves No Shadow.* Publisher and date missing.

137. Arthur Chapman, "In A Deserted Mining Camp," *Out Where the West Begins,* p. 53.

138. Sharlot M. Hall, "The Old Cow Men's Parade," *Poems of a Ranch Woman,* p. 48.

Glossary

Adiós — goodby

Backed up to a free air hose — being pregnant

Bellywash — rot gut, refers to whiskey most of the time

Big Windies — tall stories and true ones — told long and often

Borracho — drunk

Bovines — gentle, fenced, non-pugnacious cattle

Broomtails — range horse with a long bushy tail

Brushed-up — hiding in the brush

Calf out — for a cow to give birth, unless the cowboy's being funny

Caliente — warm, hot

Cavviada — or cabbiada, like remuda, but used more in the northwest than south. Horses not under saddle but exchange horses kept in a cavvy until the cowboy needed a fresh mount.

Cholla — the most vicious of all southwestern cacti. Each spine has a transparent wax-like sheath that when broken at the point, parts and allows the spine to penetrate; then like something alive, work its way into the flesh as if it loved you better than anything and wanted to stay there forever.

Chuck line — going from ranch to ranch for a free meal in winter (when most cowboys were unemployed) was riding the chuck line. This was standard practice in the old days.

Come off the rimrock — to leave touchy ground in conversation and let the talk be smooth and friendly

Dissolved with her — divorced her

Drag — to ride drag is to ride back at the end of the line behind the slowest cattle. It applies to a person who is a drag; the term originally came from the cattle industry.

Face-lickin' — a happy time, a reunion, being extra friendly

Fiddle-footed — a prancing, lively horse

Flank — to ride flank on cattle herd is to ride on the sides behind point and swing riders and in front of the drag riders

Fogging — making dust or traveling fast

Forging — Some horses, badly trained, or sloppy for other reasons will strike their back hoofs against the front ones while trotting. When said horses are shod, it sounds like the ring of iron on a forge.

Gone to Texas — gone to hell in a hand basket

Greasy sack outfit — a little operation, usually run by one man and a couple of cowboys to help at roundup

Hard-and-fast — As opposed to taking dallies, the hard-tie is a rope fixed to

243

the saddle horn with a knot, not meant to come loose, though in some instances, the saddle will. In extreme cases, *horse* and saddle.

Heeler — the fellow who ropes the cows heels by throwing the rope from his horse in a loop that catches them as they rise off the ground. The other cowboy loops the neck — they stretch the critter out then and brand him. At rodeos this is done in teams for the quickest time.

Hombre — man

Hurricane deck — the saddle of a bucking horse

Jacal — mud hut or house

Kak — slang name for saddle, sometimes spelled kack

Kidney plaster — name for an Eastern saddle with no horn, and according to the cowboys, no place to sit

Kidney pack — to put your gear, such as bedroll, slicker and whatever you're not carrying in the saddlebags, on back of the saddle over the horse's kidneys; best not to have it too heavy

Lass - lasse — to lasso

Last roundup'd — died

Leaky mouthed — a talker, one you don't tell anything to

Light a shuck — to take off, get out quick. Ramon Adams in his book, *Western Words,* describes the origin: "In the early days, corn was carried as the principal food for man and beast. It was carried unshucked in the wagon beds. Selected shucks were placed at convenient places by all fires. On leaving a fire he found the surroundings pitch black. To penetrate this blackness and give his eyes a chance to accustom themselves to it, he'd light a shuck in the fire and raise it high over his head to see."

Lizard-tailed outlaws — mean and scrawny and quick to get away

Makins — hand-rolled cigarettes, the makins being paper and loose tobacco

Malpaís — Really, mal país, meaning bad country. The worst. In the Southwest that means the old lava beds.

McClellan — a saddle named after and invented by Colonel George Brinton McClellan 1826–1885, a Union general in the Civil War.

Muley cows — ornery, mean and sullen

No breakfast forever list — refers to being dead

Open your gate — wise you up

Orejana — an unbranded calf old enough to quit its mother, weaned. Could also be a dogie, a calf with no ma and no pa and no brand of his own to distinguish him.

Packing two irons — in this case, not carrying two guns, but having two brands

Peeling broncs — riding rough horses, to tame bucking horses

Point — those who ride at the head of a string of cattle acting as leaders; point riders or riding point

Prod — on the prod, or off the prod; used to mean getting mad or cooling off

Punching the spots off each other — fighting

Querencia — homing place. There was an old Texas steer during the cattle driving days who'd lead the herd clear to the Canadian border, then they'd cut him loose and in three or four months he'd be back in Texas at the old ranch, his *querencia*.

Quien sabe? — who knows?

Reata — from the Spanish word, *reatar*, to retie. It is sometimes spelled riata, after the French *lariet*. It is made of braided rawhide, called a gut line.

Red-rumped — mad, sore

Remuda — A string of fresh horses kept by the wrangler to exchange for the cowboy's worn out, tired mount . . . first on trail rides, then later, at roundup time.

Round-rumped — fat and healthy

Sangre de Cristo — Blood of Christ

Saguaro — tallest of the Sonoran desert cactus, sometimes rising over forty feet. Related to the cordon of Mexico and Baja which has more arms and is taller yet.

Seago — a grass or hemp woven rope, known to Arizona cowboys as a yacht line

She stuff — women, girls, fillies

Soogans — belongings, bedroll and duffle

Slick eared — cattle with no ear marks or identifying brands

Swallow-fork — a mark of identification. A V-cut in the tip of a cow's ear resembling a swallow's tail.

Swing — the riders on the side in front of the flank riders, in back of the point riders

Tonsil varnish — booze, whiskey

Topscrew — foreman, owner

Tornado Juice — whiskey, booze

Vigas — the roof supports of an adobe structure that stick out beyond the walls of the house anywhere from six inches to two feet

Vented — from the Spanish, *venta*, meaning sale. When the owner sells, he vents the cattle to the buyer, placing the new owner's brand alongside his own; cow is then registered in the name of the new owner.

Bibliography

COLLECTED FOLK SONGS

Allen, Jules Verne. *Cowboy Lore.* San Antonio: The Naylor Company, 1933.

Best, Dick and Beth (ed.). *Song Fest.* New York: Crown Publishing Company, 1960.

Cazden, Norman (ed.). *A Book of Nonsense Songs.* New York: Crown Publishing Company, 1961.

Coleman, Satio N. and Adolph Bregman. *Songs of American Folks.* New York: The John Day Company, 1942.

Doerflinger, William. *Shantymen and Shantyboys.* New York: The Macmillan Company, 1951.

Fife, Austin and Alta. *Saints of Sage and Saddle.* Bloomington: Indiana University Press, 1965.

———. *Songs of the Cowboys* with Jack Thorp; Variants, Commentary Notes and Lexicon. New York: Clarkson N. Potter, 1966.

———. *Cowboy and Western Songs.* New York: Clarkson N. Potter, 1969.

———. *Heaven on Horseback; Revivalist Songs and Verse in the Cowboy Idiom.* Logan: Utah State University Press, Western Texts Society Series, vol. 1, no. 1, 1970.

Ford, Ira W. (ed.). *Traditional Music in America.* New York: E. P. Dutton and Company, 1940.

Fowke, Edith and Richard Johnson. *Folk Songs of Canada.* Ontario: Waterloo Music Company, 1954.

Gardner, Emelyn Elizabeth and G. J. Chickering. *Ballads and Songs of Southern Michigan.* Ann Arbor: University of Michigan Press, 1939.

Glazer, Tom. *A New Treasury of Folk Songs.* New York: Bantam Books, 1961.

Houston, Cisco. *900 Miles; The Ballads, Blues and Folksongs of Cisco Houston.* New York: Oak Publications, 1965.

Kennedy, Charles O'Brian. *American Ballads.* Greenwich, Connecticut: Fawcett Publications, 1962.

Kolb, Sylvia and John. *A Treasury of Folk Songs.* New York: Bantam Books, 1951.

Larkin, Margaret. *The Singing Cowboy.* New York: Oak Publications, 1963. First printing, Alfred A. Knopf, 1931.

Loesser, Arthur L. (ed.). *Humor in American Song.* Howell, Saskin, 1942.

Lomax, Alan. *Folk Songs of North America.* Garden City: Doubleday and Company, 1960.

Lomax, John A. *Cowboy Songs.* New York: Sturgis & Walton Company, 1916.

———. *Songs of the Cattle Trail and Cow Camp.* New York: Duell, Sloan & Pearce, 1950. First Edition, The Macmillan Company, 1919.

———. *American Ballads and Folk Songs.* New York: The Macmillan Company, 1934.

Lomax, John A. and Alan. *Cowboy Songs.* Revised and enlarged edition. The Macmillan Company, 1948.

Lynn, Frank. *Songs for Swingin' Housemothers.* San Francisco: Chandler Publishing Company, 1961.

———. *Songs for Singin'.* San Francisco: Chandler Publishing Company, 1961.

Ohrlin, Glenn. *The Hell-Bound Train.* Chicago: University of Illinois Press, 1973.

Randolph, Vance. *Ozark Folksongs.* Four volumes. Missouri: State Historical Society, 1946.

Sackett, S. J. (ed.). *Cowboys and the Songs They Sang.* New York: William R. Scott, 1967.

Shay, Frank. *My Pious Friends and Drunken Companions and More Pious Friends and Drunken Companions.* New York: Dover Publications, 1961. First printing, *My Pious Friends and Drunken Companions.* Macauley Company, 1927. *More Pious Friends and Drunken Companions.* Macauley Company, 1928.

Silber, Irwin, and Earl Robinson. *Songs of the Great American West.* New York: The Macmillan Company, 1967.

Thorp, N. Howard. *Songs of the Cowboys.* Estancia, New Mexico. 1908. Revised and enlarged edition. Houghton Mifflin Company, New York, 1921.

White, John I. *Git Along Little Dogies; Songs and Songmakers of the American West*. Chicago: University of Illinois Press, 1975.

FOLIOS

Autry, Gene. *Famous Cowboy and Mountain Ballads; Book #2*. Chicago: M. M. Cole Publishing Company, 1934.

Clark, Kenneth S. (ed.). *The Cowboy Sings*. New York: Paull-Pioneer Music Corp., 1932.

———. *The Happy Cowboy*. New York: Paull-Pioneer Music Corp., 1934.

———. *Buckaroo Ballads*. New York: Paull-Pioneer Music Corp., 1940.

German, George B. *Cowboy Campfire Ballads*. Yankton, South Dakota, 1929.

———. *Cowboy and Hillbilly Ballads*. Chicago: M. M. Cole Publishing Company, 1939.

Gutman, Dr. Arthur H. (ed.). *Bob Miller's Famous Folio Full of Original Cowboy Songs*. New York: Bob Miller, Inc., 1934.

Hamblen, Stuart. *Stuart Hamblen and His Lucky Stars*. Chicago: M. M. Cole Publishing Company, 1935.

Lair, John. *101 WLS Barn Dance Favorites*. Chicago: M. M. Cole Publishing Company, 1935.

Lee, Powder River Jack and Kitty. *Powder River Jack and Kitty Lee's Song Book*. New York: Southern Music Company, 1931.

———. *Cowboy Wails and Cattle Trails of the Wild West*. Butte, Montana: McKee Printing Company, 1934.

———. *Cowboy Song Book*. Los Angeles: Melrose Music, 1936.

———. *Songs of the Range*. Chicago: Chart Music Publishing House, 1937.

———. *Cowboy Song Book*. Deer Lodge, Montana: 1938.

Luboff, Norman, and Win Stracke. *Songs of Man*. New York: Bonanza Books, 1965.

McClintock, Harry K. and Sterling Sherwin. *"Mac's" Song of the Road and Range*. New York: Southern Music Publishing Company, 1932.

Maynard, Ken. *Songs of the Trail*. Chicago: M. M. Cole Publishing Company, 1935.

Montana, Patsy. *Patsy Montana Deluxe Edition of Famous Original Cowboy Songs and Mountain Ballads*. Chicago: M. M. Cole Publishing Company, 1941.

Padell Books Company. *Cowboy & Mountain Ballads*. New York: 1944.

Ritter, Tex. *Tex Ritter's Cowboy Song Book*. Chicago: M. M. Cole Publishing Company, 1941.

Sherwin, Sterling. *Singing In the Saddle*. New York: Boston Music Company, 1944.

———. *Bad Man Songs of the Wild and Wooly West*. New York: Sam Fox Publishing Company.

Sterwin, Sterling, and Henri Klickman. *Songs of the Roundup*. New York: Robbins Music Corporation, 1934.

———. *Saddle Songs*. London: Frances, Day & Hunter, Ltd., 1948.

Silber, Irwin (ed.). *Sing Out Magazine*. New York: Sing Out, Inc. (A subsidiary of Folkways Records), 1959.

University Club of Denver. *A Golden Treasury*. Denver: 1953.

Van Stone, Mary R. *Spanish Folk Songs of New Mexico*. Chicago: Ralph Fletcher Seymour, 1926.

Williams, Marc. *Collection of Favorite Songs*. New York: Bob Miller, Inc., 1937.

COLLECTIONS

The Gordon Collection of Folk Songs. Library of Congress.

Billy and Betty Simon, *Private Collection of Songs and Verse*.

Foster Cayce, *Private Collection of Folios, Recordings & Books*.

Ben and Betty Perkins, *Private Collection of Songs and Verse*.

BACKGROUND

Abbott, E. D. "Teddy Blue" and Helena Huntington Smith. *We Pointed Them North. Recollections of a Cow Puncher*. Norman: University of Oklahoma Press, 1971. First printing; New York: Farrar & Rinehart, 1939.

Adams, Ramon. *Come and Get It*. Norman: University of Oklahoma Press, 1952.

———. *Western Words*. Norman: University of Oklahoma Press. 1944.

Arnold, Elliot. *The Time of the Gringo*. New York: Alfred A. Knopf, 1967.

Bos-Ross, Lillian. *The Stranger*. New York: William Morrow, 1942.

———. *Blaze Allen*. New York: William Morrow, 1944.

Botkin, B. A. (ed.). *A Treasury of American Folklore: Stories, Ballads, and Traditions of the American People*. With a foreword by Carl Sandburg. New York: Crown Publishers, 1944.

———. *A Treasury of Western Folklore*. With a foreword by Bernard De Voto. New York: Crown Publishers, 1951.

Burt, Struthers. *Diary of a Dude Wrangler*. New York: Charles Scribner's Sons, 1924.

Carpenter, Will Tom. *Lucky 7: A Cowman's Autobiography*. Austin, Texas Press, 1957.

Cook, James H. *Fifty Years on the Old Frontier as Cowboy, Hunter, Guide, Scout and Ranchman*. With a foreword by J. Frank Dobie. Norman: University of Oklahoma Press, 1957.

Dearing, Frank V. (ed.). *Best Novels and Stories of Eugene Manlove Rhodes*. Boston: Houghton Mifflin Company, 1949.

Dobie, J. Frank. *The Longhorns*. Boston: Little, Brown and Company, 1941.

———. *Tales of Old-Time Texas*. Illustrated by Barbara Latham. Boston: Little, Brown, 1955.

Dorson, Richard M. *America In Legend*. New York: Pantheon Books, 1973.

Ellison, Glen R. "Slim". *Cowboys Under the Mogollon Rim*. Tucson: University of Arizona Press, 1968.

Emerson, Ralph Waldo. *The Writings of Ralph Waldo Emerson*. New York: Random House Modern Library Series, 1950.

Fenwick, Red. *Alfred Packer: The True Story of the Man Eater*. Denver: The Denver Post, 1963.

Gipson, Frederick Benjamin. *Cowhand: The Story of a Working Cowboy*. New York: Bantam Books, 1958.

Greenway, John. *Folklore of the Great West*. Palo Alto, California: American West Publishing Company, 1969.

Hale, Will. *Twenty-four Years a Cowboy and Ranchman in Southern Texas and Old Mexico*. With an introduction by A. M. Gibson. Norman: University of Oklahoma Press, 1959.

Haley, James Evetts. *Charles S. Goodnight, Cowman and Plainsman*. With illustrations by Harold Bugbee. Boston: Houghton Mifflin Company, 1936.

Hoig, Stan. *The Humor of the American Cowboy*. Caldwell, Idaho: The Caxton Printers, 1958.

Hough, Emerson. *Story of the Cowboy*. New York: Appleton Modern Literature Series, 1925.

Katz, William Loren. *The Black West*. Garden City: Doubleday & Company, 1971.

King, Frank Marion. *Wranglin' the Past*. Drawings by Charles M. Russell, First revised edition. Pasadena, California: Trails End Publishing Company, 1946.

Laughlin, Ruth. *The Wind Leaves No Shadows*. n.d.

Lawless, Ray M. *Folksingers and Folksongs in America*. New York: Duell, Sloan & Pierce, 1960.

Malone, Bill C. *Country Music, U.S.A.* Austin: For the American Folklore Society by the University of Texas Press, 1968.

McMurtry, Larry. *In A Narrow Grave*. New York: A Touchstone Book Published by Simon & Schuster, 1971.

Paredes, Américo. *With His Pistol in His Hand*. Austin: Texas Press, 1958.

Pocock, Capt. Roger. *Curley; A Tale of the Arizona Desert*. Boston: Little Brown, Co., 1905.

Price, doughBelly. *Wisdom & Insanity*. Taos, New Mexico. 1954.

———. *Short Stirrups, The Saga of doughBelly Price*. Los Angeles: Westernlore Press, 1960.

Rhodes, Eugene Manlove. *Little World Waddies*. Printed at The Pass on the Rio Bravo (El Paso) by Carl Hertzog, 1946.

Russell, Charles M. *Trails Plowed Under*. New York: Doubleday & Company, 1951.

Sandoz, Mari. *The Buffalo Hunters*. New York: Hastings House, 1954.

———. *Old Jules*. Lincoln: University of Nebraska Press, 1962.

Santee, Ross. *The Bubbling Spring*. New York: Charles Scribner's Sons, 1949.

———. *Cowboy*. New York: Ace Books, 1964.

———. *Lost Pony Tracks*. New York: Bantam Books, 1956.

Siringo, Charles A. *A Texas Cowboy: or Fifteen Years on the Hurricane Deck of a Spanish Pony*. Introduction by J. Frank Dobie. Drawings by Tom Lea. New York: Sloane, 1950.

———. *Riata and Spurs*. Boston: Houghton Mifflin Company, 1927.

Sonnichsen, C. L. *Ten Texas Feuds*. Albuquerque: University of New Mexico Press, 1971.

Stegner, Wallace. *Beyond the One Hundredth Meridian*. Boston: Houghton Mifflin, 1953.

——. *Mormon Country*. New York: Bonanza Books, 1942.

Stevens, Robert C. (ed.). *Echoes of the Past — Tales of Old Yavapai, Vol. 2.* Prescott, Arizona: The Yavapai Cowbelles Incorporated, 1964.

Throp, Howard N. *Pardner of the Wind.* Caldwell, Idaho: The Caxton Printers, 1945.

Vernam, Glenn R. *Man on Horseback.* Lincoln: University of Nebraska Press, 1972. First Printing, Harper and Row, 1964.

Webb, Walter Prescott. *The Great Plains.* Boston: Houghton Mifflin, 1934.

Wellman, Paul I. *The Story of the Cattle Range in America.* New York: Carrick & Evans, 1939.

——. *The Trampling Herd.* New York: Carrick & Evans, 1939.

Westermeier, Clifford. *Trailing the Cowboy.* Caldwell, Idaho: The Caxton Printers, 1955.

White, Stewart Edward. *Arizona Nights.* New York: Ballantine Books, 1973. First published, 1907.

Winther, Oscar O. *Via Western Express and Stagecoach.* Stanford, California: Stanford University Press, 1945.

COLLECTED VERSE

Barker, S. Omar. *Buckaroo Ballads.* Santa Fe: New Mexico Publishing Company, 1928.

——. *Songs of the Saddlemen.* Denver: Sage Books, 1954.

——. *Rawhide Rhymes.* Garden City: Doubleday, 1968.

Brininstool, E. A. *Trail Dust of a Maverick.* New York: Dodd, Mead & Company, 1914. Reprinted by Mr. Brininstool at Los Angeles in 1921.

Chapman, Arthur. *Out Where the West Begins.* Boston: Houghton Mifflin Company, 1916.

Chittenden, Larry. *Ranch Verses.* New York: G. P. Putnam's Sons, 1893.

Clark, Charles Badger. *Grass Grown Trails.* Boston: Richard G. Badger, 1917.

——. *Sun and Saddle Leather.* Boston: Chapman & Grimes, 1952. First printing, 1915.

——. *Sun and Saddle Leather.* Tucson: Westerners International (P. O. Box 3941), 1962. This edition, illustrated with etchings by Edward Borein, was printed by Lawton Kennedy of San Francisco.

Crawford, Capt. Jack. *The Poet Scout.* New York: Funk & Wagnalls, 1886.

Fletcher, Curley W. *Songs of the Sage.* Los Angeles: Frontier Publishing Company, 1931.

Gardner, Gail I. *Orejana Bull.* Prescott, Arizona: Published by Gail I. Gardner, 1935, 1950, 1960, 1965.

George, David L. (ed.). *Family Book of Best Loved Poems.* New York: Hanover House, 1952.

Hall, Sharlot M. *Poems of a Ranch Woman.* Prescott, Ariz.: Sharlot Hall Historical Society of Northern Arizona, n.d.

Hanson, Joseph Mills. *Frontier Ballads.* Chicago: A. C. McClurg & Company, 1910.

Hersey, Harold. *Singing Rawhide.* New York: George H. Doran Company, 1926.

Jeffers, Robinson. *Selected Poetry of Robinson Jeffers.* New York: Random House, 1937.

Knibbs, Henry Herbert. *Songs of the Outlands.* Boston and New York: Houghton Mifflin Company, 1914.

——. *Riders of the Stars. Ibid.,* 1916.

——. *Songs of the Trail. Ibid.,* 1920.

——. *Saddle Songs. Ibid.,* 1922.

——. *Songs of the Lost Frontier. Ibid.,* 1930.

Lee, Powder River Jack. *Stampede.* Greensburg: Standardized Press, n.d.

Lincoln, Elliott C. *The Ranch.* Boston: Houghton Mifflin Company, 1924.

Mackenzie, Richard (ed.). *New Home Book of Best Loved Poems.* Toronto: The Blackstone Company, 1946.

Milburn, George. *The Hobo's Hornbook.* New York: Ives Washburn, 1930.

Stevenson, Burton Egbert (ed.). *New Home Book of Verse.* New York: Henry Holt & Company, 1954.

Thing, Walter E. (ed.). *Best Loved Story Poems.* Garden City: Garden City Publishing, 1941.

Acknowledgments

IN NINETEEN FIFTY-FOUR I wrote an article about cowboy songs for *Arizona Highways*. Nineteen sixty, Ray Carlson published it. The spring of that year brought a letter from Alfred A. Knopf, publishers; would I consider doing a book on the subject? It never occurred to me that I could, but I set about trying. Ten years and three re-writes later I got the idea they'd made a ghastly mistake, yet they are the first people I want to thank . . . for *not* publishing it. I learned that, as in any other art, omission is the essence of refinement and style, that practice time is a valid teacher, that a new idea is welcome only if it can be stuffed into an old mold, and finally, what other thousands before me have learned — if you do not write about the West like an easterner, you become an unpublished foreigner.

Carl Brandt, literary agent and neighbor of Mr. Knopf in the cement canyons of New York, came to Aspen, Colorado the summer of sixty-four and said he felt sure he could sell my book back there. He tried. God knows, he tried. I got some of the biggest laughs of my career from letters written by those publishing dudes, like: "Can we leave out the music?" "Could we delete the lyrics, or the poems?" Whimsical folks.

Those closest to us in time of frustration receive the most flack, having to wade through bad temper, self-pity and outrage to keep us stimulated. Bruce Berger — cloud-sitter poet, fellow backpacker and traveler — read all versions from start to finish, kept an objective view and told me when I reached too far, allowed as how I'd never learn to spell, but that's what editors were for, and when the great day came, a champagne party. Su Lum, author in the meantime of *Fisher the Fixer*, proof read and persisted with her kind and gentle words, "Hurry up, dipshit, I want to know what happens with Buck and Old Dolores. Get the next chapter over here so I can proof it." Peggy Clifford, whose writing I so admire (*Aspen Dreams and Dilemmas*) read and told me to hang on to what I had without making too many changes "to suit the fancy of the publishers." Army Armstrong sliced away unnecessary sentences, keeping trivia at a minimum.

My admirer, fan, and friend, the infamous Fred (The Red) Rodell, Yale Law Professor, has not merely made encouraging noises, but shouted them from table-tops (and under them) since our first meeting over one in 1964. Nor is Janet, his wife, any *silent* partner. They put their money where my mouth was when the beans were lean and publishers cool. I'm in *his* book (*Her Infinite Variety*, Doubleday, 1966) — he's in *mine*.

Then, along came Brandy. Or, to be more accurate, I ran into Brandy at Bahia de Los Angeles in Baja California, May of 1968, and married him in Las Vegas, July of 1969, under a bower of plastic roses, laughing. Edwin C. Brandelius could live, they said, for three years. Emphysema. With a superior intellect, a photographic memory and sharpness of wit unexcelled, he was my dictionary, encyclopedia and rogusthisorus, as he called it. He told me I'd already invested too much time to quit. As an inveterate waste-hater, I had to go along with that. The filming of *The Last Wagon* series was also Brandy's idea, and he helped write some of the narrative. He ate meals at weird hours, rubbed my back, fed the cat, and kept pushing me back to the finger machine, saying, "Come on, Misskittylu, I haven't got much time." With Brandy's encouragement, his own great store of courage, and his love to lean on, it finally came together. He saw the movie preview, beat the doctors' predictions by two years. But I can't hand him the book and say what I want to: "Here, luv, this is as much yours as it is mine."

My mother, Ruth Lee Vozack and my dad, Zanna Park Lee won't see it for the same reasons. Yet, somehow, they both knew the book would make it one day, for they spoke always with that end in mind . . . two people who never did anything but encourage me (often to the point of depriving themselves) in whatever artistic venture I was undertaking. With that sort of background it's hard to be a loser.

Luckily we're not alone in the business of "readin' sign" — like old Fremont, other trackers have gone before. I'd have been at a loss many times without the help of Austin and Alta Fife, Department of Languages at Utah State. Themselves authors of several books on cowboy and Western songs, they have generously shared their knowledge and opened their files to unearth data. Likewise John I. White (*Git Along Little Dogies*) writer and ex-radio singer, now of Chatham, New Jersey. His correspondence file is the fattest one in my cabinet; including copies of old sheet music, and magazine articles so rare as to be collectors items. And Ray M. Lawless, author of *Folksingers and Folksongs in America*, who must have been a masochist to have so painstakingly catalogued the folksingers and their material back in the early sixties. When he contacted me for his second edition, he said he was giving up after this because he couldn't stay abreast, there were getting to be too many of us. A goodly portion of my discography came from him.

S. Omar Barker has generously given me permission to "random quote" his fine rhymes, thus adding strong support to a text that would have been less effective, by far, without them. To say nothing of what his verse has done for the cowboys over the years!

Forster Cayce (the R is silent like the Y in pumphandle) Copper State Record Company, Tucson, has a bunch of old song folios, books and records in his library which he generously let me browse through from time to time. Fred Rosenstock, a rather famous character and rare book dealer in Denver, told me I didn't have to *buy* all those books in which I found things I needed. "Just bring your own pencil and pad, there's never enough of them around here." And Jake Zeitlin, another rare book dealer (Zeitlin & Ver Brugge, Hollywood), knew me when I first started my career as a folksinger, showed me where to find things, and how, introduced me to Carl Sandburg, and produced a son (David) who taught me licks on the guitar.

A kind of belated thanks goes to Ray Carlson, way-back-then-editor of *Arizona Highways*, for roasting my second MS, telling me I blew it (using all those dirty words like Ten Thousand *Goddam* Cattle) and thereby making me so mad I persevered. And to Marge Patterson, his faithful secretary, an *un*-belated thanks for consolation. A bottle of scotch for Durrett Wagner of Swallow Press for reading and rejecting, but insisting the *right* publisher would do right by it. And to dear old Angus Cameron (Knopf) for all the nice letters he's written over the years, saying, NO.

Those of the exposure media — without them. Pooff! Time and again faithful Red Fenwick of the Denver Post has penned articles on the book-in-progress, the film, my recordings, and continuously asked, "when can I say, 'she has *writ* that book' instead of 'she's a-writin' it?' " Rhat now, Red. Dick Johnson on the city desk of that same paper, holds a Ph.D. in creative writing. He very kindly gave me an in-depth analysis and breakdown of chapters so that I could see the trees in the forest. Blessings on Studs Terkel, an exceptionally fine writer (*Division Street, Working*) and long-time member of the WFMT radio staff in Chicago, for the many interviews and airings given over to my endeavors. My agents, rare birds with whom I never sign contracts: Len Rosenfeld, New York, Bud Goldstein, Minneapolis, Bill Fegan, Mt. View, Arkansas, are friends first of all, a kind of private cheering section.

It goes so far back I'm sure I have forgotten the contributions of many kind souls who have assisted in one way or another, but let me thank those I do remember. Burl Ives, who did not help with this book, but sowed some seeds from which it grew. Josh White, who nourished the plant when it wilted. An "I care" at the right time can keep the whole project from sinking into oblivion. These people cared enough to read and offer constructive suggestions: Jackson Rippey, Brownville, Nebraska; J. Frank Wright, Blanding, Utah; Steve Pendleton, Warwick and Helen Thompkins, Dr. Stanley and Isobella Leland — Sherman Oaks, Hollywood, Laguna Hills, California; Douglas Anderson and Mable, Denver; Howard Welch and Bill Webb of Big Sur and Carmel; Mary and Mack Shroyer of La Paz, Baja California; A. V. Bryan, Phoenix; Bob and Laurie McLeod, Black Canyon; Budge Ruffner, Dick and Marion Sprang, Prescott, Arizona; Gina Gerometta, Ogden Dunes, Indiana. And an ex-mother-in-law, Doris Bush, Fair Haven, New Jersey.

When William R. Cox, a past president of Western Writers of America, told me he'd look over my #3 manuscript to advise possible revisions, I never expected he and his wife Lee would invite me to spend two weeks at their home while he red-penciled it. Having written fifty books and screen plays himself, I decided things were looking up. They were. When I pondered what I could do for him in return for his labor of love he said, "Pass it on, Katie, that's all we can ever do, just pass it on."

A special thanks to Leland D. Case, President Emeritus and Keeper of the Pitchfork of Westerners International for the use of numerous quotations from poetry by Charles Badger Clark, Jr. The copyrighted verses presented here are by special permission.

Do I thank the Museum of New Mexico and the Folk Art Museum, both in Santa Fe? Of course I do. And the Arizona Historical Society, Tucson? No, they thank me because I gave them many of these songs for their tape archives, then didn't have enough sense to go check their record files and manuscripts for rare jewels. But thanks is no word for the blessed encounter I had with their editor of publications, Dr. Leland Sonnichsen. Leland is like a bubbling spring. He is selfless and richly endowed with wit and wisdom. I'm sure you could wall the city of Tucson with the aspiring authors he has helped along their way. And Leland can spell and knows about that mad jumble of mumbles at the back of the book called a bib-lee-ogg-raff-y, which I HATE! and which he put in order, to say nothing of the hours he spent editing the manuscript that went to Northland.

Robert Roberts, fine musician and composer in his own right, did a masterful job of the scores. No Magical Musical Machine for him! He pen and inked every note from cassette tapes, set the keys, supplied guitar cords and hand lettered the lyrics so beautifully they resemble old classic ballad parchments.

As for my publisher, Paul Weaver, and my editors, Jim Howard and Rick Stetter, they've been here all along, close by, and I didn't even know it. Which proves again, if you listen to the inner ear, you *can* come home again.

KATIE LEE